D1524277

State, Class, and Bureaucracy
Canadian Unemployment Insurance
and Public Policy

Recent explanations of public policy have increasingly focused on "state-centred" theories which emphasize internal state dynamics as opposed to "society-centred" theories which concentrate on external forces such as interest group pressure. *State, Class, and Bureaucracy* assesses the fruitfulness of these approaches by comparing neo-Marxist and neo-pluralist explanations (society-centred) with explanations that emphasize the effects of bureaucracy and federalism (state-centred). Unemployment insurance (UI) was chosen as a case study because of its importance to employer and employee groups; if any program or policy is susceptible to a society-centred explanation, UI should be.

In reviewing the history of Canadian UI, Leslie Pal shows that while capital and labour had substantial disagreements over policy, their representations to state officials rarely had any decisive impact on policy development. He suggests that bureaucratic forces, including organizational ideology and inter-agency conflict, provide a much richer basis for understanding UI policy evolution. The actuarial ideology of the Commission explains the conservative dynamic in UI development, while bureaucratic rivalry, which culminated in victory by the Department of Labour, explains the expansionary thrust, particularly the addition of social welfare aspects.

In his discussion of federalism, Pal shows that intergovernmental bargaining has had a surprising effect: by the mid-1970s representations from the provinces counted for as much as, if not more than, those from employers and employees. Analysis of UI thus favours state-centred explanations over society-centred ones and suggests that we have overestimated the degree to which government simply responds to external pressures in making policy. Autonomous and distinct forces within the state also greatly affect policy evolution.

Leslie A. Pal is a member of the Department of Political Science at the University of Calgary.

State, Class, and Bureaucracy

Canadian Unemployment Insurance and Public Policy

LESLIE A. PAL

McGill-Queen's University Press
Kingston and Montreal

© McGill-Queen's University Press 1988
ISBN 0-7735-0623-3

Legal deposit first quarter 1988
Bibliothèque nationale du Québec

Printed in Canada on acid-free paper

This book has been published with the help of a grant
from the Social Science Federation of Canada, using
funds provided by the Social Sciences and Humanities
Research Council of Canada.

Canadian Cataloguing in Publication Data

Pal, Leslie Alexander, 1954-
    State, class and bureaucracy
    Includes index.
    Bibliography: p.
    ISBN 0-7735-0623-3
    1. Insurance, Unemployment – Government policy –
    Canada – Political aspects.
    2. Bureaucracy – Canada. I. Title.
    HD7096.C3P34 1988   368.4'4'00971   C87-090198-2

Contents

Tables

Acknowledgments

This book gained immeasurably from the help of several individuals and organizations. James Struthers offered valuable advice on an early version of the manuscript, along with lodgings in Ottawa as my research dollars dwindled. Jack Grove and Neil Nevitte helped sharpen my treatment of the issues raised in chapter one. Anonymous referees for the Social Science Federation of Canada and McGill-Queen's University Press persuaded me to rethink some of the theoretical arguments and to add new material in several chapters. If any part of this book persists in error, it is I, of course, who must bear responsibility.

Most of the research base for this book is documentary, and I received valuable assistance from several people in navigating through the available sources. The staff of the Public Archives of Canada was exemplary in its courtesy and zeal. I wish to thank in particular John Smart, for his help with the files of the Department of Labour and the Unemployment Insurance Commission. The Access to Information staff at Employment and Immigration Canada was equally helpful, especially in light of the strain my information requests placed on its resources. Sean O'Heagarty's Irish wit and common sense eased the process considerably. I am grateful also to the officials and politicians who patiently submitted to interviews. Some have allowed their names to be cited; to the others who must remain anonymous, I hope that this book's contribution to an understanding of unemployment insurance will be a partial reward.

Judi Powell typed several versions of the manuscript with marvellous efficiency and tolerated my impossible demands with grace and good humour. Philip Cercone and his staff at McGill-Queen's University Press exhibited a professionalism that is rapidly setting a new standard among university presses in this country, and for which I am deeply appreciative. I am also grateful for the permission to include in this book some material which was previously published in *Canadian Public Policy*, the *Canadian Journal of Political Science*, and *Canadian Social Welfare Policy*, edited by Jacqueline S. Ismael.

This book has been published with the help of a grant from the Social Science Federation of Canada, using funds provided by the Social Sciences and Humanities Research Council of Canada. My research was supported originally by a University of Waterloo Research Grant in 1981-2 and subsequently by several generous grants from the University of Calgary.

My wife, Mary, was the pattern of patience while I wrestled with this book, and at times her support was all that sustained me through bouts of exasperation. Our son, Matthew, was born just as I began to write the key chapters, making this book's birth coincidental with his own. It seems fitting, then, that it be dedicated to him.

CHAPTER ONE

Unemployment Insurance and Policy Analysis

This book is about unemployment insurance (UI) in Canada – the Unemployment Insurance program, its structure, growth, and development. It is not, however, a narrative history of the program. Instead, it aims to be analytical, to isolate and assess major forces that have shaped UI since the Depression. It approaches UI as a case study in public policy development, but a case study that, while in no sense being a "critical test,"[1] at least allows comparison of some rival theories and throws light on some more general issues in the social science literature pertaining to the growth and dynamics of the postwar state. This book is as much about public policy theory as it is about UI.

UI has become one of the country's most widely used and expensive programs. By 1985, for example, more than 3 million claimants per year received benefits.[2] The program is virtually universal, meaning that anyone who works for a wage or salary must make contributions and is usually eligible for benefits. Annual UI benefits now regularly exceed $10 billion, making UI the single most expensive of Canada's income security programs. Though the program has been revised considerably since its inception in 1940, UI has retained its basic principles and legislative integrity longer than any other program except some in the pension field. Despite this longevity, UI has been controversial: in the 1930s it was a critical backdrop to Dominion-provincial fiscal negotiations,[3] in the early 1970s it was relevant to various proposals to revise Canada's income security system,[4] and in the early 1980s it was seen as a major component of an integrated labour market strategy.[5] Most recently, both the 1985 Report of the Royal Commission on the Economic Union and Development Prospects for Canada (Macdonald Commission) and the 1986 Report of the Commission of Inquiry on Unemployment Insurance recognized that UI reform is critical to any redesigning of Canada's social safety net. Indeed, in light of these considerations, it seems surprising that UI has not attracted more sustained scholarly attention. The detailed analysis contained in subsequent chapters should help fill the gap.

COMPARING THEORIES

This book rests on two fundamental assumptions. The first is that scientific inquiry into public policy and the policy process is ultimately concerned with developing knowledge about the real world and the way that it works. Theories and theory formation are simply conceptual devices that, in limited and conjectural fashion, aid educated guess work. Despite the proliferation of theories in the social sciences, the ultimate goal is the identification of fruitful frameworks or directions of inquiry. This assumption has several corollaries that, until recently, were not in favour among social scientists. One is that there can and should be a measure (however small) of progress in science, from less adequate to more adequate understandings of the world. Another is that the responsibility of social scientists consists in trying, as best they can, to probe current theories for weaknesses and develop new, more promising avenues of inquiry.

The second assumption is that it is possible to compare, contrast, and probe competing theories that occupy a given scientific domain and to arrive at reasonable (not irrefutable) conclusions about which ones are more promising than others. This assumption opposes the view that theories construct facts and that, since there are no observations without theory, rival theories cannot be assessed against each other. This epistemological relativism reached its zenith in the early 1970s, with the popularity of figures such as Thomas Kuhn and Paul Feyerabend and was in large part a justified reaction against the earlier school of logical positivism, which separated facts from values and claimed the existence of a neutral, intersubjective observational language. Ironically, while the philosophy of science over the last decade has gradually rejected this relativism in favour of a modified metaphysical and epistemological realism, many social scientists still assume that something like Kuhn's understanding of paradigms is an adequate philosophy of science. Acceptance of relativism discourages, though in practice it does not entirely suppress, more rigorous comparisons of rival theories. Accordingly, a slight digression on current trends in the philosophy of science would help support the assumptions that underlie this book.

Kuhn's *The Structure of Scientific Revolutions*[6] had a profound effect on both the philosophy of science and the practice of the social sciences. Though Kuhn's ideas had been anticipated in the 1930s, his book was a brilliant salvo against logical positivism. By constructing a sociological explanation of the practices of natural science, Kuhn exploded the long-held superiority of natural over social science. Despite some allusions to scientific advances and their enduring contributions, Kuhn's analysis led him to argue that scientific communities share "paradigms" that define problems, facts, theories, and methods to such a degree that a debate between paradigms is logically impossible. Moreover, the choice among competing paradigms is a matter of community consensus and cannot be justified rationally or empirically.[7] Indeed, the definition of what is scientific and what is not varies with paradigms:

But paradigms differ in more than substance, for they are directed not only to nature but also back upon the science that produced them. They are the source of the methods, problem-field, and standards of solution accepted by any mature scientific community at any given time. As a result, the reception of a new paradigm often necessitates a redefinition of the corresponding science. Some old problems may be relegated to another science or declared entirely "unscientific." Others that were previously non-existent or trivial may, with a new paradigm, become the very archetypes of significant scientific achievement.[8]

While Kuhn, under critical pressure, significantly modified his earlier views,[9] Paul Feyerabend's similar conclusions became increasingly extreme. Feyerabend thus expresses, perhaps in its clearest form, the precepts of a thorough-going epistemological relativism. Feyerabend argued that not only was "the description of every single fact dependent on *some* theory" but also the unearthing of new "facts" depended on new theories.[10] He thus encouraged a methodological pluralism wherein "anything goes" in order to maximize the clash of theories. Since Feyerabend rejected a correspondence theory of truth (i.e. that our knowledge somehow corresponds to a real, independent world), the success of theories against their rivals could not be empirically based. Indeed, "successful" theories often are nothing more than oppressive ideologies.[11] Science, in its essentials, is similar to myth, religion, magic, and witchcraft.[12] The methodological principle of "anything goes" rejected, it seems, all conceivable standards of success or progress, though implicit political standards such as the development of human potentiality may have been relevant.[13]

The Weltanschauungen views of Kuhn, Feyerabend, and others are no longer considered serious contenders for a viable philosophy of science. As Suppe puts it:

Further, contemporary work in philosophy of science increasingly subscribes to the position that it is a central aim of science to come to knowledge of how the world *really* is, that correspondence between theories and reality is a central aim of science as an epistemic enterprise and crucial to whatever objectivity scientific knowledge enjoys – in sharp repudiation of the "sociological" views of knowledge found in the more extreme *Weltanschauungen* analyses while acknowledging the defects of positivistic and earlier empiricist treatments.[14]

Building on the work of Lakatos, Toulmin, and especially Shapere, Suppe highlights the importance of the context of justification in the growth of scientific knowledge, in particular the reliance on "good reasons" to determine the likelihood of truth claims. In this conception of science, there is little talk of "verification," "induction," or "falsification" of theories, in part because it is now seen that practising scientists rarely "test" theory in any rigid or uniform way. Rather,

it is commonplace for scientists working on it to suppose that the present version of the theory is defective in various respects, which is to say that it is literally false, at best being only an approximation to the truth or a promising candidate; and if one is convinced this is so, it would be pointless to attempt to either refute or inductively confirm the theory. What *is* to the point is to use observation and experiment to discover shortcomings in the theory, to determine how to improve the theory, and to discover how to eliminate known artificialities, distortions, over-simplifications, and errors in the descriptions, explanations, and predictions of reality that the theory affords.[15]

Social scientists have, on the whole, neglected these recent developments in the philosophy of science. Insofar as they reflect on these issues, they rightly despair of postivistic as well as Popperian recipes for theory testing.[16] Nevertheless, the *practice* of the social sciences, including political science, is in large part characterized by attempts to compare and contrast the usefulness, fecundity, appropriateness, or truth of rival theories. Social science consists of much more than this, of course – the generation of new theories and concepts and the exploration and extension of old ones – but comparison of theories is an essential phase in the arduous growth of knowledge.

It should be clear that few theories, even in the natural sciences, can be rigorously tested or "falsified." Modern theoretical physics, for example, traditionally seen as the model for "true science," is seriously considering theories of time and space that approach the fantastical.[17] But this does not preclude probing theories for their fruitfulness and comparing them as reasonable bases for further research and development. This book proposes to review a limited number of theories about the policy process and gauge their usefulness in these terms. The comparison does not con-stitute a "test" in the traditional, falsificationist sense of the term. Rather, it will attempt to gauge the likelihood that one or another theory may lead to more interesting research and perhaps, ultimately, to more reliable knowledge.

The range of alternative theories or approaches of the policy process is embarrassingly wide, indeed there is even disagreement on how best to organize and define the available rivals. In a recent study, Doern and Phidd isolate the rational model, incrementalism, public choice, and class analysis, as well as systems theory, interest group pluralism, and elite theories, as the main alternatives in the field.[18] Atkinson and Chandler suggest that there are "two general images of the state" that may form the basis of any analysis: neo-Marxist and pluralist. In addition, however, researchers may adopt one or more of four "strategies" in studying and explaining public policy. They may look at the determinants of policy, the types of policies, policy instruments, and policy impact.[19] Wilson discerns five different conceptions of the policy process in which policy is the dependent variable: neo-Marxist studies, systems analysis, public choice, organizational capacity or technology, and neo-institutionalism, which stresses the interplay of ideas, interests and institutions.[20] Aucoin isolates four major approaches: incrementalism, public choice, Marxism, and environmentalism.[21] Finally, in an early attempt to canvass and synthesize the literature, Simeon identified five general approaches to explaining policy variations: environment, distribution of power, ideas, institutions, and processes of decision-making.[22] These categorizations, with some terminological changes, are presented in Table 1.

TABLE 1
Alternative Theories of the Policy Process

	Doern and Phidd	Atkinson and Chandler	Wilson	Aucoin	Simeon
Neo-Marxism/class	X	X	X	X	X[1]
Pluralism/interest groups	X	X	X[2]	X[3]	X
Public choice-bureaucracy	X		X	X	X[4]
Institutions	X		X		X
Environment				X	X
Ideas	X			X	X

1 Classed as "power."
2 Classed as "system."
3 Classed as "incremental."
4 Classed as "process of decision-making."

Table 1's usefulness is compromised by the overlap in categories and definitions used by the respective authors. How are "ideas" different from "interests"? Where is the demarcation between "institutions" and "bureaucracy"? Simeon underscored this problem of boundaries when remarking, "I lean strongly towards 'ideas' and differences in dominant ideas from country to country as the basis for explaining policy differences, though I would place more stress on the link between ideas and interests and influence of different groups."[23] He suggested treating the approaches as complementary in that they explained different *levels* of a policy, from its general features to its specific ones. This may indeed be the best way to proceed, but the fact remains that those who use these approaches tend to stress their incompatibility, since at least the major ones purport to provide relatively complete models of the way in which the political system operates and policy is made.

How then to proceed? Deciding which theories are the most important is largely a matter of judgment, though judgments may be measured against what students of policy themselves are doing. Table 1 provides some guidance. All the authors, in almost identical language, list neo-Marxism or class analysis, and pluralism or interest group conflict, as major competing approaches. Public choice or the independent effect of bureaucratic decision-making, institutions, and ideas closely followed. Environmental determinants, such as demography and level of gross national product (GNP) are so broad that it is difficult to gauge precisely their effects on public policy.[24] Ideas, as an independent variable, have rarely been used unconnected to interests or group conflict.[25]

From these clues, it appears that the main alternatives are the Marxist, pluralist, bureaucratic, and institutionalist approaches to public policy. Indeed, these alternatives may be placed into two broad categories of explanation that recently have been the focus of debate within the policy literature. The first category, exemplified by both Marxist and pluralist approaches, is society-centred. Within this perspective, as Skocpol puts it, government is considered simply as "an arena within which economic interest groups or normative social movements contended or allied with one another to shape the making of public policy decisions."[26] Modern variants of both Marxism and pluralism occasionally recognize instances of independent state action but usually tend to argue that public policy is the simple resultant of social forces and conflicts.

The second category of explanation is state-centred and grants a large degree of autonomy to the state in its formation of public policy. The state is an independent, and often dominant, actor in the policy process, pursuing its own interests. These interests may contradict those of even the most powerful societal actors, such as capital or labour. Moreover, it is the state and its structure that may ultimately determine the capacity of societal actors to organize their own interests and press them within the political system. As yet, this approach represents only a shift in perspective, though one so fundamental to the study of public policy that Skocpol rightly terms it an "intellectual sea change." Examples of state-centred theories include those that emphasize internal state bureaucratic processes and such institutional features as federalism or executive/legislative structure.

It may seem somewhat odd to lump pluralism and Marxism into the same category, since traditionally they have been sworn intellectual enemies. The debate between them has been long but inconclusive, not least because its antagonists have themselves never been clearly united. On the Marxist side, there are structuralists,[27] instrumentalists,[28] and followers of the Frankfurt school[29] and of the "capital logic" school.[30] The pluralist camp has been just as fragmented, if not more so. There were the early differences, for example, between those, like Dahl, who emphasized pluralist competition among elites[31] and those, like Bentley and Truman, who gave virtually all groups equal weight in the policy process.[32] National differences in pluralist theory have also been observed between Britain and the United States.[33] Despite these divisions, pluralism as a whole – with its alleged defence of the status quo and fondness for American-style democracy – was on the defensive in the 1960s. Understandably, since battle lines were usually indistinct and shifting, the pluralist counterattack was not always satisfying, even to adherents. As one observer noted, the pluralist position seemed at times to mean no more than that all people have *some* kind of input on at least some decisions and that power in Western democracies is decentralized and complex.[34]

The pluralists nonetheless made some telling points against their Marxist adversaries by exposing the occasional brittleness and reductionism of radical theories of power. Simultaneously, European Marxism was generating theories more congenial to complex causation.[35] One result of these exchanges has been mutual tolerance and some degree of acceptance of opposing views. A general trend in recent pluralist writings, for example, has been recognition of the unique power and importance of producer groups in capitalist democracies, groups that bear strong similarities to what Marxists have described as "classes in action."[36] Indeed, the symbiotic relations between producer groups and the state are seen by some as the emerging form of interest intermediation in capitalist democracies.[37] Scholars who have usually been identified with the pluralist tradition, such as Charles Lindblom, now argue the hegemonic role of business in capitalist democracy.[38] Even Robert Dahl, the doyen of pluralist political science, has recently pointed to the importance of producer groups in modern polyarchies.[39] As well, analyses conducted within a Marxist framework have appeared that focus on intergroup conflicts in a way highly reminiscent of pluralism.[40]

Pluralism never denied the fact of inequality, and neo-Marxism has not been blind to the everyday influence of non-class actors or the fragmentation of class interests. While strong differences remain, both approaches now appear to stress the importance of organized interests, particularly producer groups, in the political process. In this respect, despite the differences between neo-pluralism[41] and neo-Marxism, both are society-centred explanations in that they highlight the role of producer groups in the policy process. This book will test the strength of these society-centred explanations by asking, first, whether there was a substantial, class-based disagreement over UI and, second, whether and to what degree policy-makers responded to these preferences.

This book will also probe the fruitfulness of state-centred approaches to the understanding of public policy. In contrast to the emphasis that neo-pluralists and neo-Marxists place on producer groups, state-centred explanations focus on the internal dynamics of the state system itself. As argued earlier, the most popular variants of state-centred approaches in the current policy literature focus on bureaucratic forces and institutional arrangements.

The bureaucratic model focuses on the internal dynamics of the state and in particular on the conflicts among bureaucrats over income, prestige, and organizational integrity. It is always possible, of course, to argue that these internal conflicts simply reflect class struggles or ideologies secreted by a capitalist society. Bureaux, in other words, conflict either because they "really" represent conflicting classes or class fractions[42] or because competition and the pursuit of self-interest are endemic to capitalism. While there certainly is a measure of truth in these assertions, they make the comparison of alternative theories difficult, if not impossible. The "public choice" school and organization theory have taken a different road, stressing the autonomous interests of bureaucratic actors and the effects these have on policy.[43] To what extent was UI shaped by departmental philosophy, administrative practices, and organizational imperatives?

The institutionalist approach to public policy is enjoying a revival from its heyday before the behavioural revolution of the 1950s. While it is now widely accepted that political parties and legislatures have a relatively minor effect on policy outcomes,[44] other institutional features of the state continue to attract attention. In Canada the single most important of these institutional features is federalism, the constitutional division of sovereignty between federal and provincial governments. The institutional structure creates sets of actors (the eleven governments), encourages some types of behaviour and discourages others, and forces certain patterns of political interaction that may ultimately have dramatic effects on public policy.

Federalism may, of course, be itself reduced to broad social and cultural forces, and it is true that many federal states differ dramatically from each other in terms of policy outputs. It is possible, nonetheless, to view federalism as an autonomous feature of the state system that itself has important effects on public policy. In the UI case, for example, did federalism impede the program's adoption? And once it was adopted, was conflict over the program organized or mobilized in a particular way because of the structure of Canadian federalism?

Neo-pluralism, neo-Marxism, bureaucratic politics, and institutionalism are among the main rivals currently entertained by students of public policy. While some global theories such as Marxism purport consistently to incorporate all of them, as well as a few others, when used singly the rivals are usually seen as mutually exclusive. Each offers a sufficiently clear set of propositions about the main influences in the policy process, and so we may confront those propositions with the available evidence from the historical record. We know the characteristics of UI policy, or the "output" of the policy process, and so we may probe the historical record to see which forces were most decisive, and hence which theory most fruitful, in explaining its development. Ultimately, this book seeks to weigh the merits of society-centred as opposed to state-centred explanations of public policy.

What is meant by "policy" in this context? UI, strictly speaking, is a program that gives effect to a variety of policy goals having to do with labour market flows and income security. In this respect, it might even be said that there is no such thing as "UI policy," only labour policy or income security policy, the latter two defined in terms of their aims. While there is some merit to this distinction between policy and program, it saps most of the life and vigour from policy analysis, reducing it to the study of highly general and abstract ideas. In practice, policy-makers themselves rarely use the distinction; they see policy issues imbedded in questions of program design and see no contradiction in having a policy about a program. Policy, therefore, in this study refers to the concrete design features of the UI program, including the timing of the introduction of those features and their relation to each other in the program.

UI AS A CASE STUDY

This book seeks to contribute to the disciplined explanation of public policy by trying to judge which of a number of key theories, representing two broad perspectives, is most fruitful in explaining a particular case. If the case were unique or rare, then the effort might be largely wasted, since what holds for UI may not hold for anything else. The existence of distinctive "policy communities" and "types" of policy is now widely accepted, with the clear implication that there is no single policy process but many processes characterized by different ideas, groups, and agencies.[45] Even if this were indisputably true, there is still some merit in seeking to understand general forces that may cut across distinct policy arenas. Indeed, the successful search for such forces may ultimately reveal that the differences among policy arenas are more apparent than real.

Nonetheless, UI needs to be a "suitable" case study in two senses. First, it should be reasonably accommodating to the theories being compared; it must not be, by definition, insulated from one or another of the sets of forces outlined in the theories. UI meets this criterion. Neo-pluralism and neo-Marxism stress the influence of producer interests, particularly business, on public policy, and UI does attract political pressures from both business and labour because it affects the balance of power in the labour market. Indeed, UI is the only income security program in which the prime beneficiaries – employers and employees – have a formal administrative role. If any policy attracts and is susceptible to producer interests, UI is. As well, however, UI has all the ingredients that should make it susceptible to bureaucratic policy explanations: complex rules, multiple goals, and high costs. Admittedly, an institutionalist explanation in terms of federalism seems the least likely, but in fact it is not implausible. UI, while now an exclusively federal jurisdiction, had to be transferred from the provinces in 1940 by constitutional amendment. It is so closely bound to the rest of the income security framework that provinces have always retained keen interest in it.

In its second sense, "suitable" means reasonably representative of other policy areas. Until recently, it has been thought that case studies are inappropriate to the search for general explanations. Yin points out, however, that explanatory research characteristically asks "how" and "why" questions, which often are best pursued through case studies.[46] A case study has the "ability to deal with a full variety of evidence – documents, artifacts, interviews, and observations."[47] Of central importance is whether this evidence allows "external validity" or generalization.[38] Indeed it does, but not in the traditional way associated with survey research. As Yin argues:

> The external validity problem has been a major barrier in doing case studies. Critics typically state that single cases offer a poor basis for generalizing [sic]. However, such critics are implicitly contrasting the situation to survey research, where a "sample" (if selected correctly) readily generalizes to a larger universe. *This analogy to samples and universes is incorrect when dealing with case studies.* This is because survey research relies on *statistical* generalization, whereas case studies (as with experiments) rely on *analytical* generalization.
>
> In analytical generalization, the investigator is striving to generalize a particular set of results to some broader theory.[49]

In other words, *general theories* are being applied to a suitable case, and so generalizations from the case apply to the theories. As suggested earlier, the rival theories are being compared in terms of explanatory power and fruitfulness as directions for further research and further applications.

UI is one of Canada's most complex programs. Chapter two discusses the significance of UI as an element of the Western welfare state, its international history, and its general structure. Chapter three provides an overview of the history of UI in Canada, outlining major developments and turning points, which will be returned to in greater detail in subsequent chapters.

Chapters four, five, and six form the heart of the book. They analyse the strength of neo-pluralism and neo-Marxism, of bureaucracy, and of federalism in explaining UI policy development. Since several objections may be anticipated to the logic and structure of this book's argument, chapter seven concludes with a brief reprise and considers some key criticisms. It also reconsiders the external validity of this case study and implications for society-centred and state-centred research agendas.

History

Unemployment Insurance in the Welfare State

This chapter seeks to set the stage for the ensuing discussion of Canadian UI by addressing several key questions. First, what is UI's relation to the welfare state as a whole, and upon what conceptual innovations does it rely? Second, what was the nineteenth- and twentieth- century history of UI, particularly in the United States and Britain, which served as benchmarks for Canada's program? Third, what is the anatomy of UI, and what rationales normally underlie its key features?

UI AND THE WELFARE STATE

Though the term *welfare state* came into popular use in Britain only during the Second World War, the phenomenon it describes is the result of fundamental socioeconomic forces released in the erosion and disappearance of feudalism. Flora and Heidenheimer argue that the welfare state is the result of several long developmental processes.[1] One is a secular increase in demands for socioeconomic equality, largely a consequence of the dynamics and growth of modern capitalism, which, while it increases the total stock of wealth, tends to accentuate if not create an unequal distribution of this wealth. Another major force in Western societies has been the extension of the franchise and citizenship rights, culminating in mass democracy shortly after the turn of this century.[2] Finally, perhaps as a consequence of capitalism or of a more fundamental process of social differentiation that progressively unbinds individuals from the social fabric, there has been a historical striving for socioeconomic security.

Combined, these forces have contributed broadly to that framework or structure of policies, ideas, and prejudices termed the welfare state. In each country, of course, depending on historical circumstances and opportunities, the steps along the road have been small or large, hesitant or bold, forward or backward. But despite these critical national differences, the ways in which social problems are defined, debated, and resolved are remarkably similar across democratic-capitalist and communist states, at least in the West.[3] In all of these countries over the last 200 years, provisions against threats to livelihood have progressively been transferred from the private realm of the family and voluntary associations to public institutions; this public provision is everywhere considered a basic right not lightly reneged; its uniform thrust, if not real effect, is to equalize income and in some measure wealth.

UI has clearly been part of this historical process; indeed, as one of the four major social insurance programs (retirement, disability, and health being the others), it has helped distinguish the modern welfare state from its immediate, Poor Law-based predecessor. The insurance aspects of UI will be discussed below, but as a general means of delivering benefits, social insurance may be seen to have the following important components.[4] First, social insurance tries to prevent destitution through routine measures, rather than extraordinary or emergency ones. Second, it tries to maintain earned income rather than respond only to need. Third, it focuses on the male labourer, rather than women and children. Finally, it usually compels potential beneficiaries to contribute to the financing of the program. We may add that social insurance confers a stronger claim to benefits because of its contributory structure but also because it typically has much wider coverage and hence is less stigmatizing.

These broad historical forces, of which the development of social insurance is a part, explain only the context within which UI was possible. UI itself, as a specific response to a specific problem, had to await a conceptual revolution. Problems addressed by the welfare state have first to be *defined as problems*, to be recognized as issues requiring social and political mobilization. This conceptual process operates in three critical ways. It must first isolate a phenomenon as a problem rather than an uncontroversial element in the stream of events. In the early stages of the industrial revolution, for example, child labour was commonplace and unremarkable. Only with time was this phenomenon defined as a social problem. Second, this problem must be conceptually transported from the private realm to the public realm; it must be defined as a social problem. Referring to children once again, it was widely agreed at the turn of this century that many children were deprived because of their parents' poverty but that it remained the parents' duty to care for those children. Family allowances were based on an alternate view that the poverty of children was a social problem insofar as it had negative societal consequences. Finally, social causation has to replace or at least supplement private causation. One of the key conceptual foundations of the modern welfare state is that private distress is not only often considered a social problem but is assumed to be socially caused.

Unemployment had to undergo this conceptual transformation before it could become an object of social and economic policy. It is important to remember that UI is only one of the instruments available for dealing with unemployment or with the broader issue of labour markets. The modern history of UI has always been entwined with questions about the efficient functioning of these markets in terms of supply and demand for labour, its price, and its mobility. Early Western societies did not, however, have a concept of unemployment comparable to ours. The Greeks, for example, did have wandering, unemployed tradesmen and surplus populations, but since most common labour was slave labour, unemployment was a private expense of slave-owners, not a social problem as we would understand it.[5] More pointedly, medieval society could not "think" the concept of unemployment because of the widespread system of obligations between worker and master, serf and lord. There was an obligation to maintain employment and to proffer it, thus underscoring how the modern concept of unemployment assumes a free labourer able to sell labour power on the market.

By the nineteenth century unemployment did have a name – idleness. In Britain this term had none of its early Christian connotation of a state of grace; it now implied a private failing or absence of initiative. Rural insurrection in 1830 led to the establishment of the Royal Commission on the Poor Laws, whose 1834 Report laid the foundation for a new system of workhouses and punitive "relief." Workhouse discipline would be so severe that it would drive away all but the incorrigibly idle.[6] This principle of "less eligibility" broke down under the trade depressions of the 1860s and 1870s and the scandals of workhouse mistreatment and abuse. The number of unemployed increased so dramatically in the late nineteenth century, as industrialism began to dominate the rhythms of the British economy, that it became difficult to blame the lack of work on simple idleness.[7]

Classical economic theory had by this time, however, generated an explanation of unemployment that still rooted it in individual motivation. Nineteenth- and early-twentieth-century political economy, following Say's Law, assumed that supply would create its own demand insofar as an excess of the former would, if competition were unrestrained, lower prices and clear the market. J.S. Mill put the argument succinctly in 1848: "Goods can only be lowered in price by competition, to the point which calls forth buyers sufficient to take them off; and wages can only be lowered by competition until room is made to admit all the laborers to a share in the distribution of the wages-fund."[8] This argument was reproduced and extended in A. Pigou's classic treatment of the subject, *A Theory of Unemployment* (1933). Unemployment was analysed not as a general feature of the industrial system but as an oversupply of labour in terms of a given price. If labourers would lower their price they could reduce or erase their unemployment.

J.M. Keynes is often inaccurately credited with having forced the first major breach in this theory. While he did purport to show that Say's Law was an inappropriate basis for a theory of unemployment,[9] he had many distinguished predecessors, including most socialists after Marx. It was William Beveridge, however, who popularized the idea that unemployment was, in part, a systemic problem. Beveridge had joined the British Board of Trade on a temporary basis in July 1908 and a year later became the director of labour exchanges. It was in that capacity that he helped design the first British UI program in 1911.

Beveridge's contribution came in his 1909 book *Unemployment, A Problem of Industry*. The title suggested its theme, since Beveridge was determined to analyse the "maladjustment between the supply of and the demand for labour" from the point of view of the industrial system rather than the Poor Law or charitable administration. He asserted that unemployment "is not to be explained away as the idleness of the unemployable."[10] The weight of Beveridge's explanation of unemployment fell on temporary labour market adjustment imperfections, such as declining trades and seasonal cycles, but more importantly on each trade's normal need for labour reserves to meet economic fluctuations evident even in prosperous times.[11] Industrialism produced unemployment as a necessary consequence of its own dynamism but also needed reserve pools of labour that could flow into new endeavours.

Beveridge's arguments led him to conclude that the problem of unemployment was essentially one of organization: the unemployed should be assisted and supported while shifting from one sector or trade to another. His solutions focused on better labour market information and placement services, along with a UI scheme. Whereas Keynes was to argue that a capitalist economy could settle at a low employment equilibrium, Beveridge saw unemployment as largely frictional. Nevertheless, he took the mainstream discussion of unemployment beyond the level of individual failing to that of a feature of the industrial system itself. Beveridge's conceptual revolution only echoed or slightly preceded similar changes in Europe and North America.[12]

Despite this significant change of view, UI remains one of the most controversial social programs in the modern welfare state. There are perhaps two reasons for this, both essential for grasping the conceptual foundations of UI. The first is that UI was the first social program that supported those otherwise physically capable of and available for work. Programs for the elderly, single mothers, children, and the handicapped are generally tolerated because it is widely assumed that these groups cannot easily support themselves. There is a lingering suspicion, however, that a large portion of those on UI are simply unwilling to work.[13] One of the most extensive surveys of Canadian attitudes to UI found, for example, that 80 per cent of the respondents believed that the program was being abused.[14]

A more sophisticated and less accusatory version of this view is that UI, like other insurance programs, increases the incidence of the risk being insured, since the cost of incurring the risk is reduced.[15]

The second reason why UI has been and will remain controversial is its unique relationship to the productive process and the role of employers and employees in that process. J.M. Becker, a leading student of American UI programs, said that a

reason for the distinctive position of unemployment insurance in the social security scheme is that it is more closely intertwined than other programs, even than workmen's compensation, in the competitive market process and comes closer to being an integral part of the industrial machine. Unemployment insurance pays benefits to potential workers – rather than to widows, children, the aged, the sick, the disabled – and this, besides raising the difficult problems of maintaining initiative, affects the bargaining power of labor. It affects the bargaining power of labor by affecting the main brake on the use of that power, unemployment. Unemployment benefits diminish, as they are intended to diminish, the pressure on the unemployed to take other, less desirable jobs. Unemployment benefits also diminish a social pressure that tends to limit strikes, namely the dissatisfaction of those thrown out of work by the strikes of others.[16]

These features of UI help explain why it was one of the last major social insurance programs introduced by the Western welfare state. It also suggests why UI has been an object of such animated debate and even conflict between employers and employees. As we will note in a subsequent chapter, UI was perceived to convey advantages to both the unemployed and the working classes generally in Canada, because of the ways in which it altered the balance of power in the labour market.

To recapitulate, UI is a fundamental product of the broad historical development of the Western welfare state; indeed, as a social insurance program that perhaps more than others favours labour over capital, it may be one of its best expressions. On another plane of development, however, UI had to await the twentieth-century concept of "involuntary unemployment," or unemployment created by the natural rhythms of an advanced industrial economy. The concept's victory was never complete, and so UI remains a controversial and contested program because of its support of the able-bodied.

INTERNATIONAL HISTORY

The development of UI in Europe and North America exemplifies the broader forces mentioned in the preceding section. This development passed through two distinct phases, the first being UI's pre-history to roughly 1920, and the second, its history from that date to the present. The first period was distinguished by substantial social experimentation. Trade unions, municipalities, and industrial employers devised various schemes to compensate the unemployed. The second phase has seen the emergence of national plans – UI underwent its conceptual revolution and became a state program. The national plans constructed in the second phase built upon the early experimentation in the nineteenth century.

The first recorded UI program was in Basle, Switzerland, in 1789. It was a municipal system inspired by the town's lacemakers, but it collapsed after a few years.[17] For almost a century afterwards, the only UI plans in Europe were provided directly by trade unions. The first was established by the English foundrymen's union in 1831 and soon became a model for others of its type in Europe.[18] In the United States, the New York Printers' Local devised a similar union plan in the same year, but it did not spread much beyond the printing, baking, and lace trades, where the incidence of unemployment was quite low and wages were sufficiently high to support reasonable contributions.[19] The British "friendly societies" had trouble establishing programs because better-paid workers were reluctant to join, leaving a membership of "high-risk" contributors.[20] An essential principle behind UI was "risk pooling," but it was difficult to devise plans attractive to both low- and high-risk contributors.

These limitations in trade union plans led to limited public support through municipally aided voluntary schemes. The first such scheme was in Berne, Switzerland, in 1893. The municipal authorities established a fund to which any worker, unionized or not, could make voluntary contributions. This system spread through Switzerland and to Germany, but it was not widely adopted because its voluntary character disproportionately attracted high risks. In 1895 the Swiss municipality of St Gall instituted the first compulsory UI scheme, whereby all workers earning less than a stated amount were required to affiliate and contribute. Regularly employed workers were reluctant to join, and the plan was bankrupt by 1897.

Other European municipalities tried a different approach in subsidizing private UI schemes established by trade unions. Dijon and Limoges implemented such schemes in 1896 and 1897, but the most widely copied model was devised by the Belgian town of Ghent in 1901. Under the "Ghent system," towns granted annual subsidies amounting to as much as 75 per cent of benefits distributed under private UI plans in the previous year. The trade unions administered the plans, even to the point of verifying the genuineness of the unemployment. The "Ghent system" spread throughout Europe, until gradually provincial and state governments provided subsidies as well. In 1905, France became the first country to apply the Ghent system at the national level, with national subsidies.

Nationally subsidized voluntary plans along the Ghent model were the favoured vehicle in Europe until the 1920s. France's legislation in 1905 was followed by Norway (1906), Denmark (1907), the Netherlands (1916), Finland (1917), Spain (1919), Belgium (1920), and Switzerland (1924). Sweden and Iceland implemented voluntary plans in 1934 and 1936, respectively. Subsidies generally amounted to between one-half and two-thirds of benefits. The plans in all these countries were frequently amended, especially during the Depression. All the countries, except Sweden, Denmark, and Finland, eventually adopted compulsory programs. Switzerland has a mixed system; the large majority of cantons operate compulsory plans while a few have voluntary schemes. The chronology of these developments is summarized in the Figure.

Britain was the first country in the world to implement a national, compulsory UI program, in 1911, and with some lag and some changes, its legislation became the model for all national plans except the Scandinavian ones, which clung to the voluntary approach. Britain's lead was not followed until 1919 (by Italy), but thereafter most plans were compulsory: Austria (1920), the Soviet Union (1922), Poland (1924), Bulgaria (1925), Germany (1927), Yugoslavia (1927), the United States (1935), South Africa (1937), Canada (1940), Greece (1945), and Japan (1947). Since Canada's UI program was strongly influenced by British and to a lesser extent American experience, some description of these plans would be useful.

Britain's scheme was established by part II of the National Insurance Act of 1911; part I contained provisions for sickness and disability insurance. While sickness insurance met with opposition from the medical profession and the friendly societies, the UI portion of the act was less controversial.[21] This was partly because of the establishment, in 1908, of a national system of labour exchanges, which seemed a natural first step towards a broader labour market strategy. While the German sickness funds were the model for Britain's National Insurance Act, the UI portion of the act was less derivative, because Germany had no UI program at the time. The British plan cautiously built upon the experience of the trade unions and friendly societies, relying on them for actuarial estimates and even some administration. Initially the program covered only seven skilled trades with approximately 2.5 million workers. Contributions came from employees, employers, and the state. Benefits were paid on a flat rate (German sickness benefits were graduated, or earnings-related), and various devices such as waiting periods, relatively short duration of benefits, and penalties for voluntary quits and refusals to find work were included to discourage malingering.

Once in place, the British UI program did not face fundamental challenge until the 1920s. The legislative response in those years eventually bankrupted and discredited the scheme, and these lessons were later carefully noted in Canada. As unemployment increased in the post-First World

FIRST UNEMPLOYMENT BENEFIT LAW THIRTY-SIX SELECTED COUNTRIES

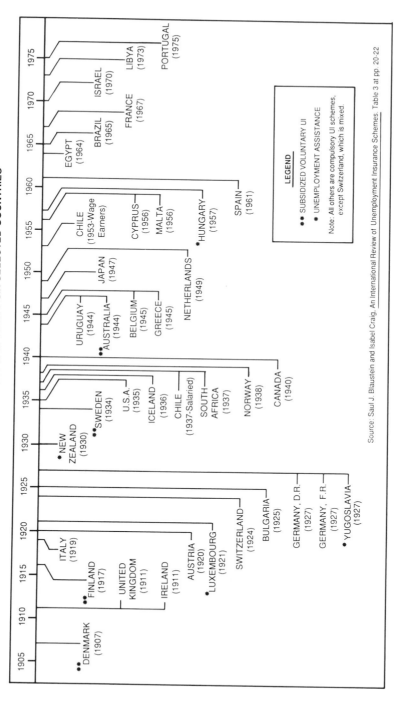

LEGEND

** SUBSIDIZED VOLUNTARY UI

* UNEMPLOYMENT ASSISTANCE

Note: All others are compulsory UI schemes, except Switzerland, which is mixed.

DENMARK (1907) **
FINLAND (1917) **
UNITED KINGDOM (1911)
ITALY (1919)
IRELAND (1911)
AUSTRIA (1920)
LUXEMBOURG (1921) *
SWITZERLAND (1924)
BULGARIA (1925)
GERMANY, D.R. (1927)
GERMANY, F.R. (1927)
YUGOSLAVIA (1927) *
NEW ZEALAND (1930) *
SWEDEN (1934) **
U.S.A. (1935)
ICELAND (1936)
CHILE (1937-Salaried)
SOUTH AFRICA (1937)
NORWAY (1938)
CANADA (1940)
URUGUAY (1944)
AUSTRALIA (1944) **
JAPAN (1947)
BELGIUM (1945)
GREECE (1945)
NETHERLANDS (1949)
CHILE (1953-Wage Earners)
CYPRUS (1956)
MALTA (1956)
HUNGARY (1957) *
SPAIN (1961)
EGYPT (1964)
BRAZIL (1965)
FRANCE (1967)
ISRAEL (1970)
LIBYA (1973)
PORTUGAL (1975)

1905 1910 1915 1920 1925 1930 1935 1940 1945 1950 1955 1960 1965 1970 1975

Source: Saul J. Blaustein and Isabel Craig, An International Review of Unemployment Insurance Schemes. Table 3 at pp. 20-22.

War recession, Britain's UI program was broadened and extended until it could no longer bear the weight of its new responsibilities. In 1920 coverage was greatly extended to include all manual workers except domestics, agricultural labourers, and all non-manual workers earning more than a certain minimum. In 1921 the flat-rate benefit was extended to provide special payments for dependants. In the same year, the government authorized "uncovenanted benefits," whereby those with inadequate contributions or those who had exhausted their previous benefits would receive some means-tested assistance on the assumption that they would "repay" the plan later when working again. This was a major departure from insurance principles and eventually resulted in 1933 in the plan supporting more claimants under the means-tested portion than under the insurance portion.[22] On the recommendation of the Royal Commission on Unemployment Insurance, the British government in 1934 specifically limited UI to short-term unemployment and created a separate, means-tested unemployment assistance program for the long-term or chronically unemployed. This remained the framework for British policy thereafter.

The American experience with UI was instructive to Canada as well, though less influential than Britain's. Unlike Britain, the United States implemented its UI program (in 1935) in the face of high unemployment and at a time when voluntary relief agencies, cities, and even state governments were financially burdened.[23] Like Canada, the American federal government had to extend financial assistance, first through loans from the Reconstruction Finance Corporation and then through the direct financing of relief by the Federal Emergency Relief Administration. The American antecedents to UI were quite different from Britain's. Whereas as many as 680 British trade unions were paying unemployment benefits in 1908, in April 1931 the American Bureau of Labor Statistics found only 3 national unions and 45 local unions with established unemployment benefit plans. There were some joint employer-employee plans, but these were not widespread.

In the United States, as in Canada before the 1940 constitutional amendment, UI was not an area of federal jurisdiction. Legislative development therefore had to await action at the state level. UI legislation was introduced in 1916 in the Massachusetts legislature and in New York in 1921. But the first state UI program to be implemented was Wisconsin's, in 1932; various UI bills had been introduced in the legislature since 1921, all similar to that state's workers' compensation program.[24] Wisconsin's 1932 legislation set a pattern, stimulating a flurry of 52 bills in 17 states.

Despite this activity, few states actually passed bills into law, since it was widely argued that any one state that imposed a UI scheme on employers would lose investment to states without such plans. Many states would not proceed until others had, and this paralysed movement. Washington, DC's, negligible interest in the UI issue also stalled state initiatives. By 1928, however, the Senate Committee on Education and Labor was holding hearings on UI, and in 1931 the Senate agreed to appoint a Select Committee on Unemployment Insurance. UI was debated for the next four years, with disagreements focused primarily on whether the federal government had the constitutional authority to impose a national plan on the states. Moreover, the American Federation of Labor had to be won over from its traditional distrust of government social security legislation and its official position that the best remedy for unemployment was reduction of the work day.[25]

The 1935 Social Security Act neatly circumvented some of the traditional problems facing UI implementation in the United States. Adopting a ploy used in the 1926 Federal Estate Tax, title IX of the act provided for an excise tax on employers equal to 1 per cent in 1936, 2 per cent in 1937, and 3 per cent in 1938 and thereafter. However, up to 90 per cent of this tax could be written off against equal contributions to a state UI plan that met certain minimal national standards. Washington was also prepared, under title III of the act, to make grants to the states to assist them with administration. In one stroke, the federal government removed the major impediment to single states embarking on UI programs. This structure remains to this day, and each state has its own UI program.

Canada learned from British and American experience, as it did from other European schemes. Canadian policy-makers were aware, by the 1930s, of the failures of the St Gall and British compulsory programs, the US debates over constitutional responsibility, and the need to have a national dimension to UI. When Canada's turn came, voluntary plans were not seriously considered, since the trade union base for their implementation did not exist. It was primarily the British design and the American example of the New Deal that influenced Canadian developments.

DESIGN AND STRUCTURE

To this point, I have avoided detailed discussion of generic features of UI in favour of outlining its conceptual and historical foundations. Subsequent chapters, however, will address shifts and changes in the Canadian legislation, as well as the sometimes technical arguments that supported or opposed these changes. We therefore need some means of usefully organizing the most important program features of UI.

UI is, in theory, only one way of dealing with unemployment and the financial losses that it causes. Alternatives range from work relief and special cash payments to retraining and fiscal stimulus to the economy. Typically, however, the key alternatives are work relief (or in modern parlance, job creation) and special payments. These are usually distinguished from UI by their emergency and ad hoc character, their generally lower level of wage replacement, and, at least for special payments or poor relief, their punitive administration. Finally, the state is usually entirely or predominantly responsible for these programs.[26]

UI's prime goal, as social insurance, is to alleviate hardship experienced by workers during periods of unemployment. It insures against a particular and specific risk: the loss of wages due to involuntary unemployment. UI does not insure against unemployment per se, since many people, such as students, retirees, and homemakers, are voluntarily unemployed in the sense that they are not participating in the wage economy. By insuring income lost due to unemployment, all UI programs assume that the claimant is still in search of remunerative work. All UI programs insure against this risk as a matter of right, so that if claimants meet certain qualifying conditions they receive benefits without regard to their real financial circumstances or needs. This means that claimants sometimes receive more in UI benefits than they would be granted under a means-tested program. In theory, the provision of benefits as a matter of right should remove the stigma of charity attached to a means-tested program.

One other special characteristic of UI deserves mention: the principle of "risk pooling." This is a basic feature of most social insurance and refers simply to the inclusion of both high- and low-risk individuals within the program. Without this pooling, UI programs with disproportionate coverage of high-risk categories face bankruptcy, as in Berne and St Gall in the nineteenth century. An interesting corollary to this principle is that UI programs have an expansionist dynamic, insofar as more stable and generous programs may be founded on broader coverage. This dynamic may conflict with other principles that would restrict UI to selected occupations.

UI programs have come to contain a number of sometimes inconsistent policy goals. UI is both an income security program and a labour market program. That it has been so from its early history is clear from the close association between UI and state-run employment offices. Generous income maintenance can, however, contradict some labour market goals, insofar as it may impede the labour mobility desired by the other.

Modern UI programs across the world may be seen to have four broad sets of goals.[27] The first is to assist individual, unemployed workers. UI should provide orderly and reliable cash subsistence that adequately replaces wages lost due to unemployment. It should permit the unemployed worker to take full advantage of accumulated skills and experience, by not having to accept a job out of desperation. UI is, in terms of these goals, meant to be a temporary means of support. The very poor, the chronically unemployed, and the incapable should be supported by other programs.[28]

A second set of goals is to improve manpower use, or at least not to hinder the mobility and supply of labour. These goals are met by limiting the duration and level of benefits, exposing unemployed workers to job opportunities, and using UI more deliberately to retrain workers. These goals have become more important within the last decade in Canada and elsewhere, as Western economies face substantial geographical and occupational shifts in their labour forces. A recent development has been to use UI funds, originally conceived as income maintenance, to pay employed workers or retrain unemployed ones.[29]

A third set of goals is stabilization of the use and supply of labour. Most UI schemes contain devices designed to encourage employers to retain underemployed labour instead of laying it off. These devices, such as experience rating, are usually quite weak, but some countries (principally the United States) rely on them extensively. Conversely, UI can retain pools of labour for seasonal or irregular employment where its absence would induce unemployed workers to seek jobs elsewhere. This goal may not be entirely accepted, but the high re-employment rates of many UI recipients seems to bear out its existence.[30]

Finally, UI tries to achieve goals of economic stability. Until recently it was assumed that UI benefits, because they are typically contra-cyclical (increasing during downturns and decreasing during upswings), help sustain purchasing power and may actually serve as an "automatic stabilizer" pushing the economy back along a growth path.[31] More recent economic analysis suggests that UI has relatively small contra-cyclical effects, and more attention is being paid to labour market disincentives than to economic stabilization effects.

All UI programs, voluntary or compulsory, early or recent, may be analysed in terms of five features: coverage, eligibility, benefits, financing, and administration.

Coverage

As mentioned, there are advantages to wide coverage, because both low and high risks can be pooled to improve the actuarial basis of a plan.[32] The early history of all UI programs, however, saw quite restricted coverage, to either selected industries or occupations, with wider and finally universal coverage coming only gradually. While one part of the explanation for this is the administrative challenge of full coverage, there were also reasons of principle.

Workers under a wage contract face the possibility that their contract might be terminated, and so wage employees are a category eligible for coverage. Self-employed individuals are not, however, since at least in theory their employment depends entirely on their own efforts. In the early stages of UI, almost all countries extended coverage to employees in basic industries such as manufacturing, mining, and commerce (though some countries had separate UI plans for some occupational groups such as railwaymen or miners). The seasonality, dispersion, and small incomes of agricultural employees led to their exclusion from most early plans and many current ones.

There are several other principles of exclusion that served at one time to restrict coverage. Relatively permanent or stable categories of employment such as government service or teaching were excluded in many early plans because there seemed little risk to insure against. Highly paid employment was often excluded as well, on the view that individuals in this category were less likely to be unemployed and more likely to have sufficient private means to sustain themselves during unemployment. Seasonal, occasional, and part-time workers were often excluded because of the difficulty of establishing whether unemployment was really involuntary.

In terms of coverage, by 1955 Canada's UI program was one of a group of more restrictive ones in a sample of 15 countries with compulsory plans.[33] The lack of comparative coverage statistics makes judgments hazardous, but it would seem that at least half of the 15 countries had more liberal provisions in 1955. By 1975, however, in a sample of 22 countries, Canada's UI program was among the 5 with the fewest restrictions.[34]

Eligibility

Simple coverage of an occupational group or industry is not enough to guarantee that its employees are eligible to receive benefits. As mentioned earlier, people may be unemployed for a variety of reasons, and UI does not insure against all of these. UI's guiding principle is that only wage loss due to involuntary unemployment is insurable under the program. This principle is the foundation for the following eligibility requirements.

First, claimants should be physically able to work, since UI programs presume that if a claimant is offered a suitable job at any time during a period of unemployment he or she will be able to perform it. In practice, as UI programs in Canada and elsewhere evolved, they have sometimes come to include sickness or maternity benefits, but the bulk of claimants still must meet this criterion.

Second, the claimant must be willing to work and available for work. These are, to a degree, psychological variables and therefore difficult to verify, but most UI programs insist that claimants actively seek work. The verification problems for this eligibility criterion are formidable and are the foundation of much of the discretionary and at times punitive administration of UI programs. The best way to verify that a worker is able, willing, and available on a continuing basis is through registration at an employment exchange and insistence on a minimum number of job searches. However, the claimant has some discretion, too: no UI program insists that claimants simply take *any* job. The usual phrase is "suitable employment," meaning a job that pays roughly what the claimant's previous job did and involving roughly the same skills and tasks. This is intended to protect workers from exploitation but also to conserve societal investments in human resources by trying, within reason, to match skills with requirements in the labour market.

Third, there must be adequate contributions within some qualifying period of time. Contribution formulae can be quite complex, specifying a minimum number of weeks or hours of contributions within a given reference period (e.g. 10 weeks of contributions within the last 52 weeks), but the principles are universal. Since UI is social insurance, some employee contribution is expected in most programs, but the actual formula is also meant to verify that claimants are indeed regular, or "attached," members of the labour force. Though this principle has to some extent been eroded over the last 40 years, most UI programs still hold that it only makes sense to insure the "loss" of employment to those who previously were regularly employed.

These three major eligibility criteria suggest the typical grounds for disqualification under most UI programs. Voluntarily quitting a job (unless there is "just cause" as defined by legislation or regulation) is one. Dismissal because of misconduct may also forfeit a claim. In both these situations, the condition of unemployment is not entirely involuntary and thus may not (at least not in whole) be insured. Labour disputes create problems as well. Normally, striking workers or those who stand to gain directly from a work stoppage are disqualified, while workers further removed who are unemployed as a consequence of a strike may be eligible. Refusal to accept suitable work or working while on claim may also be grounds for disqualification.

It is vital to note that all these disqualifications inevitably contain substantial scope for interpretation and discretion. The notion that UI, as a social insurance program, confers benefits as a matter of *right* is only partially true. This right is constrained by numerous conditions, the meanings of which are determined by program administrators.

Benefits

The most important UI benefits have historically been cash payments and the assistance of employment exchanges in finding jobs. More recently, UI programs have started to support retraining and even job creation. The three key aspects of UI benefits are rates, duration, and waiting periods.

Benefit rates under UI programs are of two types, either flat-rate or graduated. The British system originally provided only flat-rate benefits, meaning that all claimants, regardless of previous earnings, received the same amount. Graduated, or earnings-related benefits, which now predominate, replace a given percentage (to a limit) of a claimant's wage or salary. Claimants will thus receive differing amounts depending on past earnings. Canada has always had a graduated scheme, with its attendant formulae determining the replacement rate itself, the means of calculating the claimant's previous average earnings, and any ceilings that might apply. To complicate matters further, Canada's early legislation also used a "wage class" method that divided earnings into a number of categories, each with its own replacement rate. Various supplementary benefits were also part of this complex structure, as they were in other countries. The ceilings on benefits usually are determined by limiting the previous employment earnings to be insured. In Canada, some maximum of "insurable earnings" has from time to time been designated, and replacement rates apply to this figure.

The duration of benefits is another critical point. Canada, like most countries, has had variable duration periods, depending on previous employment and contributions. Maximum duration is reserved for those with maximum attachment to the labour force, though in the 1970s the Canadian UI program began to consider national and regional unemployment rates. The paradox of rewarding long attachment with long UI benefit duration is that those who have greatest difficulty securing and retaining employment may receive the lowest benefits for the shortest time.

All UI programs have a waiting period before benefits are payable. In 1955 Canada's was typical of the rest in requiring approximately one week. By 1975 the Canadian waiting period of two weeks was the longest in the world. The waiting period has been compared to the deductible portion of most private insurance plans but also absolves UI from covering short spells of unemployment, which in the aggregate amount to a significant portion of the overall unemployment rate. This saves money as well as administrative energy.

Financing

As mentioned earlier, a key financing principle of UI is "risk pooling," which presumes that the financial stability of a plan can be buttressed by including low-risk as well as high-risk contributors. Unfortunately, few occupations are immune to unemployment, and so in theory even low-risk individuals may wish to enrol in plans. In practice, low-risk occupations usually have to be coerced to join.

There are usually three sources of revenue for UI plans: employees, employers, and the state. Some small additional revenue might be generated by investments of the UI fund. The United States is the only country to base its plan exclusively on employer contributions.[35] All others have a tripartite structure, usually with equal employer and employee contributions making up the bulk of UI funds. Employee contributions affirm the "insurance" character of UI but are likely to be regressive, bearing more heavily on low-income earners. Employer contributions, in some schemes, can act as an incentive to maintain employment, since an increase in layoffs may result in higher contributions. The state's financial contributions may be justified on the grounds that some part of unemployment is the result of deliberate policies aimed at economic goals that benefit the entire community, such as lowered inflation. One group in society therefore suffers in order that the rest benefit, and the collectivity has some responsibility to repay the sacrifice.

At another level, contributions establish a proprietary claim on the program. The state, for example, could hardly justify unilaterally altering a UI program completely funded by employers and employees. This underlines a pertinent point about UI: even as a state program, it is rooted more than most in initiatives and support from employers and employees. In the debates leading to the Canadian plan, for example, some trade unionists demanded a non-contributory plan, funded entirely by the state through a tax on wealth. They reasoned that since unemployment was the product of capitalism, let those who enjoy the fruits of that system pay for its dysfunctions. Another and ultimately dominant line of trade union thinking was that through contributions workers would in effect "buy" a right to control the program.

The form and specific rate of contribution need not detain us here. It is enough to know that employees are assessed a contribution that is some percentage of their earnings and that employer contributions are then set as a proportion of employee contributions within the firm. Normally the state pays some fixed portion of total employer and employee contributions. After 1971 the Canadian formula became more subtle, with Ottawa paying in whole for some benefits, in part for others, and not at all for the rest.

Administration

Countries face a range of choices on how to administer and implement their UI programs. The key variable in all of them is the degree of state control. Most countries, since they have national programs with national scope, administer UI through a national agency, department, or commission. Whatever form is used, the administrative agency responsible for UI is usually also responsible for employment offices. The decentralization and visibility of employment offices and UI administration are second only to schools and post offices. When Canada embarked on UI in 1940, it was well aware of the administrative challenges that lay ahead.

Canada, unlike Britain, decided to give administrative responsibility for

UI to a commission, which would report to the minister of labour. This was intended to insulate the program from political pressures similar to the ones that bankrupted the British UI program in the 1920s. The chairman of the commission has always been appointed by the government, with one representative each from employers and employees. A little-appreciated aspect of Canadian UI is that this commission structure was to reflect the fact that the program was managed by the state but substantially "owned" by employers and employees. A major but almost unnoticed development in Canadian UI has been the state's capture of the program, to the point where the commission acts largely as an advisory body on major policy decisions.

Conclusion

These five elements of UI – coverage, eligibility, benefits, financing, and administration – universally define its character as a social insurance program. In some ways UI resembles private insurance, which also pools risks, demands contributions, and assesses eligibility. UI is in some respects more lenient than private insurance, as with dependant's allowances and other benefits that address claimant's needs rather than simple contributions, but UI is also tougher in some respects, as in the variation of benefits depending on previous employment.

The next chapter sketches the legislative and regulative history of UI in Canada. More details will be provided in subsequent chapters as the different explanations for these developments are probed. Readers familiar with the program's history may wish simply to review the appendix, which gives a chronology of major developments.

CHAPTER THREE

Unemployment Insurance in Canada

The history of UI in Canada echoes the broader themes discussed in the previous chapter but also reflects unique Canadian circumstances. The early, pre-program debates focused on unemployment itself, whether it was a mass, involuntary phenomenon calling for state action. A further complication was jurisdiction: even if unemployment were admitted as a social, rather than an individual, problem, was insurance against unemployment a federal or a provincial responsibility?

The political dynamics of the program changed significantly after its establishment in 1940. With the program in place, few debated the need for UI. Instead, the question became how far the program could be extended without compromising its insurance principles. In fact, the history of UI in Canada is one of almost unbroken expansion and liberalization between 1940 and 1975, followed, however, by steady retrenchment. Two other themes in the program's post-1940 history were UI's relation to other labour market and income security programs and the effects of UI expansion or retrenchment on provincial social policy budgets.

EARLY EVOLUTION: 1914-40

Unemployment, in the modern sense, is a relatively recent feature of Canadian history. According to H.C. Pentland, permanent reserves of labour emerged only after the 1840s as a consequence of immigration, population increase, and the growth of a domestic market for manufactured products.[1] The depression in the later 1870s saw thousands out of work, many of them destitute because of the limited scope of public and voluntary assistance programs.[2] While the British North America (BNA) Act had little to say about those activities that now comprise the welfare state, by tradition municipalities were responsible for "relief," or aid to the poor and the unemployed. The early history of Canadian efforts to aid the indigent is thus a history of local institutions, voluntary charitable groups, and occasional, emergency assistance from provincial and federal governments. The emergence and eventual acceptance of UI had a double significance, centralizing a good deal of "relief" at the federal level and making it a regular and normal entitlement.

The First World War fuelled these developments insofar as it "expanded the government's responsibility for unemployment."[3] Unemployment rose dramatically in the 1913-14 depression, but Canadian governments argued that responsibility for relief, such as it was, should remain with municipalities. The war, however, induced Ottawa to establish a national system of employment offices, while Ontario appointed a Royal Commission on Unemployment in December 1914. Ottawa's action reflected the need for national coordination of war industries and their manpower requirements. Ontario's initiative stemmed from the widely held assumption that labour matters – and hence unemployment relief – were under provincial jurisdiction.

The Ontario commission's interim report recommended a strategy aimed at "organization of the Labour market."[4] It urged a provincial Department of Labour and system of employment offices, better occupational training in public schools, and a voluntary UI system. It estimated the average period of unemployment in 1914 for formerly fully employed workers at about 15 weeks. In the commission's view, the compulsory 1911 British UI system was possible there because labour union data permitted calculation of risk. No such data existed for Ontario, and so the interim report suggested that the provincial government provide subsidies equal to 20 per cent of unemployment benefits paid by voluntary associations of workingmen to their members. This followed the Danish and French models rather than the British, though the commission suggested that the newly appointed Department of Labour collect statistics on the causes and risks of unemployment.

The commission's 1916 final report fleshed out the details of its earlier proposals, providing data on unemployment and destitution in Ontario, relief methods, and unemployment in specific occupations. These investigations were influenced by William Beveridge's *Unemployment, A Problem of Industry* (1909), particularly in the firm distinction between the personal and impersonal causes of unemployment: "For unemployment resulting from trade depression, or the temporary dislocation of business, workingmen are not responsible."[5] The final report repeated the earlier recommendation on voluntary UI.

The war eased unemployment by 1916, but when it ended and the soldiers returned, the economy began once again to slide into recession. Ottawa responded with a Soldier Resettlement scheme and the 1918 Employment Offices Co-ordination Act.[6] The latter was a cost-shared program with the federal government subsidizing provincial employment offices (through a $150,000 annual grant and 50-50 sharing of costs of expanding provincial systems) and co-ordinating their activities on a national basis. According to Struthers, the Employment Service marked a turning point in Ottawa's view of unemployment as a temporary and essentially provincial problem to an industrial problem, national in scope. The Employment Service was to provide employment data and advice, a task zealously undertaken by its energetic first director, Bryce Stewart. The issue of employment offices became important later in the 1930s when UI was being considered seriously in Ottawa. First, the fact that these offices were provincially run reinforced a jurisdictional claim over the labour field. Second, most informed observers between the wars held that UI without co-ordinated labour market programs, administered through national employment offices, would be unworkable.

Three events in 1919 propelled UI briefly to the top of the political agenda. Canada signed a draft recommendation favouring state UI at the first International Labour Conference in Washington, DC; Canada's new Royal Commission on Industrial Relations supported UI in its majority report; and the Canadian Liberal party endorsed UI at its first national convention. The international agreement helped those urging adoption of UI in Canada against those (like William Lyon Mackenzie King) who resisted it. The royal commission, chaired by the chief justice of Manitoba, T.G. Mathers, was appointed in April 1919 to investigate industrial unrest across the country. Its July report listed ten causes, and chief among them were "unemployment and the fear of unemployment."[7] The committee's major recommendation was that the government consider "the question of making some provision by a system of State Social Insurance for those who through no fault of their own are unable to work, whether the inability arises from lack of opportunity, sickness, invalidity or old age. Such insurance would remove the spectre of fear which now haunts the wage earner and make him a more contented and better citizen."[8]

The report's other recommendations were also far-reaching: profit-sharing, minimum wages, a standard eight-hour day, the right to organize and bargain collectively, a scheme to elect more labourers to the federal legislature, better housing, and voluntary industry councils along the lines of the British Whitely Plan. A minority report argued that unemployment was largely a problem of the distribution of labour and recommended against UI because of its corrosive effect on initiative.[9]

The Liberal party was probably influenced by the Mathers Commission's report, released only five weeks before its own convention. Nonetheless, the Liberal Advisory Committee had been working independently on a UI resolution as early as 1916. Mackenzie King, who would win the party leadership and in 1921 form a minority government (relying on the Progressives), helped draft the historic Liberal resolution on social insurance: "So far as may be practicable having regard for Canada's financial position ... an adequate system of insurance against unemployment, sickness, dependence in old age, and other disability, which would include old age pensions, widows' pensions, and maternity benefits, should be instituted by the Federal Government in conjunction with the Governments of the several provinces."[10]

The momentum of 1919 was sustained briefly when Prime Minister Robert Borden instructed the Department of Labour to study UI. The department supported UI but was uncertain about Ottawa's authority to implement it. Its reservations echoed Arthur Meighen's, who succeeded Borden as prime minister in 1920. The deepening recession forestalled a new, untried, and costly program. Nevertheless, action was needed, and so in December 1920 the Meighen government proposed to pay one-third of municipal direct relief costs. The program was temporary, aimed at what Ottawa called a war-related employment crisis. Later, in January 1922, the new King government increased the level of assistance slightly, but the program was discontinued that summer.[11] At a Dominion-provincial conference later that year, both Ottawa and the provinces agreed that the crisis justifying their assistance was over. In normal times, unemployment was a municipal, not a provincial or federal problem. The Liberal government also reduced its Employment Service funding to a minimum in a general drive for fiscal restraint. By mid-decade, UI was far less favourably viewed in government circles than it had been immediately after the war. Ottawa continued throughout the 1920s to reject any permanent responsibility for unemployment relief.[12]

The issue refused to die, however, and on 16 March 1927, A.A. Heaps, a labour representative in Parliament, moved that the Commons Committee on Industrial and International Relations investigate the feasibility of social insurance for Canada. Defeated that year, the motion passed in 1928, and the committee addressed insurance against unemployment, sickness, and invalidity. Its 1928 report argued that UI was inevitable and endorsed a compulsory, contributory plan, provincially administered but supported by federal grants. Advised by the Justice Department that UI was a provincial matter, the committee urged consultations with the provinces.[13] The investigation continued in 1929, but the final report for that year revealed that "the provinces, on being consulted by the Department of Labour with regard to their attitude towards the establishment of a general scheme, do not appear to be prepared to take immediate action."[14]

Mackenzie King was defeated by R.B. Bennett's Conservatives in 1930, partly because Bennett had promised greater federal action against unemployment, which was once again on the rise and would remain high for 10 years. Bennett's key economic policies were increased tariff protection and the Relief Act of 1930. The latter promised $20 million to assist direct municipal relief, but only as long as municipalities paid 50 per cent and the provinces 25 per cent.[15] The act was to be a temporary response to a brief surge in unemployment; it acknowledged no continuing federal responsibility for the unemployed. Rather than diminish, the jobless ranks grew, and so relief acts were passed annually. The details varied, but as the unemployment problem grew, so did Ottawa's share of relief expenditures and so did the calls for UI, which seemed a way out of the impasse. Prime Minister Bennett encouraged some of this pressure by promising in 1931 and 1932 to implement UI. A Dominion-provincial conference was held on 17 January 1933 on the question of a constitutional amendment to give Ottawa jurisdiction over UI. The conference failed.[16]

The example of the American New Deal persuaded Bennett and his advisers that a change of course was necessary, and so Ottawa reduced, under provincial objections, its contributions to relief in 1934-5 in order to implement federal public works and UI. A UI scheme was drawn up, and the provinces were approached for their support on a constitutional amendment, but Quebec and Ontario refused. In January 1935 Bennett delivered a series of radio broadcasts, and in June the Employment and Social Insurance Act was passed. The act established a UI scheme and took preliminary steps towards health insurance. Modelled on the recently revised British UI legislation, the act proposed a flat-rate benefit scheme, based on worker, employer, and state contributions. Approximately one-third of the labour force would have been ineligible under the program, principally from seasonal and low-skill industries. A commission, with employee and employer representatives, was to administer the program. The commission was appointed and began to organize the program, but these steps were discontinued after 1935, when the Bennett government was defeated and Mackenzie King returned to power.

King had been careful over the years not to oppose UI on principle – he scarcely had any choice, since his own party had, with his help, endorsed it. His objections were constitutional: UI was a provincial responsibility and no federal government could unilaterally impose it. Bennett had had his doubts as well, but in public (during the radio broadcasts) argued that Ottawa had sufficient powers under the BNA Act's peace, order, and good government clause and in taxation. King disagreed and referred the Employment and Social Insurance Act along with the rest of the "Bennett New Deal" legislation to the Supreme Court of Canada in 1936. The complicated set of eight laws, ranging from the Limitations of Hours of Work Act to the Natural Products Marketing Act, was not disallowed in toto by the court. Some laws (e.g. the Farmers Credit Arrangement Act and the Dominion Trade and Industry Commission Act) were upheld in whole or in part, but others, including the Employment and Social Insurance Act, were struck down. Ottawa appealed to the Judicial Committee of the Privy Council in London, which in 1937 upheld the Supreme Court judgments.[17]

This decision affirmed provincial authority over UI and made constitutional amendment necessary if Ottawa were to implement the program.

King continued the relief acts but wanted better accountability for federal expenditures. He established the National Employment Commission in April 1936 to review provincial expenditures, attach conditions to federal subsidies, and generally find ways to reduce relief expenditures. Despite its conservative members and mandate, the commission in 1938 surprised almost everyone, and certainly Mackenzie King, with its strong recommendation that Ottawa assume responsibility for relief *and* UI. Its 1937 interim report had urged home and farm improvement programs, assistance for low-rental housing, and training grants, but also reduced expenditures on public works and firm conditions on federal relief grants to "employables."[18]

The commission's 1938 final report was substantially different. Ottawa had been negotiating with the provinces since 1937, and so the commission's endorsement of UI was not radical; the report also argued, however, "that the establishment of a national system of Unemployment Insurance would necessitate a supplementary system of Unemployment Aid to meet those phases of unemployment need which experience abroad has shown cannot be covered by Unemployment Insurance."[19] In short, a coherent UI scheme implied a co-ordinated labour market and relief system under national control. This would have widened Ottawa's responsibilities and expenditures well beyond anything contemplated by King or Bennett.

King had appointed the Royal Commission on Dominion-Provincial Relations in April 1937 and knew that it too was considering UI. Correspondence with the provinces had revealed opposition from premiers Dysart (New Brunswick), Duplessis (Quebec), and Aberhart (Alberta). By 1940, with Duplessis replaced by a Liberal government, King was able to negotiate a unanimous provincial agreement on a constitutional amendment to the BNA Act transferring authority over UI. The National Employment Commission and the Royal Commission on Dominion-Provincial Relations had simply served to express what had become widely accepted by the end of the Depression: unemployment was national in scope, UI would deal with it in a more humane and efficient manner than relief, and Ottawa should be in charge of UI.

ESTABLISHMENT AND EXTENSION: 1940 TO DATE

As the preceding suggests, UI's prehistory in Canada was marked by debates over the proper balance of federal and provincial authority in the labour field, as well as over the technical design of a UI scheme that would confer advantages to the work-force without bankrupting business or the country. The details of these debates will be discussed in subsequent chapters.

After 1940 the nature of the debate changed and narrowed somewhat, since Ottawa had assumed responsibility for UI and a concrete plan was in place. The central issue was the program's insurance character: how far could coverage be extended, benefits increased, and eligibility requirements relaxed before the program became welfare, not insurance?

In July 1940 the British Parliament passed an amendment to the BNA Act placing UI among the list of federal powers by the addition of section 91.2.a. After committee review and discussion of the proposed bill in July, the Canadian House of Commons debated and passed the Unemployment Insurance Act in August 1940.[20] It took some time to establish the administrative machinery, since provincial employment offices were transferred to the new Unemployment Insurance Commission, and so contributions became payable only on 1 July 1941, while benefits could be collected only as of 27 January 1942. The main features of the 1940 UI act may be summarized with the criteria developed in chapter two: coverage, eligibility, benefits, financing, and administration.

Coverage

As in most other UI schemes, the Canadian legislation began by stating that all private-sector employment and all public-sector employment (provincial employees with the consent of the provincial government), as well as some forms of employment outside Canada (by insured employees for Canadian employers), were insurable. It then listed 21 specific types of employment that were exempted from coverage, the most prominent being agriculture, horticulture and forestry, fishing, most lumbering and logging, transportation by water or by air, domestic service, hospital employees, teachers, Government of Canada employees appointed under the Civil Service Act or certified as permanent, municipal and provincial employees unless their employers agreed, and generally any employment earning more than $2,000 per year. Roughly 42 per cent of the labour force was covered; the rest fell into the exempted categories. The Unemployment Insurance Commission was empowered to include exempted categories of employment for insurance coverage if the continued exemption created anomalies.

Eligibility

In order to collect benefits, insured workers had to demonstrate that they were indeed unemployed, capable, and available for suitable work and that they had made proper contributions in insured employment for at least 180 days during the two years immediately preceding the claim. Sixty of these contributions had to be made since the last day of previous benefit in the twelve-month period immediately preceding the current claim. Claimants were not eligible for benefits if they had an interest in or participated in a work stoppage and could also be disqualified for up to six weeks if they were fired for misconduct, quit voluntarily without just cause, or refused suitable employment.

Benefits

The conceptual basis of benefits under the 1940 act was that only wage loss due to inability to find suitable work could be compensated. Wage loss due to illness, injury, pregnancy, or retirement was not. The plan did pay slightly higher benefits to those with dependants, however, even though contributions were determined solely by wage levels. The regular weekly benefit rate was 34 times the average weekly contributions made by the claimant; the rate for those with dependants was set at 40 times the average contribution. Wage earners were divided into eight income classes for purposes of contributions and seven for benefits (class "0" had its contributions paid on its behalf by the employer). The weekly benefit rate for single persons ranged from $4.08 for "class 1" employees to $12.24 for "class 7" employees. The respective rates for those with dependants were $4.80 per week and $14.40 per week. These graduated benefits mirrored the different standards of living among classes of employees. On average, the lowest-paid workers could expect UI benefits to replace 63 per cent of their previous earnings, while the highest-income class had 37 per cent of its earnings replaced. Since higher-paid employees made larger UI contributions, redistribution across income classes was built into the program. There was a nine-day waiting period, and no benefits were payable for the first day of a week unless unemployment lasted the full week. The maximum benefit duration was one day of benefits for each five daily contributions in the last five years, or one year for someone with five years of continuous employment. This maximum was reduced by one day for each three days of benefit received in the previous three years.

Financing

Employers and employees each, in aggregate, contributed equally to the plan. The government's share was 20 per cent of total private-sector premiums and all administrative costs. Contributions went into a special account of the Consolidated Revenue Fund entitled the Unemployment Insurance Fund. Surplus monies from the fund could be invested, and shortfalls could be covered by government advances.

Administration

The 1940 act was administered by an Unemployment Insurance Commission reporting to the minister of labour. It consisted of three commissioners appointed by cabinet: a chief commissioner and one representative each for employers and employees. The commission was empowered to make regulations to enforce the act, and it also administered the newly created network of national employment offices. The cabinet appointed, in addition to the commission, an Unemployment Insurance Advisory Committee consisting of a chairman and four to six other members. The advisory committee's major responsibilities were to report annually on the financial condition of the fund, on any changes required to bring it into balance, and on eligibility criteria and benefit and contribution rates. Finally, the act provided appeal procedures for claimants with grievances against the commission: there were to be regional courts of referees (with employer and employee representatives and a chairman) to which claimants could appeal commission decisions; if not satisfied, they could appeal to the umpire, appointed from among the ranks of the judges of the Exchequer Court of Canada and the provincial superior courts.

The original act was frequently amended, and it was completely overhauled in 1955.[21] The 1955 changes consolidated previous amendments and made some technical changes as well. Supplementary benefits (introduced in a 1950 amendment to assist seasonal workers) were integrated as seasonal benefits; the entrance requirement was slightly relaxed, as were requalifying conditions. The maximum benefit duration was reduced from one year to 36 weeks, but the minimum benefit period was increased from 6 to 15 weeks. The benefit rate averaged 50 per cent across all earnings categories, with higher rates for lower categories. By 1955, slightly more than 75 per cent of wage and salary earners in Canada were covered by UI.[22] In large part this broader coverage was the result of gradual inclusion of seasonal workers, something that the commission generally opposed but that was demanded by the government.

The 1955 act liberalized the UI program modestly. Passed in a period of relatively low unemployment (the average annual rate since 1946 had been 3 per cent), it was consequently strained during the 1957-62 recession (when average annual rates reached 7 per cent). High unemployment and more liberal provisions eventually reduced the UI fund to a slim reserve of $874,881 in 1964.[23] Government advances kept the fund solvent, but in 1961 a Committee of Inquiry into the Unemployment Insurance Act, chaired by E.C. Gill (an insurance executive), was appointed. Its report raised the curtain on almost a decade of investigation into the program. An interdepartmental review, including Finance, Labour, and Health and Welfare, submitted a report to the minister of labour on 25 March 1966.[24] Some of its recommendations were incorporated into the commission's 1968 report on the program.[25]

Though business and labour groups appeared before the Gill Committee, the program review conducted in the 1960s was largely internal to the federal government and took place within the context of developing an appropriate manpower policy. It was widely thought after the 1957-62 recession that manpower training and placement should be given higher priority in economic management.[26] Accordingly, the employment services formerly administered by the commission were transferred in 1966 to the newly created Department of Manpower and Immigration. By 1970, however, policy-makers were coming to see UI in the context of social policy as well.[27]

Proposed revisions were announced on 17 June 1970 in a White Paper entitled *Unemployment Insurance in the 70's*. The White Paper was referred to the Commons Standing Committee on Labour, Manpower and Immigration, which held 30 meetings from September to November 1970, received 53 submissions, and heard from 33 organizations. The new Unemployment Insurance Act, 1971, differed little from the White Paper, which contained the legislation's philosophical roots.

The White Paper was built on two premises. The first was that, in "keeping with a more realistic approach to social policy,"[28] a new UI act would have to contribute to a more equitable distribution of income in Canada, as well as offer services and not just cash benefits. Simple "welfare" through cash payments was not enough; the White Paper used the concept of the "service state." The second premiss was the imminence of "post-industrialism," an economic system marked by rapid technological change and labour market instability. Even formerly secure employment could be drawn into the vortex of rapid economic change. Automation would increase the incidence of unexpected, temporary layoffs. Public servants, teachers, skilled, and semi-skilled alike would be threatened. Aggregate unemployment rates would not increase much, but turnover within the ranks of the unemployed would accelerate.

The program deduced from these premisses would be more generous, with easier terms and wider services. UI was to be a more active program, assisting workers and encouraging them to deal with labour market adjustments: "A reoriented unemployment insurance program, however, can keep the door to the mainstream of society open. The combination of financial aid, plus complementary services provided by other government agencies designed to assist the worker to be reabsorbed quickly into the labour force, will help to save him from sinking into the quicksands of chronic unemployment."[29] The proposed revisions worried critics, principally because a more generous program could be more expensive and because higher UI benefits might reduce work incentives. The government responded by emphasizing the new mandatory provision of two interviews per claimant and cost estimates that suggested that the new program would not be any more expensive than the old.[30]

The Unemployment Insurance Act, 1971, was passed by the House of Commons on 14 June 1971. Benefit provisions took effect 27 June 1971, while coverage was extended as of 2 January 1972. A review of the key elements of the new act suggests that it substantially liberalized UI in Canada.

Coverage

Coverage was almost universal, at 96 per cent of the wage/salary-earning labour force, compared to 80 per cent before.

Eligibility

The new minimum entrance requirement for those without a previous claim was 8 insurable weeks in the last 52; for those with a previous claim, 8 insurable weeks since the beginning of the previous benefit week. This contrasted with the 1955 requirement of 30 insurable weeks in the last two years, 8 in the year preceding the claim.

Benefits

These were increased from an average of 43 per cent of insurable earnings, with an upper limit of $53 per week, to 66.6 per cent of insurable earnings, up to $100 per week. Benefits became taxable, and contributions tax-deductible. Minimum benefits of $20 per week were instituted, and a dependant's benefit rate of 75 per cent was paid to all claimants in extended benefit phases and to low-income earners in the initial phases. Sickness, maternity, and retirement benefits were payable to claimants with at least 20 weeks of insurable employment in the qualifying period. The new act had a complex five-phase structure that depended on previous contributions and the prevailing national and regional unemployment rates. In the initial benefit period a maximum of 8 weeks' benefit was available for claimants with 8 to 15 weeks of insurable employment; those claimants with up to 19 weeks' insurable employment received additional benefit weeks; those with 20 insurable weeks or more were eligible for a maximum of 15 weeks of benefits. If one were still unemployed after this initial phase, a second re-establishment phase of 10 benefit weeks automatically applied. The other three phases depended on labour force attachment, the regional unemployment rate, and the national unemployment rate. The maximum benefit duration was 51 weeks.

Financing

The old formula whereby the federal government paid 20 per cent of combined employer/employee contributions into a fund was replaced by an Unemployment Insurance Account. Private-sector contributions were to pay for administrative costs, sickness, maternity, and retirement benefits, as well as regular benefits in the first two phases up to a national unemployment rate of 4 per cent. The federal government was to pay, out of the Consolidated Revenue Fund, for all extended benefits and some regular benefits for national unemployment rates over 4 per cent. The act authorized the government to make advances of up to $800 million to the account.

Administration

At the time the act was passed there were no administrative changes. The commission continued to be responsible for the program, though it had to adopt more sophisticated procedures and computer technologies to enable it to deal with the more complex legislation. Later, in 1972, the commission began reporting to the minister of manpower and immigration, rather than the minister of labour, and this reflected the prevailing view that UI was an intimate part of labour market strategies.

This brief summary of the main features of the 1971 act shows that UI was considerably enhanced. Entrance requirements were relaxed, redistribution across income classes and regions was explicitly fostered, and various "income security" provisions (e.g. the dependants' rate and special benefits) were included, softening the strict insurance aspects of the program. These changes were accepted largely because they were thought to add no net costs to the government.

Various devices were included in the act to ensure that costs would not escalate. The waiting period was increased from one to two weeks, and the legislation made a distinction between "major attachment" claimants (with at least 20 weeks of insurable employment) and "minor attachment" claimants (with 8 to 19 weeks). Only major attachment claimants were eligible for special benefits, some extended benefits, and advance benefit payments (a lump sum payment of three weeks' benefits that the claimant could keep regardless of how quickly employment was found). And as mentioned earlier, mandatory interviews also served as a check.

Despite these features, the coercive aspects of the 1971 act were not prominent. The disqualification for voluntary quits, misconduct, job refusals, and other infractions was lowered from a maximum of six weeks to three (though benefits were deemed to have been paid for any weeks of disqualification).

The program was in trouble almost immediately. It received some criticism in the fall of 1971, with the Toronto *Globe and Mail* (6 September) going so far as to call it "immoral and stupid."[31] As evidence of cost miscalculations began to accumulate in the late summer and fall of 1972, however, the tone of public criticism sharpened. In the federal election campaign under way at about the same time, Prime Minister Trudeau himself denounced "freeloading." All through September and October, Bryce Mackasey, the minister of labour, defended UI in the newspapers and on the platform.[32] The Liberals were returned as a minority government, and some MPs blamed UI for the results.[33]

Legislative action had to be taken, but because the House was not sitting, Mackasey in October 1972 obtained a governor-general's warrant for $234 million for the UI account. On 17 January 1973, Robert Andras, the new minister of manpower and immigration, introduced Bill C-124 to remove the $800 million ceiling on government advances. He also introduced Bill C-125, to tighten up program administration, curb abuse, and raise entrance requirements for voluntary quits, misconduct firings, and job refusals. Bill C-125 was withdrawn on 29 October 1973 because of lack of support from the New Democratic Party (NDP) (the Liberals relied on the NDP to keep them in power).

Its parliamentary weakness and reliance on the NDP limited the government's ability to tighten the program through legislation. This was accomplished instead by the commission through its regulatory powers. The 1973 replacement of the separation certificate by the record of employment was one technique to this end,[34] as was the doubling of benefit control officers in the same year.[35] The average monthly disqualification rate jumped from 9.1 per cent of claims in 1972 to 12.2 per cent in 1973 and 14.5 per cent in 1974.[36]

In 1975 the commission intensified its control procedures by adding the Special Job Finding and Placement Drive (calling for mandatory interviews with claimants in occupations in high demand), mandatory preregistration with Canada Manpower offices to receive benefits, a new record of employment, and extended employer audits.[37]

Between 1975 and 1978, with its parliamentary majority restored in the 1974 federal election, the government introduced and passed three major revisions to the 1971 act. The first was Bill C-69, introduced in the House by Robert Andras in July 1975 and given royal assent in December. Its key features were the elimination of the 75 per cent dependency rate in favour of a standard benefit rate of 66.6 per cent, an end to the advanced benefit payment, doubling of the maximum disqualification rate to six weeks, and a new financing formula whereby the threshold for government contributions was set at a moving average of monthly national unemployment rates over the previous eight years.

The next major legislative revision was Bill C-27, introduced by Bud Cullen, the new minister of manpower and immigration, in December 1976 and finally passed in the House, under closure, on 19 July 1977, receiving royal assent the same month. This was a complex and far-reaching bill that not only sought to amend UI but also proposed the creation of a new Department of Employment and Immigration out of the former Unemployment Insurance Commission and Department of Manpower and Immigration. Commission and Manpower offices were combined into Canada Employment Centres, and the Unemployment Insurance Commission was replaced by the Canada Employment and Immigration Commission. The major UI amendments were the introduction of the variable entrance requirement, whereby the minimum period of insurable weeks needed to qualify for benefits was raised to a range of 10 to 14 weeks, depending on the regional unemployment rate; a reduction of the five phases of benefits to three, with the third, extended phase now tied entirely to regional unemployment rates; a reduction in the maximum entitlement of minor attachment claimants; and the "developmental" use of the UI account for work sharing and job creation.[38]

Bill C-14 was the last of the major amendments in the 1970s. Introduced by Bud Cullen in his new capacity as minister of employment and immigration in November 1978, it was passed by the House in December (under closure), receiving royal assent the same day. Its major amendments were a change in the minimum insurability formula to an hours basis rather than an incomes basis, thus reducing claims from people working few hours but at high rates; higher entrance requirements for repeaters, new entrants, and re-entrants; a reduction in the benefit rate to 60 per cent from 66.6 per cent; a shift of part of extended benefit costs from government to employers and employees; and a provision whereby high-income earners would pay back a portion of UI benefits received in the previous year.

At the close of the 1970s the program was once again under review, by both the commission and a departmental task force on unemployment insurance established by the minister. This review was undertaken in the context of developing a new manpower policy for the 1980s, and so the UI task force was twinned with one on labour markets. Both task forces reported in 1981.[39] The UI task force made several recommendations, all with the general goal of strengthening the labour market objectives of the program. This confirmed the emphasis of previous amendments in the 1970s. The task force recommendations were not implemented, however, because of the severe recession that gripped Canada 1980-3. The only major innovations were in work sharing; any substantial cuts in the program would have been difficult to defend in the face of rapidly rising unemployment rates. As well, the assumption underlying the recommendations that UI should assist and encourage labour flows from dying industries and occupations to growing ones was negated by an economy that seemed to be uniformly in decline.

In 1985 the Mulroney government appointed a Commission of Inquiry on Unemployment Insurance, headed by Claude Forget. The Forget Commission was embroiled in controversy immediately upon the release of its recommendations in December 1986, as four of its commissioners (the two labour and the two business representatives) issued dissents. The business dissents were minor, but the labour dissent amounted to an attack of the main report and Forget himself. The unprecedented ferocity of this dissent is explained by the magnitude of Forget's proposals. The majority report wished to restore to UI "its integrity as an insurance program."[40] It argued that the current program was inequitable because it treated claimants differently depending on where they lived (e.g. regionally extended benefits and the variable entrance requirement) and tried to do too many things, from creating jobs to supporting fishermen. Forget's guiding philosophy was that UI should be refocused on major attached claimants and treat them the same regardless of region. Monies saved would be redirected to job creation and income supplementation programs, which in Forget's view were better means for dealing with the special problems of young workers and the unemployed in depressed regions.

The most important of the commission's 53 recommendations were a new commitment to a human resource development strategy, which would include full employment as well as education and training; elimination of regionally extended benefits, to be replaced by income supplementation schemes; "annualization," a new method of calculating benefits whereby they would equal 66.6 per cent of total insurable earnings in the previous year and be paid in 50 weekly instalments, or less if employment were found; development of a cumulative employment account which would permit long-term attached claimants to build up certain UI "credits" to be used in specified circumstances; elimination of fishermen's benefits, to be replaced by a special income supplementation program; reconstitution of the commission as an autonomous crown corporation, at arm's length from government. These and other changes would save $3 billion, $2.8 billion of which would come from elimination of regionally extended benefits. While the cuts would affect all regions, Quebec and the Maritimes would suffer disproportionately.

Within hours of tabling the report, Employment Minister Benoît Bouchard announced that the government did not endorse the Forget proposals.[41] Instead, he asked the Commons Standing Committee on Labour, Employment and Immigration to review the Forget report. The committee submitted its report on 19 March 1987, and its 90 recommendations departed somewhat from Forget's approach. The minister responded on 15 May that the government would make no fundamental changes to UI.

PROGRAM TRENDS

Subsequent chapters will flesh out the preceding narrative and deal with explanations for major changes in Canadian UI over its more than 40-year history. But what trends underlie the events described above? In addition to legislative developments, what other features of the program deserve attention?

Table 2 summarizes some of the key features of the unemployment insurance acts of 1940, 1955, and 1971. This is a static representation that obscures many of the details, but it does afford an overview of the successive legislative regimes. Three defining features of UI are benefits, contributions, and disqualifications. Table 2 displays the different dimensions of these features.

TABLE 2
Comparison of Canadian UI Legislation, 1940, 1955, 1971

	Benefits				Contributions			Disqualifications		
Level[1]	Limit	Duration	Principle of calculation		Coverage	Principle of calculation	Source of income (%) Employees/Employers/State	Waiting period (days)	Maximum disqual. period	Qualifying period (wks)
1940 31.4% in	34 times average contrib.	1 day of benefit for each 5 daily contributions in last 5 years	7 wage classes Graduated		42% of labour force	8 wage classes Graduated (3.2% of lowest wage to 0.94% of highest)	40 40 20	9	6	180 daily contribs. in last 2 years of which 60 in last year
1949	for single 40 times average contrib. for dep.							1st day of week unless unemployed for full week		
1955 30.4% in	$23/wk for single	Min: 15 wks Max: 36 wks	9 wage classes		75% of labour force	10 wage classes	40 40 20	6	6	30 weekly contribs. in last 2 years of which 8 in last year
1961	$30/wk for dep. seasonal benefits		Graduated			Graduated (close to 1% of wage for all classes)				

TABLE 2 (Continued)

Benefits				Contributions			Disqualifications		
Level[1] Limit		Duration	Principle of calculation	Coverage	Principle of calculation	Source of income (%) Employees/Employers/State	Waiting period (days)	Maximum disqual. period	Qualifying period (wks)
1971 41.4% in		Max: 51 wks	5 phase benefit structure:	96% of labour force	Employee contrib. set at 0.90 cents a week for every $100 a week insurable earnings	Employer/employee: Regular benefits in first two phases for national unemployment rate up to 4%	14	3	8 weeks in last 52
1972	66.6% of insurable earnings for single 75% of insurable for dep.		(1) Initial benefits (8-15 wks) (2) Re-established initial benefit period (automatic 10 more wks) (3) Labour force extended benefits (up to 18 more wks for major attachment claimants)'			Sickness, maternity, retirement benefits		a week of disqualifica-tion now considered a week of benefits paid	20 weeks in last 52 to qualify for special bene-fits and labour force extended benefit
	Maximum: $100/wk.		(4) National extended benefits (up to 8 wks if national unemp. > 5%) (5) Regional extended benefit (up to 18 wks if regional unemp. rate > national		Employer contrib. set at 1.4 times employees'	Administration			
					Tax deduct-ible	Government: Regular benefits in first two phases for national unemployment rate over 4%			
						All extended benefits Training benefits Self-employed fisherman's benefits			

[1]Average weekly UI payments as percentage of average weekly wages and salaries

Benefits may be measured in a number of ways. For example, average UI payments per claimant tripled in real terms between 1949 and 1976. This represents a substantial increase when viewed within the terms of the program itself. When examined in relation to average wages and salaries, however, the trend is less clear. In 1949 average weekly UI payments per claimant were 31.4 per cent of the average weekly wage. They remained at this level or slightly above it until the end of the 1960s, when, partly as a consequence of the 1971 legislation, they increased to 41.4 per cent. The trend in the mid- and late 1970s was for this ratio to decline. The explanation for this stability is that while UI benefits were increasing in real terms, real wages and salaries were increasing too, at roughly the same rate. Only with the 1971 legislation did this "replacement ratio" grow dramatically.

The formula by which benefits are calculated has changed with every act. In spite of this, only the 1971 changes made a major difference to the replacement ratio. Earlier changes, while they increased benefit levels in real terms, only kept payments up with increases in wages and salaries. The 1971 changes, however, outpaced increases in wages and salaries and put Canada among the ranks of the world's most generous UI programs. The maximum benefit duration also increased from 36 weeks in 1955 to 51 weeks in 1971. Though the 1971 act had a lower minimum duration of 8 weeks as opposed to 15 weeks in 1955, the qualifying period was shorter. Since most unemployment is short-term, the minimum duration of UI benefits is a more important program indicator than maximum duration.

Another important program indicator is coverage. The original 1940 act covered about 42 per cent of the Canadian labour force. By 1955, both through intervening amendments and because of changes in the new act itself, that proportion had risen to 75 per cent. Shortly before the 1971 act was passed, UI coverage was close to 80 per cent. Essentially, UI had been growing over the years from a program that protected lower- and middle-income groups to one that covered upper-income groups as well (apart from the self-employed). The 1971 act simply ratified this development by extending UI coverage to previously exempt occupations such as government employment and teachers. At the time these were still relatively stable occupations, and policy-makers thought that they could use the contributions of these new groups to pay for the higher benefits payable under the program.

In addition to coverage, the other important feature of contributions is the formula and balance of private-sector and government financing for the program. Under both the 1940 and 1955 acts, the split had been 40 per cent from each of employers and employees and 20 per cent from the government. The 1971 act worked on the principle that Ottawa should be particularly responsible for unemployment above a given figure (originally 4 per cent) and for long-term unemployment. Regular and other benefits could be supported entirely from employer/employee contributions. This principle was thought to reflect a renewed government commitment to attaining full employment.

Finally, disqualifications have generally relaxed since 1940. The original act had a nine-day waiting period and a maximum of six weeks' disqualification. The 1955 act reduced the waiting period but kept the disqualification period intact. The 1971 act increased the waiting period to two weeks, among the longest in the world, but halved the disqualification period. It also made the grounds of disqualification clearer and less arbitrary.

Glancing back then across the history of Canadian UI, it seems clear that the program was considerably liberalized between 1940 and 1971. Benefits were higher, easier to get, and more varied. Virtually the entire working population came to be covered under the program. As a proportion of GNP, UI payments rose from 0.4 per cent in 1949 to slightly over 2 per cent by 1975. UI makes up a larger share of GNP in Canada than it does in most European countries and is relatively more important to the Canadian income security system. It became more closely aligned with manpower and labour market policies to the point where it is now a crucial feature of federal economic policy.

These are the long-term trends. Within them, however, there are numerous shifts and discontinuities. The passage of the 1940 act itself broke with almost two decades of procrastination. In 1956 Ottawa passed the Unemployment Assistance Act by which it made conditional grants to the provinces for a certain portion of their social assistance payments. The conceptual framework of manpower policy changed in the 1960s and coincided with a re-evaluation of UI that eventually led to the 1971 act. The mid-1970s saw major changes to UI that on the whole served to reduce benefits and increase disqualifications.

The following chapters will endeavour to explain the long-term as well as short-term trends with the help of society-centred and state-centred theories of the policy process.

PART TWO

Three Theories

CHAPTER FOUR

Capital v. Labour

The most influential society-centred theories of the policy process are neo-pluralism and neo-Marxism. They both stress the importance of organized economic interests – especially employer and employee groups – in the initiation, definition, and implementation of public policies. In this view, the content of public policy is explained best by tracing it back to the balance of political power among interested groups. The state more or less "registers" this balance of power and interests in the form of public policy. These approaches do not deny the play of other forces such as ideas and institutions, but they tend to stress group conflict.

While neo-pluralism and neo-Marxism share a common focus on the influence of producer groups, they have obvious and important differences. Marxism traditionally stressed the importance of economic factors and had an elaborate theory of classes and class struggle that illuminated at least those conflicts within which there was a discernible class interest. In North America, and to a lesser extent in Europe, Marxist political economy was opposed by theories emphasizing electoral or group politics. Electoral models of the political process argued the critical role of elections and party conflict in policy making. Theories of group politics, while not dismissing the occasional salience of economic or class conflict, argued the broad role and balance among myriad groups in the political process. Relying perhaps on American experience, those theories defended the pluralism of modern Western democracies and the absence of stable concentrations of power and interest basic to a Marxist understanding. The interest group model asserted, in other words, that most people had and could have some effect on politics through group activity. Marxism tended to argue that economic groups, and employers and capitalists particularly, dominated the political system.

Over the years there has been some rapprochement between these two frameworks, in part due to developments within Marxist political analysis that emphasized the divisions and conflicts within capitalist classes.[1] Developments within interest group theory, in part stemming from Mancur Olson's work, have also been important. Olson noted that all organizations exist to provide public or collective goods for their members, goods from which no member may be excluded. This raises the problem of "free riders," since a rational individual would prefer to receive a benefit without paying for it. Small groups, wherein benefits are concentrated among a few members, each of whom stands to gain substantially if the collective benefit is provided, are more likely voluntarily to pursue their goals than larger groups, where benefits are diffuse and organizational costs high. Olson drew an important conclusion about interest group politics from these principles:

Industries will normally be small enough to organize voluntarily to provide themselves with an active lobby – with the political power that "naturally and necessarily" flows to those that control the business and property of the country. Whereas almost every occupational group involves thousands of workers, and whereas almost any subdivision of agriculture also involves thousands of people, the business interests of the country normally are congregated in oligopoly-sized groups or industries ... The multitude of workers, consumers, white-collar workers, farmers, and so on are organized only in special circumstances, but business interests are organized as a general rule.[2]

Thus public choice theory, of which Olson's work is an important part, has proposed the dominance of economic and business interests in the political process. As Mark Sproule-Jones has noted, public choice theory "shares many of the conclusions of Marxist and neo-Marxist political economy. The approach would agree, for instance, that many governmental officials possess preferences and ideologies in common with corporate and organized interests."[3] Doern and Phidd argue that non-producer associations such as labour unions and consumer and environmental groups, while active in the political system, have, on the whole, an organized political base "much weaker, less stable and less coherent than producer associations."[4] Thompson and Stanbury sum up the literature on the role of interest groups in Canadian public policy as follows: "Indeed, much of the evidence on interest-group activity does no more than demonstrate the extent of *business* groups' influence on public policy. It seems likely that business officials have always had a privileged role in the policy-formulation process, benefiting not only from the care with which government satisfies business interests in general but also from the privileged roles they enjoy as participants in policy deliberations."[5]

UI lends itself well to an exploration of the neo-pluralist and neo-Marxist approaches because in Canada, as in many other countries, the program directly involves employers and employees in its organization and financing. More fundamentally, as noted in chapter two, UI is one of the most visible and expensive income security programs, and the welfare state has been contentious for economic groups to the extent that it has altered the balance of power among classes and their organizational representatives. One might argue, with Schlozman and Verba, that "the politics of unemployment is actually a case study in class politics" because lower-class groups suffer the greatest when unemployment is high.[6] If unemployment is in general terms a class issue, so is UI.

One school of thought casts the class component of UI in terms of its general labour market function. This function is to discipline and organize the labour force and is accomplished through the employment offices normally responsible for administering UI and through the fact that benefits are conditional on a host of requirements, not the least being demonstrated willingness to work. Kincaid, for example, sees UI in Britain as part of a social security system that "keeps people at work, or prevents them from improving their position by walking out of a job or by going on strike."[7] Brunelle makes a similar argument in claiming that the function of UI is to maintain a "reserve army" of workers. Benefits are kept low to keep low-wage labour attractive, and UI traps people in the reserve army by tying present benefits to past and future wage labour.[8] Perhaps the most succinct version of this argument was made in 1940, in a report to Britain's Fabian Society:

The system must be such that it does not reduce the supply of labour willing to work at a low wage; it must not interfere with the individual's natural inclination to provide for future misfortune (even if that inclination results in present poverty); and it must generally be consistent with the idea that men only work in order to earn their living, and with the incentive of insecurity. The advantage of such a system is that it enables the Government to satisfy its natural humanitarian impulses and at the same time to ensure that the excess labour supply shall be immediately available when required.[9]

UI is also sometimes seen as a mechanism, applied in concert with social assistance programs, for dividing the working classes into "deserving" and "undeserving" segments. The "deserving" are provided with UI as a consequence of their labour force attachment, while the "undeserving" are stigmatized and coerced by social or unemployment assistance programs. Those in the first category resist slipping into the second, and so general discipline is maintained. This is an old argument, as demonstrated by an analysis of Canadian UI by J.L. Cohen in 1935. Cohen maintained that a contributory UI program relegated the less well-off to charity and relief, thereby blunting the recognition of the right of all workers to employment. Cohen also suggested that UI depressed the wage level by offering benefits geared to the lowest-paying employment and by forcing the unemployed into low-wage labour by threats to cut benefits.[10]

The class character of UI may be seen more directly as a consequence of its effects on the relationship between employee and employer, worker and capitalist.[11] Analysts have noted the controversy over UI stemming from "conflict between management and labor on many aspects of the program"[12] and the extent to which "labor and management are lined up against each other on practically every substantive change proposed in unemployment insurance laws."[13] Few survey data exist on employer/employee attitudes to UI, but what there is supports the conclusion that employers are generally suspicious of UI and desire lower benefits of shorter duration, while employee representatives support UI but want expanded benefits with more relaxed rules.[14]

Canadian survey data support these findings. In 1981, Canadians approved of the concept of UI by a two-to-one ratio, though 68 per cent desired changes in the program, generally in the direction of tighter controls and restrictions.[15] Canadian employers, in contrast, were evenly split over support of the program, and 90 per cent of them believed that there is at least some abuse by those collecting benefits.[16] These data are tentative, but they echo much earlier findings from a survey conducted in 1968, before the program expansions in 1971. In that survey, for example, higher-income occupational groups were most concerned with abuses and cheating. Professionals, managers, and owners were less likely to support increased benefits and longer benefit duration than were skilled and unskilled labourers.[17]

Most studies of Canadian UI give some prominence to employer/employee differences over the program because it is in some senses "owned" by the private sector. Struthers, for example, underscores business opposition to UI through the 1920s and 1930s as an important impediment to implementation.[18] Pelletier offers a Marxist interpretation of recent UI developments that focuses on its role in stabilizing capitalism. While the broad economic rhythms of capitalism are the fundamental backdrop for his analysis, he suggests that the post-1975 changes were in large part a result of new contours of class struggle. Business was demanding cutbacks because of the high costs of the 1971 program, and, more generally, because of a desire to reduce state intervention. Workers, for their part, were beginning to circumvent the wage discipline strategy that Pelletier believes was central to the 1971 act and were engaging in more frequent strikes.[19]

In perhaps the most consistent application of a society-centred perspective, Carl Cuneo examined the balance of employer and employee interests leading to the 1940 act.[20] He compared the efficacy of instrumental versus structural Marxist theories of the capitalist state, the latter positing a relative autonomy of the capitalist state that permits it to contravene the immediate interests of capitalists. Cuneo argued that UI was introduced in 1940 to "help keep the peace between labour and capital."[21] In this case, however, employers' interest in capital accumulation and labour's interest in wage subsistence were eclipsed by the state's general interest in social control. This eclipse was possible because, during the Depression, the capitalist class was weak and divided. The issue of state autonomy will be taken up in the next chapter; all that need be noted here is that for Cuneo, and to a lesser extent Struthers and Pelletier, UI policy developments are cast against a backdrop of conflicts among economic groups.

This chapter will deliberately ignore some of the debates over whether "classes" or "interest groups" are the most valid unit of analysis. In practice, even Marxist analyses such as those by Pelletier and Cuneo depend on submissions and representations by recognized, formal associations of producer and labour groups. These include, on the employer side, such organizations as the Canadian Manufacturers' Association (CMA), the Canadian Chamber of Commerce (CCC), various provincial employers' associations, and municipal boards of trade. On the labour side, there were the Trades and Labour Congress (TLC) and the Canadian Congress of Labour (CCL), which amalgamated in 1956 to form the Canadian Labour Congress (CLC), and some large individual unions such as the United Auto Workers of America (UAW) and the Steelworkers Union. These and other organizations like them may be considered "classes-in-action" or as simple interest groups, but both Marxist and non-Marxist political economists identify these organizations as key economic actors.

We shall assume in this chapter that neo-pluralist and neo-Marxist explanations of public policy, as society-centred approaches, trace changes and developments in that policy back to the interests and balance of power among key economic groups. Also, as we noted with Olson, Sproule-Jones, and Thompson and Stanbury, business interests seem to dominate the public policy process. This may seem too stark an approach to be realistic; it makes the state into a cipher, a simple instrument of employer interests. In fact, though the approach used here is deliberately stripped of nuance so as better to assess its strength, even in this version the government need not be entirely passive. It may resist pressures; it may attempt compromise between two or more widely differing positions; it may succeed in changing the minds of the powerful. These and other issues of the state's autonomy will be taken up in subsequent chapters.

For this chapter, we concentrate on the economic interests surrounding UI. The program is an excellent case study for this approach, because employer and employee associations presumably have strong and opposed views on UI, which themselves reflect UI's potential effects on the capitalist relations of production. Unlike some income security programs such as health and pensions, UI directly affects the labour process and the labour market. If any public policy is susceptible to an explanation that stresses conflict among producer groups, UI is.

We would expect to find a number of things, were such an approach valid for understanding the evolution of Canadian UI. First, there should be differences in views between employers and employees, over both the philosophy of the program and its specific provisions. While there may be debates within each camp, these are either transitory or outweighed by larger differences between the groups. One would expect also these differences to be stable, since otherwise one could not draw any general conclusions about the policy process in any given field. The other studies mentioned earlier examined only segments of UI's history in Canada; this chapter will review the program's entire history.

Second, policy-makers (politicians and bureaucrats) will be aware of these differences. There should be independent evidence showing not only that the differences exist but also that they are politically salient. Political salience has various dimensions. The differences in views have to exist in action or practice; that is, they must be more than simple expressions of support or rejection found in trade magazines or association speeches. They should appear in the political arena, as speeches, submissions, and formal and informal contacts. Next, it should be clear that these differences are known to policy-makers, that they are conscious of them. This should extend beyond simply categorizing a general "business" or "labour" view, to discerning specific positions on specific program changes. Ideally, it would include both.

Third, and most crucial, policy-makers will tend to respond to the interests and views of the most powerful group, and, as we noted above, neo-pluralist and neo-Marxist literature has argued that business interests tend to prevail in most public policy issues. There are weak and strong versions of this hypothesis. The weak one suggests only that policy-makers work within constraints imposed by powerful interests. The strong version suggests that specific policy decisions may be traced back directly to the demands of one or another group. In the course of this chapter, we will assess evidence for both versions. Clearly there may be times when policy-makers seem quite autonomous and other times when they seem to respond to direct demands. A case study with a narrow time horizon, such as Cuneo's, may misread the real nature of the relationships; examining UI over a longer period should get closer to the truth. For this reason as well, it should provide a better grasp of labour's effect on UI, since its apparent strengths during the Depression may have waned in the postwar period.

The number of submissions and representations from business, labour, and other organizations on UI from the 1920s to 1981 is very large. To make the discussion more manageable, I will concentrate on positions taken in the great periods of change for UI: the early agitation to establish a program; the debate through the 1960s, crystallized by the Gill Committee; and the 1970s, which saw repeated, substantial program changes. The discussion will be based on formal submissions to parliamentary committees, internal government memoranda, and occasionally correspondence, much of it from the Depression period and the Bennett and Mackenzie King Papers. It might be argued that such a concentration on formal, public sources risks missing the "real," behind-the-scenes machinations of interest groups and policy-makers. In an isolated case study this might be true, but we can control for possible bias by reviewing all major submissions for the history of the program. Groups may lie in public, but it seems unlikely that they would (or could) lie and lie consistently for half a century. Another useful control is internal govenment documents for the same period – any substantial discrepancies between rhetoric and reality would show up there eventually.

DEBATES OVER PRINCIPLE:
1915-40

Employees' Positions

Unlike organized labour in the United States, which did not support national UI until shortly before 1935, Canadian trade unions approved of it even before the First World War.[22] In 1915, for example, labour representatives appearing before the Ontario Commission on Unemployment argued against government labour exchanges, which they thought could be used as strike-breaking weapons, but supported state-assisted voluntary UI programs run by unions themselves.[23] The commission recommended a voluntary UI scheme, but this was not pursued. UI nonetheless was gathering momentum, as shown by the 1919 International Labour Conference recommendation supporting the program and the Liberal party platform's adoption of UI in the same year. In 1920 the federal Department of Labour produced a draft UI scheme modelled on the British plan.[24]

This momentum died quickly, however, partly as a result of labour's weakness. The defeat of the 1919 Winnipeg General Strike left labour organizations demoralized and gave business and agrarian interests the opportunity to attack UI. Reform-minded ministers and bureaucrats left the government, prosperity returned for the rest of the decade, and so attention shifted from UI to labour exchanges and relief. UI remained dormant on the political agenda, however, ready to be revived with the onslaught of the Depression.[25]

The first major opportunity that interested parties had to represent their views on UI to the government occurred in the 1928 sessions of the House of Commons Select Standing Committee on Industrial and International Relations. Three labour unions were represented in those hearings: the Catholic Workers' Union of Canada (CWUC), based in Quebec; the All-Canadian Congress of Labour (ACCL), formed in 1927 for national unionism and primarily a vehicle for the Canadian Brotherhood of Railway Employees; and the TLC.

All three organizations strongly supported UI in principle, though, contrary to the Ontario Commission on Unemployment slightly more than a decade earlier, all assumed that the plan should be compulsory and state-managed. Throughout the 1920s, beginning with the aborted Borden government scheme, Canadian UI proposals were consciously modelled after the British plan, which was national in scope and compulsory.

The three trade unions agreed on another point as well: if possible the UI program should be federally managed. At this time it was widely assumed that UI lay in provincial jurisdiction, by virtue of control over property and civil rights.[26] Even the Commons committee assumed that Ottawa's role in UI would be largely financial, modelled after conditional grants for Old Age Pensions. Under this 1927 program, the provinces voluntarily administered the program within their borders, while Ottawa contributed half the costs.

Pierre Beaule, president of the CWUC, assumed that a UI program would probably parallel Old Age Pensions but urged that should provinces – possibly Quebec – refuse to participate, Ottawa should establish a program to which employers and employees could contribute.[27] He did indicate a preference, however, for a federally run scheme. The ACCL and TLC positions are easy to understand: as national unions, active in each province, both wanted to ensure that any UI program be available to all their members. As Tom Moore, president of the TLC, put it: "All social legislation of the nature now being dealt with should be of a Federal character as otherwise many workers are denied the benefits of the same because of the difficulty of establishing the requisite provincial residence qualifications etc., owing to the transient nature of their employment."[28] A.R. Mosher, president of the ACCL, echoed this sentiment.[29] Moore cited the International Labour Conference agreement and the report of Canada's Royal Commission on Industrial Relations, both in 1919, as evidence for his views.

Financing was a major issue in both the ACCL and the TLC testimony. Mosher and Moore each argued that workers should not be expected to contribute to the program. In effect, they were suggesting a "non-contributory" UI scheme. Mosher argued that workers had a prior claim to maintenance when unemployed and that industry had an obligation to meet this claim. In any case, wages were too low to support contributions.[30] As far as the ACCL was concerned, it did not matter how UI funds were collected or calculated as long as they came completely out of industry's pocket.

Moore argued that "the responsibility for unemployment thus rests largely with industry" and that "the cost of unemployment insurance should be placed primarily on industry though it is recognized that Government has also some responsibility to participate."[31] When challenged on this point,

Moore replied that the general policy of organized labour "has been to support the view that when industry contributes, the workers are contributing as well as the employers, industry being composed of both their efforts."[32] With a separate contribution, workers would be contributing twice. The TLC argued that since Ottawa controlled immigration, it indirectly controlled unemployment and so should be responsible.

Moore went on, however, to articulate what he described as a minority view in the labour movement, that workers should contribute towards a UI fund. Contributing would give workers "a much greater right to participate in the management of the funds. It would remove the stigma of charity, and place it as a purely insurance jointly managed fund rather than a charity fund in any respect."[33] Mosher, while preferring a non-contributory scheme, stated that many workers would be prepared to contribute if that were the only way to get a program started. In his words, "Any scheme will be better than no scheme at all."[34]

This compromise position on contributions became the official stance of Canadian organized labour in the 1930s but did not reflect simple conservatism.[35] As Moore had suggested, organized labour realized that workers' UI contributions would establish a proprietary claim not just to benefits but also to management of the program itself. Without such contributions, the program would "belong" to employers. While in one sense the willingness to contribute to UI was a concession, organized labour recognized that it might thereby protect its future interest and control over the program.

The first report of the Commons committee recommended a UI system modelled on Old Age Pensions and suggested that Ottawa approach the provinces to gather support. Its 1929 report noted that this support had not been forthcoming and therefore suggested a Dominion-provincial conference and meetings with employer and employee groups. No such conference was held until 17 January 1933. In the mean time, the country sank rapidly into the Depression, with the number of unemployed rising monthly to reach perhaps as much as 25 per cent of the labour force (only rough estimates are possible for this period). The Bennett Conservatives won the 1930 election on an activist program to end unemployment but became enmeshed in the annual relief acts, whereby Ottawa assisted the provinces in dealing with the enormous number of unemployed. Prime Minister Bennett, goaded by the Opposition and frustrated with the limited success of relief, promised on 29 April 1931 and again on 22 November 1932 to introduce UI once data were collected to permit actuarial calculations.

The Depression and indignities of relief spurred workers across the country to press vigorously for UI. The Workers' Unity League of Canada (WUL), set up by the Communist party of Canada in 1929, agitated vigorously from 1931 to 1935 for a non-contributory UI program, through petitions, letter-writing campaigns, and telegrams. The WUL's call for non-contributory UI was linked to demands for a seven-hour day, a five-day week, a guaranteed working week, and a minimum wage of $25 per week. Its draft UI bill called for universal coverage, no waiting period, maternity benefits, a fund established by diverting armament expenditures and sustained by a steeply progressive income tax on incomes over $5,000 per year, and administration of the fund by administrative councils with majority trade union and unemployed council's representation.[36] The WUL presented this draft bill and a petition with 94,136 signatures to the prime minister on 15 April 1931.[37] Bennett, of course, was aware that the WUL had communist affiliations and was unsympathetic.[38] Indeed, it is unlikely that he had ever thought seriously of mounting UI on a non-contributory basis. In a letter dated 18 August 1930, for example, he stated: "Unemployment Insurance is not a difficult matter for it merely means fixing a rate of premium on an actuarial basis."[39] In his promise to the House to introduce UI, Bennett made the same point: any plan would have to be actuarially sound.[40] The WUL and affiliated organizations continued to deluge Bennett's office with telegrams and petitions, particularly before the 1933 Dominion-provincial conference, but they had little direct impact.[41] The last product of this wing of the labour movement was the Workers' Social and Unemployment Insurance Bill, identical in all important respects to its predecessors, presented to the federal government on 18 February 1935, shortly before Bennett's own legislation was introduced.[42]

Planning for the 1935 act had been under way for some time. The Dominion Bureau of Statistics had been gathering the available spotty data to assess the number of unemployed since 1931. A Dominion-provincial conference was held on 17 January 1933 to discuss UI and relief. Bennett's position was that Ottawa could implement UI only upon transfer of constitutional authority. The conference failed to agree to such a transfer, possibly because Bennett himself was not in favour of it.[43] Canada's superintendent of insurance had considered the issue in December 1932 and advised cautious study before proceeding on such a major, costly program.[44] Bennett's chief private secretary, R.K. Finlayson, had personally consulted British officials in 1933 on Britain's new Unemployment Bill, and while Canadian policy-makers were sensitive to differences between the two countries, they were nonetheless strongly influenced by the British experience.[45] A team of officials and experts was assembled in January 1934 to work out the details of a UI program, and a draft bill was ready by the end of that year, allowing the prime minister to promise immediate action on the program in his famous radio speeches of January 1935. In August 1934 Bennett prepared to negotiate the needed transfer of powers from the provinces but, realizing the opposition he faced from Quebec and Ontario, decided simply to claim federal jurisdiction over UI and pass the bill anyway.[46]

Once the bill was prepared, Finlayson sought a meeting with Tom Moore of the TLC in December 1934 to get organized labour's reaction. Moore made some detailed points, but his major objections were about administration and contributions.[47] The TLC could not support a program funded entirely by employers and employees; his suggestion was a three-way split of contributions: government 30 per cent, employees 30 per cent, and employers 40 per cent. He suggested also that the UI fund carry the costs of administration and that the commission, rather than being appointed at large, have one representative each from labour and industry. Finally, he suggested a slight relaxation of entrance requirements and a slight increase in benefits, as well as inclusion of coal miners and construction workers.

It is clear that beyond increasing the program's generosity, Moore was keenly concerned with establishing labour's proprietary interest in the program. The Employment and Social Insurance Act, 1935, departed from the British scheme in establishing a commission to manage UI, beyond direct government influence. A direct voice for labour on the commission, balanced by a voice for industry, would effectively make UI a program run by its beneficiaries. While Moore's suggestions on entrance requirements and benefits were not taken up, his key demands for a tripartite contributory and administrative structure were.[48] These remain features of Canadian UI to the present.

Despite its passage in June 1935, and the establishment of the commission, the new act was placed in limbo later that year by Mackenzie King's newly elected Liberal government. King had had reservations about UI, in particular about Ottawa's jurisdictional authority to embark on the program, and so referred this act, along with the other major pieces of Bennett's "New Deal" legislation, to the Supreme Court and then the Judicial Committee of the Privy Council. The latter decided in 1937 that UI was ultra vires the federal power, and so King had to approach the provinces that year to seek their consent for a constitutional amendment. Lacking unanimous support, he dropped the issue until 1940, when the introduction of UI looked useful for the war effort.

The draft UI bill of 1940 was similar to the 1935 version; indeed, it was designed by many of the same people involved in the earlier effort. Work on the program continued sporadically through 1938 and 1939, and the May 1940 Throne Speech announced the intention to proceed with a constitutional amendment. Agreement was reached with the provinces in June, and the British Parliament amended the BNA Act in July to include UI as a federal power (sec. 91.2.a). A special committee of the House of Commons was appointed 17 July 1940 to hear witnesses and submissions regarding the bill. Among those appearing were Tom Moore for the TLC and N.D. Dowd for the ACCL, as well as representatives of railway workers and Catholic workers.

All the labour representatives were generally pleased with the legislation and appeared to prefer it to the 1935 act. There were no objections to any of its principles, though the ACCL raised the question of non-contributory funding. The principles of suitable work, entry requirements, commission structure, contributions, and waiting periods were not challenged. Moore and Dowd, along with A. Charpentier (la Fédération des travailleurs catholiques du Canada) all pressed for broader coverage, however. Moore and Charpentier wanted the income ceiling to be raised from $2,000 per year to $2,500 per year, while Dowd argued for its complete removal and universal coverage.[49] Moore suggested a shorter list of exempted industries and also thought the waiting period of nine days too long. Only Dowd for the ACCL argued that UI costs should be completely borne by employers, though he admitted that it would be "impracticable to ask industry, as now organized," to bear the full costs and that employee contributions might place "a hardship upon low-paid workers."[50] Dowd was shrewd enough to realize that some of these technical points could be addressed by the newly established commission.

Thus Canadian organized labour supported the 1940 UI act, though it would have preferred a more generous design. This wing of the labour movement had supported the principle of state UI through the 1920s and 1930s but had never played a proactive role. Instead, it tended to react to government proposals, particularly the two draft bills in 1935 and 1940. It was ambivalent about contributions, since at least the TLC believed that employee contributions might strengthen labour's claim to a say in UI administration. The WUL and its affiliated organizations kept the pressure on for a non-contributory plan, but this was never seriously considered by the government. Though formal labour representations in 1928, 1935, and 1940 had no apparent effect on legislation, on occasion – as with Tom Moore's reaction to the draft 1935 bill – labour leaders could influence some provisions. In one sense, these minor influences were eclipsed by the social unrest and discontent of the 1930s. But the effect even of the latter on the timing and character of UI legislation was minimal.

Employers' Positions

Both Cuneo and Struthers have documented some of the business opinion on, and later reaction to, UI. They point out that the leading Canadian business organizations were divided on the issue, many opposing even the principle of UI, but a significant minority, especially later in the Depression when there seemed the need to sustain purchasing power, cautiously supporting it. In the 1920s the CMA was the most clearly interested party, since it represented the manufacturing sector. But even as late as 1928, before the Commons Select Standing Committee on Industrial and International Relations, the CMA seemed unsure of its position. William C. Coulter, chairman of the CMA's Industrial Relations Committee, admitted that his organization had no position on UI because it had not thought that UI, or social insurance in general, would become an issue in the near future. In what was to become a common refrain in business statements on UI over the next decade, Coulter argued that introduction of UI would be "untimely" because the United States, Canada's major economic competitor, did not have it. The leading cause of unemployment in Canada was seasonal fluctuation, and UI could not remove this.[51]

With the Depression, however, the business community could ill afford such inarticulate and unsubstantiated views. UI was in the air after 1930, and the prime minister's almost yearly promises to introduce it, in combination with highly visible WUL tactics, stimulated a stream of letters, briefs, and formal submissions to him from individual businessmen and organizations. These documents suggest some substantial divisions within the business community, as well as shifts in opinion over time. On the whole, however, the weight of this opinion preceding the 1940 act was negative.[52]

Most of the letters that Bennett received from businessmen before 1935 opposed UI on principle, though some, like that from J.C. Kyle (a Winnipeg investment dealer), noted that the Tories might have to introduce it to forestall a Liberal/Labour alliance or, worse, revolution.[53] Bennett was warned vaguely that UI was "a dangerous thing"[54] and that it was not "ever going to be satisfactory."[55] A prevailing worry was the additional cost of a contributory program, though many of these objections seemed based on a rejection of social insurance per se. A more sophisticated ambivalence was expressed by Sir Thomas White (vice-president, Canadian Bank of Commerce), who worried about the "political pressure" on a program paying weekly benefits, which might lead to "grave and increasing abuse."[56]

The most intense opposition to UI came from the CMA. In a letter to Bennett, J.E. Walsh (general manager, CMA) pointed out that the CMA was on record opposing UI in 1928, 1930, and 1932 and that it still believed that "it would not be wise to introduce a system of unemployment insurance in this country."[57] The CMA estimated that UI costs, at $150 million per annum, would be "prohibitive." Direct relief would still be needed, even with UI, since an actuarially sound program could cover only a small portion of the labour force. Pointing to Britain and Australia, the CMA argued that the "universal tendency of unemployment insurance cost is to rise." Thus an expensive program would become even more expensive. Moreover, the CMA cited various insurance experts to support its view that "unemployment is not, except within very narrow limits, an insurable risk" and suggested that in addition to the "danger of sapping individual initiative which is inherent in any system of maintaining people when unemployed," UI might actually increase unemployment by making employers less reluctant to let workers go.

Most of these arguments were echoed by the Employers' Association of Manitoba in a January 1933 brief to Bennett. This group had no doubt that UI favoured workers and was an "injustice to the employer." Apart from the large, direct costs that contributory UI would impose on industry, there were problems of "morale": "The workers' spirit of independence, self-reliance, and self-respect will be destroyed and there will be no incentive for thrift. The employee who knows that if discharged he can have compensation will not be particularly interested in efficiency, and will not be alert to make good in his job; and when he is out of a job will take no steps whatever to find another."[58] The brief also warned that a UI fund would "get into the hands of politicians and political control in some way."[59]

Not all business letters and briefs opposed UI. F. Sturgeon of Sturgeon's Ltd, a member of the CMA, endorsed the "Payment of a temporary minimum wage to all unemployed," funded by general income tax and administered by an agency beyond the control of politicians.[60] The Vancouver Board of Trade supported UI, as did G. Gordon, president of the Bank of Montreal.[61] Gordon's letter summed up the reasoning of those businessmen supporting UI by 1934: "The point is being brought home more forcibly to us from day to day that the system of direct relief which is followed by the various Municipalities throughout Canada is gradually, but most assuredly, impairing the credit standing of the Municipalities, to say nothing of the added strain which is being thrown upon the treasuries of the Provinces and of the Dominion Government."[62]

Some business groups seemed ambivalent or unsure on the UI issue. The CCC, for example, had not taken a firm stand on UI even as late as 1933.[63] The Canadian Construction Association wrote to Bennett in 1933 and again in 1934, asking simply to be kept informed of any UI proposals.[64] At least one businessman wrote not to represent views but in genuine puzzlement, asking for guidance on Bennett's position.[65]

One business group that approached the UI issue constructively was the Canadian Life Insurance Officers' Association. It commissioned two studies by Hugh H. Wolfenden, who later helped design the 1935 act.[66] In a letter to Bennett dated 9 January 1933, T. Bradshaw of the association offered Wolfenden's services to the government, noting that the "Life Insurance Companies, individually or through their Association, do not seek to support any definite type of legislation. They have formed no opinions, nor have they expressed any on the subject of unemployment insurance."[67] The memorandum accompanying the letter suggested something quite different, however. First, it stressed the limited effect of UI: it would neither remove the causes of unemployment nor cover those currently employed. Second, since the contingency of unemployment was "largely and directly dependent upon the human will," rates of unemployment were rarely predictable "and then only when the rights of claimants to benefits are very carefully restricted and controlled."[68] UI was therefore "possible only for a small percentage of the population; and for those groups it would be essential to safeguard the plan carefully against exploitation, lax supervision, and amendment."[69] Thus the association was forced to doubt the practicability of UI and requested that a body of experts be appointed to discuss the matter thoroughly.

After Bennett announced that the government would definitely pass a UI bill in 1935, the tone of the business letters softened considerably. Six letters that Bennett received in January and February 1935 supported the principle of UI but asked for exemptions for their specific industry.[70] One of these was from J. Dobbs, president of the Canadian Bankers' Association asking that the original exemption for bank and trust companies under the 1935 bill, which had been removed by the Senate Banking and Finance Committee, be reinstated.[71] In 1938, when federal officials were once again proceeding to plan a new act, the association's arguments were quite scathingly dismissed as "a very poor case."[72]

As mentioned earlier, the drafting of the 1940 UI bill proceeded without consultations with employer or employee groups; they had to await the Commons Special Committee in the summer of 1940 to present their views. Employer associations were much more evident at these hearings than labour groups: four labour groups appeared, and eleven business or employer representatives. The CMA was thus not alone in its objections; each of the business organizations wished either to delay the legislation or receive an exemption. The CMA brief went somewhat further in suggesting an alternative to the UI "pooling" plan – a "savings" plan whereby employees and employers would contribute to a limited, individual account (e.g. up to $100), leaving the individual worker free to purchase interest-bearing bonds for later redemption.[73] The CMA also argued that UI unaccompanied by assistance programs for the chronically unemployed would lead to irresistible political pressures on the UI fund. The CMA preferred a program with experience rating, so that stable employers could pay less. Because of these reservations, the CMA suggested postponement of the legislation.[74]

The government was prepared for these arguments. A 1940 memorandum identified the CMA as "the principal organization opposed to the immediate establishment of a system of unemployment insurance."[75] The memorandum noted the CMA's "savings" plan and concluded: "The intention of this plan is obvious: to minimize the contribution of the employer as much as possible."[76]

The arguments and proposals of the business community were usually held in low esteem by key officials involved in the program. A good example of this comes in a memorandum written in 1943 by Eric Stangroom, the chief insurance officer in the Department of Insurance, and one of the small group who designed the 1940 act. Stangroom was commenting on a pamphlet written by Huntley R. Drummond, president of the Royal Trust Company:

I don't find this pamphlet ... impressive. He says a capitalist is a better citizen for having a stake in the country. Surely a man with a job also has a stake in the country's stability. Lloyd George said the stake provided by unemployment insurance prevented a revolution in Great Britain after the last war ... Business men should realize that if they insist on taking over again completely immediately after the war, and their ... plan of again providing "the highest material condition of social life ever known" fails, then the ... state plan, which will then be advocated, will rouse them to new but lonely heights of poetic lamentation.[77]

Most of the other employer representations at the 1940 House committee were also self-interested. The Canadian Hospital Association, the Retail Merchants Association of Canada, the Canadian Bankers' Association, and the Canadian Transit Association all vaguely approved the principle of UI but asked that their own particular industries be exempted. The CCC, like the CMA, had asked for a delay in order to "study" the plan but also argued that introducing UI during the war would divert necessary manpower and capital, would raise the costs of goods, and would induce workers to demand higher wages to recover those lost in UI premiums. Even under persistent questioning, the CCC representatives would not, however, approve of UI in principle.[78]

The 1940 act was passed despite business opposition. The opposition was generally mild, and the business community as a whole did not speak with one voice on the issue. Some associations, like the Canadian Bankers' Association and the Retail Merchants Association, saw general economic advantage in UI and so supported it in principle but did not want their industries to be covered by the plan. In any case, by the time the bill reached the Commons committee, it was far enough along that only the most extreme opposition was likely to derail it. The CMA's alternate "savings" plan was ignored, as were the plans for exemptions for bankers and retailers. While business briefs and representations had been numerous and detailed over this period, they seem to have had as little effect as those coming from labour.

AN INTERREGNUM OF
STABILITY: 1940-69

With passage of the 1940 act the debates over principle subsided, reappearing only in the 1960s and 1970s. After 1940 the issues were not about the fundamental nature of the program (e.g. contributory v. non-contributory) but about the details, such as exempted classes of employment, benefit and contribution rates, and earnings ceilings. There were few rearguard actions to dismantle the program. On the contrary, in virtually every year between 1943 and 1959, the plan was expanded and liberalized. Each step was small, most were uncontroversial, and many did not even attract public attention, but their aggregate effect was quite notable by the end of the 1950s: in 1940 the act covered approximately 42 per cent of wage and salary earners; by 1959 it covered more than 82 per cent.[79]

If UI became less controversial, the pattern of political representation and advice changed as well. Before the act established an Unemployment Insurance Commission, representation had been directed to ministers, the prime minister, and committees of inquiry. After 1940, proposals and amendments for UI tended to be either generated within or aimed at the commission, though the minister of labour and the cabinet could and did recommend changes from time to time.[80]

Table 3 shows the major program developments between 1940 and 1959. While the commission and the government occasionally acted to tighten up UI (e.g. by seasonal regulations and married women's regulations), the trend was to yearly expansion of coverage and improvement in benefits. There is little evidence in this period of strong pressure from employer groups for this expansion, though employee groups appreciated the improvements.[81] It was only at the end of the 1950s, as the UI fund began to haemorrhage, that the program came under more far-reaching examination by government and economic interest groups.

By 1960, benefit payments were outstripping contributions, and the UI fund was evaporating. In 1961 the Diefenbaker government appointed a committee of inquiry into UI, chaired by Ernest C. Gill, president of the Canada Life Assurance Company. Gill and his colleagues spent a year assessing UI, in particular its abuse or misuse and its relation to other income security programs. The committee's November 1962 report had 244 recommendations, most of which tried to re-establish UI on a solid insurance basis and develop a more concerted manpower policy. The committee tried to adapt some of the original goals of Canadian UI to current circumstances. In 1940, for example, it had been clear that UI would require a labour market dimension insofar as it would test availability for work and insofar as re-employment of beneficiaries was its ultimate aim. The Gill Committee argued that new economic conditions required greater emphasis on labour market objectives and thus recommended transferring the UI employment service to the Department of Labour.[82]

The committee's main recommendations were to develop three tiers of support for the unemployed: UI, financed by employer and employee contributions, for short-term and frictional unemployment; extended benefits, supported by general taxation for prolonged unemployment and some seasonal unemployment; and unemployment assistance, administered by local authorities on a needs-test basis.[83] Coverage would be made virtually universal. The committee's other major recommendation addressed benefit rates and duration, contributions, and seasonal employment.

The committee received 51 briefs and submissions. Most were from

TABLE 3

Major UI Program Developments, 1940-59

1942	Commission, by order-in-council, becomes branch of Dept of Labour, to administer National Selective Service regulations.
1943	New earnings ceiling of $2400 a year for some employees (R) Coverage extended to municipally operated public utilities and non-permanent employees of federal government (A) Contribution requirement relaxed slightly (A)
1945	Coverage extended to employees in charitable organizations and air transportation and professional nurses (R) UI benefits become payable to veterans under Veterans' Rehabilitation Act
1946	Coverage extended to employment in transportation by water (A) Commission becomes responsible to minister of labour (A) Seasonal regulation devised to restrict benefits in "off-season" (R) Coverage extended to logging and lumbering in British Columbia (R)
1948	Contributory earnings ceiling raised (R) Benefits increased (A) New earnings class created (A)
1950	Supplementary benefits introduced (A) Contributory earnings ceiling increased (A) Dependants' benefits increased (A) Coverage of logging and lumbering extended from British Columbia to nation (A) Special eligibility requirements for second or subsequent benefit year (A) Additional eligibility requirements for married women (R) Waiting period reduced from nine to eight days (A)
1952	Dependants' benefits increased (A) Waiting period reduced to five days (A) Supplementary benefit period extended by two weeks (A)
1953	Claimants who get ill while on claim permitted to continue to collect benefits (A)
1955	New act (see chapter three for discussion)
1956	Qualifying conditions for second or subsequent claim relaxed (A) Coverage extended to fishermen (R)
1957	Seasonal benefit period extended (A) Married women's regulation revoked (R)
1958	Seasonal benefit period extended for that year only (A)
1959	Contributions increased by 30 per cent (A) Earnings ceiling increased (A) Maximum benefit duration increased from 36 to 56 weeks (A)

Source: Dingledine, *A Chronology of Response*, pp. 17-39.
Note: "A" stands for amendments to the act; "R" stands for changes to the regulations.

employer and employee groups (roughly 33), and, rather than examine each in turn, this section will review representative ones.

The CMA's brief to the committee was the most important from the business side. The employer representative on the Unemployment Insurance Commission was traditionally, if informally, recommended by the CMA, and so this organization's opinions carried weight. It also represented the single largest group of employers to contribute to the UI fund. The CMA's brief assumed that the main problem facing the program was depletion of its fund and that this reflected weaknesses in design and administration. "It is the Association's view that the proper remedy is the restoration of sound insurance principles which will bring the outlay of the fund in line with its income and make it self-sufficient."[84] UI, in the CMA's view, was a limited means of providing income support to unemployed persons that must avoid "supplementary measures which, though good in themselves, cannot be based on sound insurance principles."[85] Seasonal benefits were a clear case of the abandonment of sound principles, since off-season unemployment was not an insurable risk, but a certainty.

The CMA therefore recommended removal of seasonal benefits, reinstitution of seasonal regulations to bar claims from employees with "regular and expected periods of inactivity each year" (this would probably have removed coverage of much of the logging, agricultural, and transportation industries), restoration of married women's regulations, no increase in employer or employee contributions, and an educational campaign to "make various segments of the public fully aware of the purpose and nature of the Unemployment Insurance Act and the fund."[86]

What impression did these and other briefs make on policy-makers? In January 1962, George Haythorne, deputy minister of labour, received a memorandum reviewing and summarizing the main submissions before the Gill Committee.[87] The memorandum noted that most of the briefs "attribute the recent depletion of the fund to two weaknesses: (1) the seasonal provision of the Act and (2) the abuses."[88] It summarized the business and labour submissions as follows:

As might be expected, the suggested remedial actions *follow along traditional lines of employers and unions*. By and large, employers suggest that a pure insurance system in line with the 1941 Act should be restored ... That is, only those workers whose unemployment risk is unpredictable should be covered by the Act ... While the unions, on the other hand, may agree that the seasonal workers have been a drain on the fund, they do not want to see any change in the present coverage of the seasonal workers under the Act. The unions suggest, however, that any deficit arising from seasonal expenditures should be provided by general revenue.[89]

Other differences of opinion between business and labour had to do with levels of contributions and benefits and with abuses. Employers believed that levels of contribution and benefit were adequate, while unions wanted the latter to be increased to two-thirds of earnings. As noted earlier, employers recommended reinstatement of married women's regulations and the counting of pensions and old age assistance as earnings for the purpose of calculating benefits. Unions disagreed with both suggestions. The memorandum noted that four business organizations (two retail and two insurance) suggested a merit rating system but commented that "this suggestion has [not] been thought out very well."[90]

Significantly, the memorandum referred to the "traditional" lines of argument taken by business and labour on UI. These lines were first established in the 1930s and were reinforced over the succeeding decades. Despite the Byzantine complexity of UI, all business and labour briefs over this period were short, usually no more than 6,000 words. Consequently, the briefs from both sides tended to focus on a narrow range of issues. Typically, employers concentrated on the costs of UI, while affirming their support for the principles behind the program. They linked this concern over costs with work incentives, since an overly generous and undisciplined plan would erode the need and hence the desire to work. Employers almost invariably suggested ceilings on benefits and urged that the program be kept true to its insurance basis. From there, briefs usually highlighted one or more egregious examples of abuse or ill-conceived benefit categories.

Labour briefs, in contrast, consistently took the opposite position. They rarely if ever mentioned abuse or costs of the program, though some urged that contributions remain stable and that employers or government – usually the latter – step in to fund improvements. They emphasized the basic problem of unemployment and UI's role in alleviating it. From that perspective, the main issue was program expansion and enhancement, and labour unions consistently pressed for higher benefits, longer benefit duration, fewer and less complex entry requirements, and other liberalizing features.

Policy-makers understood these differences of view and appreciated their stability. The lines between business and labour were consistent over a long period. The differences are precisely those suggested at the outset of this chapter and reflect the way that UI affects the capitalist labour process and labour market. Their stability meant that they were predictable; by the early 1960s and certainly afterwards, employer and employee reactions to proposed UI changes could be easily anticipated. The memorandum to Haythorne also suggests that the views on either side were held in no special regard within the civil service but were assessed on their merits, as perceived by officials close to the program.

The Gill Committee's recommendations cannot easily be traced to one or other side. The suggestion of an expanded unemployment assistance program to deal with chronic and long-term unemployment may appear to reflect the CMA's recommendations (though the idea had a long pedigree of its own), but expansion to universal coverage and introduction of government-funded extended benefits were closer to the union position. A key recommendation, separation of administration of UI from the employment service, seems to have come from within the committee itself.

It would be a mistake, however, to conclude that the Gill Committee's recommendations and those of the groups appearing before it were the deciding factor in the government's approach to UI reform. In fact, the government had at its disposal, before the Gill Committee was appointed, the report of an interdepartmental committee on UI and a cabinet committee analysis. The first was available on 1 March 1961, and the second, no doubt informed by the first, on 15 May 1961. The specifics of each of these committee reports will be discussed in the next chapter, but it is clear that cabinet had been considering several options well before the Gill Committee added its views. For example, the cabinet committee in 1961 suggested retaining seasonal benefits as part of the normal UI program, though modifying and reducing them, supplemented by unemployment assistance. It came to decisions on benefit and contribution levels (maintaining the former, increasing the latter), proposed a modest increase in coverage, and contemplated an increase in the government's share of UI funding.[91] It would be mistaken to argue that the Gill Committee reflected one or the other side of the issue and that therefore government proposals flowing from Gill reflected that side as well. The Gill Committee is not easily pigeon-holed, and, even if it were, its recommendations were filtered by the internal policy process.

The internal process continued for six years. Immediately after the release of the Gill Committee's report, another interdepartmental committee was struck to assess the recommendations, with representatives of the departments of Finance, Labour, Health and Welfare, and National Revenue and of the commission. It reported in 1963. Another interdepartmental committee advised the minister of labour on UI changes in 1966, and its analyses fed into a comprehensive review undertaken by the commission in 1968. The commission's 1969 publication, *Report on the Study for Updating the Unemployment Insurance Programme*, was an important ingredient in the government's 1970-1 proposals. Throughout this six-year period the government promised to implement some of the Gill Committee's recommendations but went ahead with only one major one – separation of the employment service from UI. The former was turned over first to the Department of Labour, effective 1965, and a year later it became the responsibility of the newly created Department of Manpower and Immigration. UI remained the ultimate responsibility of the Department of Labour.

As we noted, this particular recommendation appears to have come from within the Gill Committee itself and was not the result of strong pressures from business or labour. The government took it up in preference to the others probably because of its preoccupation in those years with a new labour market strategy that would focus more directly on the supply of labour, its mobility, and training.[92] In any event, the policy evaluation and re-evaluation conducted between 1963 and 1969 were done behind a bureaucratic curtain. Only in 1969, with publication of the commission's report, did some of these proposals get into the public arena. By this time, there was such broad agreement that UI should be redesigned that it would be improper to speak of "pressure" from interested parties forcing the government's hand.

As in the previous period we examined, there was between 1940 and 1969 no dearth of representations from employer and employee groups. Indeed, by the end of this period the positions had firmed to the point where they were quite predictable. As expected, employers urged stricter program controls, stable if not reduced costs, and work incentives. Unions wanted program expansion. The clear trend in these years was for expansion of UI coverage, better and longer benefits, and relaxed entry requirements, and to that extent it might seem that the labour interest "won" over the employer interest. This conclusion must be treated cautiously, however, because there is no strong evidence that policy-makers felt themselves being "pushed" by labour to make these changes.

THE NEW ACT

When proposed UI changes were finally announced in the 1970 White Paper entitled *Unemployment Insurance in the 70's*, they were couched not primarily in economic or labour market terms but within an income security framework.[93] From the very outset, the White Paper spoke of Canadians believing "at least as much in a more equitable distribution of our national wealth and the fulfillment of the expectations and the potential of all our people" as in economic growth.[94] It explicitly identified UI as social policy and described the UI act as providing "financial assistance to lower income workers during periods of temporary unemployment."[95] In arguing for changes to the UI program, the White Paper maintained that modern social policy had to go beyond simple monetary assistance to "being directed toward the more complete fulfillment of people".[96] It suggested, therefore:

In keeping with a more realistic approach to social policy, the government now believes that a revamped unemployment insurance program should provide higher benefits more related to earnings and with less emphasis on the employees' labour force attachment.

Persons with a short work history may have even greater problems than those who have a long term labour force attachment. Allowing workers to take early advantage of an unemployment insurance program prevents them from falling into unstable work patterns. Instead, they are effectively integrated into the productive mainstream.[97]

Ironically perhaps, in light of some later criticisms that the 1971 act was too generous and hence corrosive to the work ethic, the White Paper was arguing that a more liberal program, buttressed by various manpower services, would integrate otherwise discouraged workers into the labour market.

Chapter five contains a more detailed discussion of the White Paper, but since its labour market philosophy seemed so at odds with previous and subsequent policy, a brief explanation is warranted. Several forces contributed to the White Paper's rationale and its eventual acceptance by the government. First, the rationale reflected some currents of contemporary labour market thinking in viewing labour as "human capital" needing careful development and support.[98] To some degree, the White Paper's liberal view was common in the 1960s. Second, key officials who might have disputed the approach, principally in the commission and the Department of Finance, were either frozen out of the decision process or preoccupied with other matters.[99] Third, the White Paper had the support of left-leaning ministers such as Jean Marchand and John Munro, who happened to be influential in cabinet.[100] Finally, the White Paper's generosity was supposed to be costless, thus disarming potential criticism.

The White Paper was referred to the Commons Standing Committee on Labour, Manpower and Immigration on 17 June 1970. The committee deliberated until 18 December 1970, when it submitted its report. The committee requested representations from interested parties and received 53 briefs and 18 letters, hearing evidence from 33 organizations. The UI bill was then introduced on 10 March 1971, receiving royal assent on 23 June 1971. The bill was also referred on 21 April 1971 to the standing committee, which once again held hearings on the proposals. This second set of hearings was only with government officials, most from the commission and the Department of Labour. Groups that had submitted briefs during the first set of hearings were invited to forward comments but were not asked to appear.[101]

Tables 4 and 5 summarize the submissions before the standing committee on the White Paper. The left column in Table 4 shows the organizations that submitted briefs and presented them to the committee; the right column shows those that submitted briefs but did not defend them. Table 5 summarizes the positions of a selected sample of the first set of organizations. The sample consists of the eight largest employer associations and the six largest employee associations. These organizations' briefs were the most thorough and lengthy in their comments on the White Paper. The arguments presented in specific briefs will be discussed in detail below; for the moment we will examine whether there were any patterns among the positions.

Table 5 lists some of the White Paper's key proposals: expansion of coverage from roughly 80 per cent of the work-force to 96 per cent, excluding

TABLE 4
Briefs Submitted and Presented to the Standing Committee on Labour,
Manpower and Immigration Regarding the White Paper *Unemployment
Insurance in the 70's*, September-December 1970

Presented	Submitted
Canadian Manufacturers' Association	Aluminum Company of Canada
Canadian School Trustees Association of Canada	Burlington Northern Inc.
Retail Council of Canada	Canadian Association of Equipment Distributors
National House Builders Association	Canadian Association of Movers
Canadian Airline Pilots Association	Canadian Canvas Goods Manufacturers' Association
Canadian Railway Labour Association	Canadian Fertilizer Association
United Auto Workers	Canadian Telephone Employees' Association
International Association of Fire-Fighters	Canadian Trucking Association
William M. Mercer Ltd	C.E. Dionne, MP
Canadian Construction Association	Employers' Council of British Columbia
National Council of Women	F.W. Morneau & Associates Ltd
Ontario Mining Association	W.J. Keough, minister of labour, Newfoundland
Communist Party of Canada	John A. Kroeker, fellow, Society of Actuaries
Domtar Ltd	Ontario Hospital Services Commission
Canadian Institute of Temporary Help and Business Services	Prince Edward Island Labour-Management Relations Council
United Electrical, Radio and Machine Workers of America	Regina Chamber of Commerce
Canadian Chamber of Commerce	Social and Industrial Welfare Committee Inc; St Jean and District Labour Council
Canadian Nurses' Association	United Community Services of Greater Vancouver Area
Mining Association of Canada	Vancouver Board of Trade
Fisheries Council of Canada	Quebec Road Builders and Heavy Construction Association
Railway Association of Canada	
Canadian Health Insurance Associates	
Canadian Labour Congress	
Canadian Teachers Federation	
Canadian Welfare Council	
Professional Institute of the Public Service of Canada	
Quebec Employers Council	
Public Service Alliance of Canada	
Canadian Hospital Association	
Life Underwriters Association of Canada	
Johnson, Higgins, Willis Faber Ltd	
Quebec Woodworkers Federation	
Confederation of National Trade Unions	

Source: Canada, Parliament, House of Commons, The Standing Committee on Labour, Manpower and Immigration, *First Report Respecting the White Paper on Unemployment Insurance*, pp. 42-6.

TABLE 5
Summary of Positions of Selected Employer and Employee Groups
Regarding the White Paper *Unemployment Insurance in the 70's*

	Universal Coverage	Reduce Qualifying Period to Eight weeks	Increased Benefit Rates and Levels	Sickness Benefits	Maternity Benefits	Phased Program Structure	4% Trigger for Government Contributions	Experience Rating	Waiting Period of Two weeks
Employers									
Canadian Manufacturers' Association	A	R	AR	R	R	AR	R	R	NP
Retail Council of Canada	A	R	AR	R	R	NP	NP	R	NP
Canadian Construction Association	A	R	NP	R	R	NP	NP	R	NP
Ontario Mining Association	A	R	AR	R	R	AR	NP	A	NP
Canadian Chamber of Commerce	A	R	AR	R	R	AR	NP	A	NP
Mining Association of Canada	A	R	AR	R	R	AR	NP	A	NP
Railway Association of Canada	NP	NP	AR	R	NP	A	NP	R	NP
Quebec Employers Council	A	R	NP	R	R	NP	R	R	NP
Employees									
Canadian Railway Labour Association	A	NP	NP	A	A	NP	AR	AI	NP
United Auto Workers	A	A	AI	A	A	R	R	R	R
United Electrical, Radio and Machine Workers	A	A	AI	A	A	R	NP	NP	R
Canadian Labour Congress	A	A	A	A	A	R	R	R	R
Public Service Alliance of Canada	A	A	A	R	AR	R	R	R	R
Confederation of National Trade Unions	A	A	A	A	A	NP	AR	A	NP

Source: Submissions by listed organizations to Standing Committee on Labour, Manpower and Immigration, 1970

Notes: A = approve as is.
          AR = approve, but reduce.
          AI = approve, but increase.
          R = reject.
          NP = no postion.

the self-employed; reduction of the minimum qualifying period from 30 weeks in the last two years to 8 weeks in the last 52 weeks; an increase of benefit rates and levels from an average of 43 per cent of earnings with an upper limit of $53 per week to 66.6 per cent, with a limit of $100 per week; sickness benefits for those with at least 20 weeks of employment in the last year; maternity benefits for those with at least 20 weeks of employment in the last year; a five-phase benefit structure, with a maximum of 51 weeks of benefits; a "trigger," set at a national unemployment rate of 4 per cent, whereby the federal government would pay costs of regular benefits over that figure; experience rating, whereby employers with high lay-off rates would pay higher premiums; and an increase in the waiting period from one to two weeks. There were other features of the White Paper and legislation, but the above were the most frequently commented upon.

There are a number of striking patterns to Table 5. With the exception of the Railway Association of Canada, which expressed no position, employer and employee groups unanimously supported expansion of the program to a universal basis. The employer groups tended to justify this expansion on insurance grounds: a good insurance plan pools risks, and the bigger the pool the more sound the plan. Employee groups on the whole took a moral point of view: all people should be protected from the hardships of unemployment.

The other program feature upon which there seemed broad agreement was benefit rates and levels. All but two of the employer associations and all but one of the employee associations favoured an increase. In the case of employers, however, the specific proposal in the White Paper was too much. Many employer groups, while supporting an increase in benefits, suggested a rate of 60 per cent of previous earnings and an upper limit of $100 per week. The UAW and the United Electrical, Radio and Machine Workers approved an increase in benefits but agreed that the White Paper proposal was inadequate. The other three labour centrals simply approved the White Paper proposal.

Employer and employee associations were opposed on most other issues, however. The lowering of the minimum qualifying period to 8 weeks of employment out of the previous 52 was unanimously opposed by employers; it was unanimously approved by employees. Employers argued that this period did not indicate sufficient labour force attachment, while unions applauded the assistance this would extend to workers with unstable work histories. Sickness and maternity benefits showed the same extreme polarization: employers unanimously rejecting them, employees, with the exception of the Public Service Alliance of Canada (PSAC), approving their inclusion. Employers as a group made one consistent argument against their inclusion. They pointed out that the rationale of UI, as an insurance program, was that it covered wages lost through involuntary unemployment.

Persons collecting benefits had to demonstrate that they were available for and capable of suitable work. Sickness and maternity benefits were inconsistent with this logic. While sickness could be presumed to be involuntary in most cases, pregnancy usually was not. More important, in both cases, a sick or pregnant person could not reasonably be defined as "available for work."

Employee groups, because they placed little or no emphasis on the insurance character of the program, seeing it instead as a social or income security device, approved the inclusion of these new types of benefits. Interestingly, the PSAC, the members of which had not previously been covered by UI but would now come under the program, argued against these benefits, in part on the same grounds as employers, but also because in its view these benefits were open to abuse. A few of the employer groups, such as the Railway Association of Canada, rejected sickness and maternity benefits as part of the UI plan but suggested that they might be established as separate programs.

The differences over the phased nature of the new program were complex. Three of the eight employee associations had no position on the matter, while most of the rest approved of the phases but thought the maximum duration of benefits available through them – 51 weeks – far too long. Most of this group referred to the Gill Committee recommendations that the maximum duration of regular benefits be 26 weeks. Since most employer groups approved the discontinuation of seasonal benefits, this would effectively have become the maximum duration. Labour unions, in contrast, tended to reject the phased structure because it actually reduced the maximum duration of benefits. The UAW, for example, argued that under the pre-1971 act persons could receive up to 51 weeks of regular benefits and then, in some cases, another 25 weeks of seasonal benefits. Thus, as in other areas, employers pressed for a less generous duration while employees pressed for a more generous definition.

Surprisingly, because the White Paper itself highlighted it, most of the employer groups did not refer to the "4 per cent trigger." The two that did, the CMA and the Quebec Employers Council, recommended against it, for financial and administrative reasons. From the financial point of view, the government's contributions could come only from tax revenues, and both groups suggested that taxes were already high enough. From the administrative point of view, they worried that such a substantial government role would undermine the autonomy of the commission and reduce its authority and obligation to manage the program efficiently. The employee groups, except for the United Electrical, Radio and Machine Workers, which had no position, either rejected outright the 4 per cent trigger or approved it, but with the recommendation that the trigger be lowered. In both cases, the logic was the same. Employee groups believed that, whatever the government's disclaimers, a 4 per cent trigger that acted as the point beyond which the government acknowledged a responsibility for unemployment would become the new definition of a socially acceptable level of unemployment. Most of the employee associations preferred the Economic Council of Canada's recent definition of the full employment target as 3 per cent, while others simply upheld the old tripartite funding structure.

The last two of the White Paper's key proposals drew an interesting pattern of response. Employer associations were clearly divided on the question of experience rating, lukewarm support contrasting with adamant opposition. The CMA, the Retail Council, and the Canadian Construction Association rejected experience rating, possibly because many of their members were in seasonal industries, but the Canadian Chamber of Commerce and the Mining Association of Canada supported it. Employee associations were similarly divided, with approval coming from only the Canadian Railway Labour Association and the Confederation of National Trade Unions. The former suggested steeply graduated rates to ensure the disincentive effect; but the UAW, the CLC, and the PSAC argued against this proposal. Perhaps because of this broad opposition the government, while including experience rating in the 1971 act, never implemented it.

The White Paper proposed increasing the waiting period before benefits were paid from one to two weeks. Not one of the major employer associations mentioned this change, while all but two of the labour organizations opposed it. From the labour point of view the change was an unwarranted restriction of program benefits, and the UAW added that it opposed any removal of benefits to which workers were currently entitled. This labour opposition is less surprising than the employers' silence, but the latter may simply have been an oversight due to the other, larger changes the White Paper proposed.

In summary then, employers and employees did agree on making UI universal and increasing benefits. On the latter point employers were not prepared to go as far as the White Paper, while labour was either satisfied with the White Paper's proposals or wanted even greater increases. On virtually every other issue, however, including reduction of benefits and the phased structure of the program, labour and employers had clear, sharp differences of opinion. These differences over specifics reflected larger differences in philosophical approaches to the program.

Employer groups tended to approach the White Paper from the point of view of UI's effects on the economy and costs of production. The CMA, for example, in the first paragraph of its submission to the Standing Committee on Labour, Manpower and Immigration, argued that "in the designing or redesigning of an unemployment insurance program the amount and duration of benefits, as well as the circumstances under which they shall be paid, must be limited by a consideration as to the effect the total cost of the program will have on the job creating potential of the economy."[102] For the CMA, any drain of tax funds to support a generous UI program sapped investment and productive employment. The CCC also highlighted the cost factor, pointing to Canada's competitive position against the United States, where employers were less burdened with supporting extensive social security arrangements.

Employers consistently emphasized, aside from costs, the importance of solid insurance principles as the basis for the new program. The CCC, for example, argued that the "beneficiaries of Unemployment Insurance should be ready, willing and able to work, and the benefits should be of such a level and duration that seeking work is not discouraged."[103] The CCC also listed what it understood to be the basic insurance principles under which the Canadian program had operated: accumulation within the fund; protection against uncertainties, not certainties; benefits for involuntary and short-term unemployment; benefits not so high as to discourage work effort; and adequate verification of the statement of unemployment and the payment of contribution. The CMA made the identical point in urging that the "internal consistency of the program must be measured by the degree to which sound insurance principles are observed." Among such principles was the concept that benefits be limited to persons who are unemployed and available for work.

Taken together, the emphasis on costs and that on insurance principles help explain the employer position on the White Paper. The White Paper had not contained any cost projections for the new program, and so employers were understandably nervous about what it might entail. While some employer associations, such as the CCC, recognized that UI benefits sustained purchasing power and hence economic activity, most worked with an implicit economic model wherein a dollar of UI benefits was a dollar subtracted from investment. Thus it logically followed that lower UI costs would aid investment and competitiveness. The appeal to "sound insurance principles" had the same result, insofar as these principles could be taken to mean that sickness and maternity benefits were not properly part of UI, that strong labour force attachment (i.e. more than 8 weeks) must be demonstrated, that regular benefits be not so high as to blunt work incentives, and that UI not be directed at long-term or chronic unemployment.

The trade union representatives before the standing committee approached the question quite differently. As one would expect, they kept their attention firmly on the specific problem that UI addresses: loss of income. From this perspective, any proposal that would alleviate the problem would be received favourably. Thus, the CLC welcomed the White Paper "because it promises a greater measure of security against those contingencies which confront members of the labour force, namely, loss of income arising out of unemployment, illness or maternity."[104] The CLC also referred approvingly to insurance principles, such as requiring claimants to be capable of and available for suitable employment, but, unlike the employer groups, thought that the new entry requirement of 8 weeks out of the last 52 was sufficient to show labour force attachment. The UAW took a somewhat more radical line than the CLC, referring to the importance of UI as a social security program and the government's primary responsibility for maintaining employment. Indeed, this last point infused most of the labour submissions: unlike employers, who consistently implied that employment is the private sector's responsibility, employee associations held that it was the government's responsibility. The corollary was that unemployment could be avoided, that its cause was largely social and political, not individual. This position predisposed most employee associations to assume that the vast bulk of unemployment is involuntary and that therefore UI should not be narrow or restrictive.

The PSAC's submission to the standing committee differed from that of other labour organizations in its emphasis on the problem of abuse of UI. In this respect it was closer to employer views than to the CLC or the UAW, possibly because many of its members were coming into the program for the first time but were also least likely to be collecting benefits since public-sector employment at that time was more stable than private-sector employment. Consequently, PSAC members possibly saw themselves as paying the costs of a program without collecting direct benefits.

A final point, not noted in Table 5, deserves mention. The majority of employer and employee associations raised the issue of administration of the program, firmly arguing in favour of the old tripartite commission arrangement. The CMA recommended an "arm's length" relationship between a tripartite commission and the government, similar to that prevailing in workers' compensation boards. It urged that the program "be as far removed from direct or indirect political influence as possible." The CLC favoured a tripartite commission because that gave a direct voice in administrative matters to the two parties most directly interested in UI – employers and employees. Thus, employers seemed worried that governments might try to influence the program for political purposes – possibly expanding it to buy votes – while employees feared losing their traditional control through representation on the commission. Though the reasoning was slightly different, the conclusions were the same: keep the commission as an autonomous body responsible for UI.

According to Bryce Mackasey, minister of labour and responsible for piloting the White Paper and bill through Parliament, the government did not have major problems with employee or employer associations over the new UI program.[105] The government did shy away from experience rating, because of opposition from the construction industry and the CLC, and encountered stiff resistance from national and provincial teachers' associations over the inclusion of teachers under the act. From Mackasey's point of view, the teachers did not want to be included in any UI plan because unemployment among teachers was virtually non-existent, meaning that they would be taxed – through UI contributions – to support others. Mackasey forged ahead anyway, possibly because of the strong support for universal coverage coming from almost every other quarter. Mackasey has also said that the employer representations on the White Paper were viewed somewhat sceptically in both the standing committee and the minister's office, largely because their positions were so predictable. Employers could almost always be counted on to oppose anything that would make the program more generous, while supporting measures that tightened it up.[106]

To judge by the standing committee's report on the White Paper[107] and the act as it was introduced to Parliament shortly afterwards, the multitude of business and labour representations had no major effects. Even the standing committee's changes to the bill resulted in only technical amendments. The philosophy and main provisions of the 1971 UI act were identical to those of the White Paper.[108] In this case, it might appear that the real losers were the employer groups. The White Paper and the legislation accorded fairly well with the interests of labour unions in a richer program and ran directly against views held very strongly by such important groups as the CMA and the CCC. Yet neither side had been involved in designing the White Paper proposals – these were devised by experts and consultants within the government – and so once again a "pressure model" would be inappropriate. It would seem that the 1970-1 UI proposals arose for other reasons and that the appearance of employer and employee groups before the standing committee was little more than an elaborate but ultimately futile ritual.

The new UI program ran into trouble within months of implementation. The first difficulties were largely administrative. The commission was dealing simultaneously with two programs, because the pre-1971 provisions remained in force for those who became unemployed before the new act came into effect. The extension of coverage and the conversion to computer-based data storage compounded the difficulties. Within a year, however, and just before the 1972 federal election, concern shifted to alleged abuses of the program and its rapidly increasing costs. The two issues were linked insofar as widespread abuse led to higher program costs. It was argued in the press that the eight-week entry requirement, the high benefit rates, and special benefits such as maternity, sickness, and retirement left the program extremely vulnerable. The government's commitment to pay regular benefits for unemployment rates in excess of 4 per cent was leading, as rates rose, to alarmingly high transfers to the UI account. By 1975 the federal government was paying roughly 50 per cent of program costs.

In 1973 the minister of manpower and immigration, Robert Andras, introduced Bill C-125 to tighten up the program. It would have raised entry requirements for voluntary quits, misconduct dismissals, and failures to take suitable employment and would have increased the disqualification period from 3 to 8 weeks. As one observer has noted: "The employer community favoured more stringent disqualifications provisions. But the Bill was considered unacceptable by a number of Members of Parliament and employee representatives at a time when continuing difficulties in receiving benefits were being experienced by those with legitimate claims. The government, then in a minority position in the Commons, withdrew the Bill."[109]

An intense period of legislative amendment began in 1975 and extended through to 1978. There was a brief hiatus in 1979 (though studies were under way on possible changes), but the process began again in 1980 with the appointment of a Task Force on Unemployment Insurance. The task force's July 1981 report was the basis of consultations with the private sector that should have led to further legislative change, but the latter did not occur. The 1975-8 series of amendments to UI was contentious, partly because the changes themselves reduced the program's generosity, but also because they were implemented just as Canadian unemployment rates were increasing. Acrimony was particularly evident in the House of Commons, where Liberal Maritime MPs criticized the government's proposals as vigorously as the Opposition did. In each case as well, employer and employee groups appeared before the Standing Committee on Labour, Manpower and Immigration to press their views. Positions had not changed since 1970, though the lines had hardened somewhat; employer groups generally favoured most of the changes while employee groups opposed them. Table 6 summarizes the main changes proposed in each set of amendments.

The changes implemented in Bill C-69 (1975) were alluded to first in the Throne Speech of 30 September 1974 and then again in fuller form in the federal budget of 23 June 1975. The government had been prepared to make legislative amendments to the UI act within one year of its passage but had refrained because of its minority position in the House. The 1975 changes therefore can be traced back to 1972. They also had roots in an ongoing process of comprehensive review of UI being conducted by the commission and the development of new labour policies by the government. In his introduction to the bill, Robert Andras said:

I should like to emphasize that the changes contained in this bill which is being presented to parliament are the results of the first findings of our review of the legislation. However, as is proper with a program of such significance, this comprehensive examination is continuing, particularly in relationship to two parallel policy developments. I mentioned one, the over-all harmonization of all our social security programs. The other is the evolution of an integrated and more comprehensive manpower policy.[110]

TABLE 6
Summary of Major UI Amendments,
Bills C-69, C-27, C-14

Bill C-69 (1975)

Disqualification for voluntary quits, misconduct dismissals, job refusals increased from
   three to six weeks
Special 75 per cent dependants' benefit rate discontinued
Four per cent threshold changed to eight-year moving average
More flexible rules for sickness benefits, voluntary termination of claims, and qualifying
   period

Bill C-27 (1976–7)

UIC and Department of Manpower and Immigration amalgamated
Five phase benefit structure changed to three phases
Developmental uses of UI authorized
Variable entrance requirement (VER) of 10 to 14 weeks, depending on regional
   unemployment rate

Bill C-14 (1978)

Higher entrance requirements for new entrants, re-entrants, and program repeaters
Reduction in benefit rate from 66.6 per cent to 60 per cent
Tripartite financing of labour force extended benefits
Increase in fines and penalties for fraudulent collection of benefits
High-income claimants return 30 per cent of benefits in taxation.

The changes of Bill C-27 (1976-7) were rooted in the development of a new, comprehensive manpower policy announced by Bud Cullen, the minister of manpower and immigration, in his *Employment Strategy*. In itself, the "strategy" put old wine into a new bottle. It sought to consolidate and rationalize existing programs and in that respect reflected long-run forces discussed in more detail in the next chapter. The strategy had three broad thrusts: a job creation program, youth employment measures, and preventive measures to reduce loss of work and hasten a return to employment. The developmental uses of UI fell in the last category, but the other changes in Bill C-67 could also be seen as ways of removing obstacles in the program to labour mobility.

   Bill C-14 (1978), the amendments in which promised to save almost $1 billion in program costs by 1980-1, seems to have had its genesis in the prime minister's surprise economic restraint announcement in the summer of 1978. The minister was forced to generate new cost-cutting proposals by September, ones that he had not anticipated.[111]

   Despite the cumulative impact and magnitude of these changes between 1975 and 1978, the government solicited relatively little interest group feedback at committee stage and none at drafting stage. The CMA and the CLC presented briefs on each of the three bills, the Canadian Federation of Independent Business on two, and the Canadian Council on Social Development on one. Since 1971, business and labour stances on UI had hardened considerably. In 1970 there had been some modest consensus over extending coverage and improving benefits, but the program's problems in the intervening years had served to make the CMA's criticisms of UI more pointed and the CLC's defence more determined.

The CMA approved, in varying degrees, of all the major changes proposed in each set of amendments. It found fault with Bill C-69 for not going far enough in tightening up the program and recommended the same provisions it had put forward in 1970 regarding the White Paper and in 1962 before the Gill Committee: a 60 per cent benefit rate, a maximum benefit duration of 26 weeks, and a qualifying period of at least 20 weeks.[112] The CMA made the same suggestions a year later with reference to Bill C-27, emphasizing what it saw as the high costs of UI and the program's work disincentive. It thus approved the bill's measures, though it did not support work sharing or job creation expenditures using UI funds, worrying that these would be open to political abuse.[113] Bill C-14, which contained the most dramatic program cuts of the three bills, was applauded by the CMA for its "positive effect on cost competition" and received the association's strong support.[114]

In contrast, the CLC strongly opposed most of the measures in each of the bills. Of Bill C-69, for example, the CLC said: "The Congress, therefore, views several of the proposed amendments ... as being odious in principle and retrogressive."[115] The CLC opposed virtually every provision in Bill C-27, though it was prepared to see an amalgamation of the Department of Manpower and Immigration and the commission, as long as UI was not eclipsed in the move by an excessive focus on manpower policies. Interestingly, its only point of agreement with the CMA was the rejection of work sharing and job creation uses of UI funds.[116] The CLC appeared less worried about financial boondoggles than the political meaning of these programs: they were to be supported by funds drained from a less generous UI program.[117] Bill C-14 engendered the most bitter brief from the CLC; it strongly protested the haste with which the bill was introduced and expressed total opposition to the proposals, which in its eyes would turn UI into little more than means-tested welfare. A final notable feature of the CLC submissions on bills C-27 and C-14 was complaints about lack of consultation. In each case, the CLC claimed, the amendments had been "sprung" on the public without discussions with labour or business interests most directly affected by UI.

These sharp views from interest groups again had little effect on legislation: the standing committee's suggestions in all three cases were merely technical, and the only major revision, in Bill C-27 from a uniform 12-week entrance requirement to a variable 10-14-week requirement, was the result of internal Liberal party dissent from Maritime MPs. In inspiration and effect, however, the changes were as clearly favourable to employer interests as the White Paper proposals had been to labour interests. Once again, however, a simple pressure model must be used with caution. Bills c-69 and c-27 had their genesis in internal policy development, in which employer views may have carried some, but not dominant weight. Bill c-14 stemmed from the prime minister's quixotic decision to impose further fiscal restraints on government. Moreover, some of the legislative amendments had no employer counterparts, such as the amalgamation of the Department of Manpower and Immigration and the commission, or were explicitly opposed by the CMA, such as work sharing. Finally, while government policy was moving in the employers' direction, it was not even remotely close to some of the program recommendations in the CMA briefs. The relation between interest group positions and government policy was therefore somewhat ambiguous.

These conclusions are supported by a brief analysis of the 1980-1 Task Force on Unemployment Insurance. UI and federal labour policies had been under almost constant scrutiny since 1978, and when the Liberals were returned in 1980 they decided that a fundamental review of both aspects of policy should be undertaken. Two task forces were thus established, one to analyse labour market trends and recommend new manpower policies, the other to look at UI. The UI task force had a small, compact staff and conducted its research and formulated its recommendations without any consultations with interest groups or provinces. One reason for this "internal review" structure was that the positions of interest groups were entirely predictable and entirely opposed.[118] The review had to be detailed enough to indicate specific changes, but this would have been impossible had the report been *built* on consultation.[119] Consultation did come, however, but after the task force released its report in July 1981. The task force eventually met with over 100 employer associations, 15 labour centrals, the provinces, and women's groups. There also were interdepartmental consultations on implementing the task force "package."

The task force's report was intended to generate discussion and reaction and eventually consensus. The authors of the report decided against an "options approach," which in their view would have encouraged the mixing of elements and diluted overall impact. Rather, they presented a "package" of proposals touching on virtually every major aspect of the program. The drawback of this approach was its impression that a single package had the government's full approval. To the task force, and to the minister, these were simply suggestions; to interest groups they appeared suspiciously like a fait accompli. The task force's counter-strategy to minimize opposition was a careful balancing of proposals so that roughly half would appeal to employer associations and roughly half to employee associations. The authors knew what the reactions would be to any given proposal and were able to use this knowledge to their advantage. Far from influencing government policy-makers with strong, clear positions, employer and employee reflexes became resources that the state used to achieve its own purposes.

The task force's package was aimed at strengthening UI's "contribution to labour market objectives" and specifically at reducing barriers to "labour market adjustment now present in the program design."[120] The package also recommended changes that would reduce the program's complexity and increase the equity of treatment of claimants, particularly women. The package had ten major proposals:

1. Eliminate the special entrance requirements for new entrants, re-entrants, repeaters, and special benefits (sickness, maternity, and retirement).
2. Adopt a single entrance requirement of 15-20 weeks, depending on regional unemployment rates.
3. Reduce the three-phase benefit structure to a single phase.
4. Streamline maternity benefits.
5. Relax minimum insurability rules.
6. Extend maternity benefits to adoptive parents.
7. Double the disqualification period for voluntary quits.
8. Increase the benefit repayment rate to 50 per cent.
9. Eliminate special retirement benefits.
10. Revise the formula for determining maximum insurable earnings.[121]

The net effect of these changes would have been a saving of $220 million, but this was a result of a $295 million saving by the government added to a $75 million net increase in costs for the private sector. Most of the savings came from three items: the increased entrance requirement ($175 million), the single-phase benefit structure ($225 million), and the doubled disqualification period ($190 million). The greatest increases in expenditures were associated with the new maternity benefit structure ($140 million) and the new formula for determining maximum insurable earnings ($157 million).[122]

Employer and employee reactions to this package of proposals closely paralleled positions taken throughout the 1975-8 amendments. In a letter to Lloyd Axworthy, minister of employment and immigration, the CMA said that it supported "those Task Force proposals which reinforce the insurance aspects of the unemployment insurance program, and object to those which move the program further in a social direction."[123] Quite logically, therefore, the CMA supported as "moves in the right direction" the increased entrance requirement, shortened benefit duration under a single-phase structure, the increased disqualification period, and elimination of special retirement benefits. It still wished, however, to see a uniform, national entrance requirement of 20 weeks and a maximum benefit duration of 26 weeks. It opposed "the further extension of the program into social areas" and thus disagreed with reducing requirements for maternity and sickness benefits, as well as easing rules on insurable employment. The CMA also disagreed with the heavy share of new costs the private sector would be forced to bear. The CCC's response was virtually identical to the CMA's.[124]

This cautious approval from business contrasted with strong disapproval from labour. The CLC, for example, put the task force's report in the context of policies for full employment and what it saw as recent federal policies "exclusively devoted to the aim of bringing about a shift of national income from labour to capital".[125] The CLC supported the six task force proposals that would make the program more equitable in its eyes – such as easing and extending maternity benefits and eliminating special requirements for new entrants – but opposed the eight recommendations that were largely supported by business – such as increasing the entrance requirement. Other major employee associations took the same approach.[126]

The government was never faced with having to negotiate among these sharply opposing views because the task force's report became irrelevant almost the day it was released. The report, and its companion analysis of labour market policies in the 1980s, had assumed that the Canadian economy was in a state of fundamental transformation from traditional industries (e.g. automobiles) in traditional areas (e.g. Ontario) to new, large-scale, resource-related industries and high technology located at least in part in the West. Government programs, it was thought, should assist the coming industrial and geographic shifts. Unfortunately, the recession deepened alarmingly in the winter of 1981, and the rationale underpinning the task force's proposals collapsed.

The patterns described above seem to be reflected in the fortunes of the Forget Commission.[127] The commission's key recommendations would have revolutionized the program by eliminating regionally extended benefits, the variable entrance requirement, and fishermen's benefits and drastically reducing regular benefits for everyone except those with over 40 weeks of employment a year. Essentially, Forget's philosophy paralleled Gill's, in that he proposed separate programs for the chronically unemployed.

Of the six Forget commissioners, two represented labour and two represented business. The latter supported the majority report, which itself reflected in broad terms the business agenda on UI expressed since 1971. The minority report issued by the two labour representatives was, as we would expect, in almost complete disagreement with Forget on all key points. Does this mean that business exercised a dominant influence? As with the 1981 task force, the evidence is mixed. First, some key recommendations had few referents in any major business submissions – for example, annualization, the cumulative employment account, and elements of the human resource development strategy. Second, a little-appreciated aspect of the report was its potential to generate a number of new income supplementation programs financed through UI savings. Business on the whole is unenthusiastic about such programs, which are distinct from social assistance. Third, even if decisive business influence were conceded, this was after all merely a royal commission report. The government itself wasted no time in disassociating itself from the recommendations. Even if business groups won the battle with Forget, they lost the larger policy war.

CONCLUSION

If any government policy is susceptible to neo-pluralist and neo-Marxist explanations, then UI must be. It is deeply embedded in the capitalist labour market because it reduces the immediate need to find work if one is unemployed. It thus shifts the political as well as economic balance of power. It is also costly, for both workers and employers. One would expect to find, therefore, strongly held positions. These approaches also suggest that the views of employers – presumably critical of UI – prevail.

The first expectation is clearly upheld in the history of Canadian UI. Labour has supported UI since the First World War, and its only doubts in the 1930s were whether the program should be contributory or non-contributory. Labour consistently favoured program expansion after 1945 and broadly supported the 1971 act. It strongly opposed changes made in the 1970s to restrict the program, as well as similar proposals in the report of the 1981 task force. Canadian labour has always approached the program as a specific instrument to alleviate the distress of unemployment, an instrument moreover that Canadians may claim as a right. Economic and labour market goals have always been secondary.

Employers, in contrast, opposed UI in the 1930s, constantly suggesting delays in implementation to further "study" the program. Some employers, in private correspondence with Prime Minister Bennett, did recommend UI, because they saw it as a means of avoiding open class war or simply from sympathy with the unemployed. Employer associations came to accept the program once it was in place but opposed virtually every extension of coverage, benefits, or duration of benefits suggested in the 1950s and 1960s. By the time of the Gill Committee's hearings, the CMA was no longer opposed to universal coverage and even some improvement in benefit rates, but this was less surprising than it might seem, since coverage was already up to 80 per cent of the work-force and benefit improvements were modest. The CMA and other business groups supported most of the 1970 White Paper proposals but seemed uncomfortable doing so: they usually suggested caution and care and were unequipped to deal with finer technical points. Accordingly, when the program foundered, employer groups strongly supported retrenchment and cutbacks. If labour has focused on the *problem* of unemployment and UI as an income security measure, business has organized its arguments for 50 years around the notion of "sound insurance." It has consistently argued that sound insurance involves pooling of risks, a stable fund, and coverage of involuntary unemployment only. On these grounds, the CMA and other groups could oppose allegedly overgenerous benefits, special benefits, low entry requirements, and long benefit duration.

The second component of these explanations was also evident. Government policy-makers were clearly aware of the differences in views between employers and employees. They learned of these differences through formal and informal channels, such as letters and submissions to standing committees and correspondence. By the early 1960s, policy-makers were referring to the "traditional" stances of these groups, and by the 1970s these stances and reactions to proposed changes in UI were considered utterly predictable.

In 1980, for example, the Policy and Legislation Development (Benefit Programs) Branch of the commission produced a detailed summary of non-governmental organizations' briefs regarding UI for the 1971-9 period.[128] It noted employers' clear concern over "adherence to the insurance principle," their "overall negative attitude" to maternity and sickness benefits, their "almost unanimous opposition" to developmental uses, and their emphasis on work disincentives and high costs. Employee organizations, in contrast, focused on the need for greater government action against unemployment without penalizing the unemployed, the need for adequate and immediate access to benefits, and the protection of claimants' rights.

The evidence for the third and crucial component of the explanation is the weakest of the three. If these differences between employer and employee groups existed, and governments were aware of them, did policy respond as the literature suggests, that is, did it tend to favour the employers' views? The answer is a qualified no. First, there is evidence that employers' views on UI were treated with some disdain throughout this period. Officials in the 1930s and afterwards often commented pejoratively on what they saw as technically inadequate submissions from the CMA and others. The very predictability of the business position engendered weariness among policy-makers in the 1970s and also provided them with a resource, since proposals could be "packaged" in order to exploit business support.

Second, most of the legislative record stands as witness to the absence of business impact on policy. The 1940 legislation was passed over significant business opposition, and program development in the 1950s was undertaken despite business disapproval. The CMA endorsed the Gill Committee's recommendations, but these were not implemented, save for the separation of the National Employment Service from the commission, a recommendation on which the CMA had no strong views. On balance, the 1971 act contradicted business views. Only the changes implemented in bills C-69, C-27, and C-14 strongly reflected business sentiments, but even there business's view was not accepted in its entirety. Indeed, a dispassionate assessment would suggest that in its first 35 years of existence, UI program development met labour interests more accurately than business interests. In any case, business's views in the 1970s were entirely reactive; the key associations were not consulted on the bills.

It may be expecting too much to derive specific legislative changes from business briefs and submissions. These society-centred approaches might just as usefully outline the constraints that employer and employee groups place on government decision-makers – the limits of reform and change. It is empirically difficult to establish such limits, but examination of UI's history suggests that even this weak version of the approach fails. It is hard to imagine a more funadamental constraint than "total opposition," and yet governments passed the 1935, 1940, and 1975-8 acts over such opposition from either business groups or labour.

Another saving hypothesis might be that the real influence of interests comes through political parties that have a class base. Labour, for instance, might be impotent to influence legislation through its parliamentary briefs but might affect policy through the CCF/NDP. This seems implausible for several reasons. First, as small parties, the CCF/NDP or independent labour members could have had a decisive impact only in minority-government periods, 1921-6, 1962-8, 1972-4, and 1979-80. In the first period the Progressives, as an agrarian party, opposed UI. The NDP was ineffectual in all but the 1972-4 period, when its opposition to UI cuts forestalled legislative change, *but not regulatory change*. Second, if the CCF/NDP represents labour, then presumably the Liberals and Conservatives represent business, but, as was shown, these parties often ignored business demands.

It might be argued that governments do pay attention to the balance of class forces but that this balance is general, not specific to a given policy field. What mattered, in other words, in the 1930s was the threat of revolution; in the 1970s capital was demanding curbs on labour in exchange for investment.[129] It is this broader warfare, not specific battles, that determines a government's posture. This position has some merit but shifts the focus to internal government calculations and the ways these calculations are made. It also leaves the specifics of policy unanswered. Why make these and not other benefit provisions? Why are these occupations covered, but not others? Why choose this form of administration instead of another?

CHAPTER FIVE

Bureaucratic Politics

Modern public policy is increasingly, it appears, a bureaucratic affair, conceived and developed within the state, proposed as part of departmental agendas, and implemented by state authorities. Recent work has therefore focused on the influence of bureaucracy on public policy. This influence may be understood more broadly as the effect of autonomous state forces on public policy formation and implementation. While different models emphasize different forces, their common ground is a belief in the independence of state and political institutions – from bureaucracy to political parties – from other social forces.

This general approach stands, sometimes consciously and sometimes not, in opposition to more society-centred views of the state. The latter try to understand the state and the political process in terms of forces such as ideology, class structure, or interest group conflict. The state and its organs do not have independent interests, separate agendas, or self-sufficient routines. Instead, they reflect or echo, with varying degrees of fidelity, external social forces. The state is less an actor than an arena, more a mirror than a mover. As Stephen Krasner puts it: "Academic explanations have treated government behavior as the outcome of a series of pressures that emanate from the society. The state has been seen not as an autonomous actor, but rather as a mirror reflecting particularistic societal interests."[1] Krasner prefers what he calls a "statist paradigm" wherein the state is conceived "as a set of roles and institutions having peculiar drives, compulsions, and aims of their own that are separate and distinct from the interests of any particular societal [g]roup."[2]

Eric Nordlinger has provided a sustained critique of society-centred views of politics, which imply that bureaucrats are preoccupied with the balance of societal interest groups. In Nordlinger's view, "the democratic state is not only frequently autonomous insofar as it regularly acts upon its preferences, but also markedly autonomous in doing so even when its preferences diverge from the demands of the most powerful groups in civil society."[3] The state's "preferences" are defined as the "resource-weighted parallelogram," or resultant, of public officials' preferences, in turn shaped by career interests, organizational loyalties, and professional knowledge.[4] State preferences result from internal political conflict among public officials. Nordlinger is careful to distinguish his view from that of Krasner, who assumes not only that the state behaves differently from other institutions by acting on its own preferences but that these preferences are internally generated.[5] Nordlinger believes this to be unlikely, since all actors in a given nation-state are affected by the same environment. As well, while Nordlinger defines the state in terms of individual actors occupying a given set of roles, Krasner essentially defines it in terms of the highest and most insulated offices, in the United States, the presidency and the State Department.

Theda Skocpol also attacks the assumption that "political structure and struggles can somehow be reduced (at least 'in the last instance') to socioeconomic forces and conflicts."[6] This assumption makes it impossible, in Skocpol's view, to see the state as a structure with "a logic and interests of its own," as an "organization-for-itself."[7] Thus, whereas many students have seen the political crises that launch most social revolutions as "epiphenomenal reflections of societal strains or class contradictions," Skocpol argues that political conflict over state structures has been a central, and autonomous, force in social revolutions. The French, Russian, and Chinese revolutions were launched in large part as a consequence of "old regime crises," centred in state structures and situations.[8] While hers is a broader historical vision than Nordlinger's or Krasner's, and emphasizes coercive and military segments of state structure, Skocpol's work has made an influential contribution to the view that policy is best explained by looking inside state structures.[9]

Krasner, Nordlinger, and Skocpol tend to see the state as a single actor, with a single set of preferences, though Nordlinger is prepared to acknowledge that this unity sometimes masks internal conflict. The theme of internal conflict, of the state as a feudal coalition of competing departments, agencies, and interests, has been extensively developed within the public administration and public policy literature. From the beginning, this literature rejected the prevailing mechanistic paradigm in organization theory, which saw complex organizations as unified instruments responding to an executive's will.[10] In contrast, the new perspective stressed the politics of bureaucracy, both within organizations and across them. Bureaucratic politics was much like ordinary politics in that it entailed conflict over prestige, power, and resources. One of the earliest presentations of the argument termed the phenomenon "bureaucratic imperialism" and suggested that senior administrators were really "administrative politicians" faced with the "necessity to increase power if the agency is to survive and flourish in an administrative habitat crowded with other agencies."[11] Agency strategies depended on the incentives the agency could provide to maintain a favourable balance of constituencies. Government bureaucracies, in other words, shape social forces, as well as being ultimately determined by them. A variation of this approach suggested that while government organizations reflect political and even social forces and priorities, once in place they have an effect all their own, shaped by organizational tradition and routines and by professional standards.[12]

The salient feature of these arguments is the independence of bureaucracy and hence its disproportionate effect on public policy. Some have gone so far as to suggest that "it is in the crucible of administrative politics today that public policy is mainly hammered out, through bargaining, negotiation, and conflict among appointed rather than elected officials."[13] Bureaucracy, by mobilizing interests and constituencies, and by virtue of its control over strategic information resources and expertise, can control the development of public policy.[14] B. Guy Peters has noted these and other resources that bureaux enjoy (e.g. they can claim to be apolitical and hence above the fray; they have permanence and stability denied to most political groups) but cautions that while they permit substantial influence, they have not led to "bureaucratic government" or rule by bureaucratic elites.[15] Bureaucratic politics is restrained by a desire to maintain stability and the security of influence within a given policy sphere.

Graham Allison takes a less sanguine view of the internal rivalries and conflicts that characterize the bureaucratic policy process. To Allison, government is "a conglomerate of large organizations and political actors who differ substantially about what their government should do on any particular issue and who compete in attempting to affect both governmental decisions and the actions of their government."[16] Policy decisions are usually resolved by small groups of "senior players," whose part in the game derives from "action channels" or routines of inclusion but whose strategies flow from a host of political, organizational, and personal interests.[17] The game analogy is quite appropriate, since outcomes depend on the skill and will of participants, chance, and external constraints.

While Allison, Peters, and others who argue for a bureaucratic politics approach differ substantially from Krasner, Nordlinger, and Skocpol, they all agree on looking *inside the state* for explanations of public policy. Public opinion, elections, and interest groups have a small or insignificant place in the explanatory framework. Yet the differences among these writers are also notable. The principal fissure concerns the importance of organization versus the importance of individuals within organizations. In discussing the role of bureaucracy in policy formation, there is a tendency either to stress structural and organizational variables, such as tradition, expertise, and monopoly of information, or to highlight the individual self-interest of officials acting within the context of bureaucratic institutions. In other words, bureaucratic politics may be a matter of either the politics of bureaux or politics in bureaux. The first approach underscores those stable features that give bureaucracies a predominant role in the public policy system, while the latter tends to analyse single policy decisions.

These differences have been at least partially reconciled in the work of Buchanan, Tullock, Niskanen, and Downs. Their work represents a more deductive approach to the characteristics of modern organizations, which rests upon certain premises about individual behaviour. Though the first three writers have focused on public bureaucracy, and especially its effect on societal resource allocation, while Downs has tried to present a more general organization theory, their work may be treated as a whole for the purposes of this discussion.

The theory is grounded in assumptions about human nature. Tullock asserts that "every man is an individual with his own private ends and ambitions."[18] Public officials therefore have private interests to which organizational interests will be subordinated. Niskanen, for example, suggests that a bureaucrat's utility function is composed of the following: salary, perquisites of office, public reputation, power, patronage, output of the bureau, ease of making changes, and ease of managing the bureau.[19] Downs agrees that bureaucratic officials are "significantly – though not solely – motivated by their own self-interests."[20] "Bureaucratic officials in general have a complex set of goals including power, income, prestige, security, convenience, loyalty (to an idea, an institution, or the nation), pride in excellent work, and desire to serve the public interest ... Every official is significantly motivated by his own self-interest even when acting in a purely official capacity."[21] An important point is that officials, while being utility maximizers, need not be considered as Machiavellian manipulators of their environment: it is enough that organizational goals may be reinterpreted and understood by officials in terms of their self-interest.

The self-interest of officials is pursued within the organization or the bureau and in large measure depends upon it. All the items in Niskanen's utility function save the last two depend on the bureau's budget. Individual salary, prestige, and power rest, for the most part, on the size of the bureau, which, other things being equal, depends in turn on its budget. From this stems most of the rivalry and conflict among bureaus, noted by Allison and others. Budgetary resources are limited, and so officials are involved in constant "pulling and hauling" to ensure jurisdictional authority, legitimacy, and stable, if not growing, budgetary allocations.

Downs has developed the most elaborate version of this argument. He suggests that the functions of a given bureau take place within a "policy space."[22] The policy space surrounding each of the bureau's specific functions may in turn be divided into territorial zones, defined by the degree of dominance over social action that the bureau exercises in each portion of the space. In the "interior zone" the bureau has the dominant policy role, and this may in turn be subdivided into a "heartland," where the bureau exercises absolute control, and the interior fringe, where it is dominant but where other social agents have some influence. Beyond the interior, there is "no man's land," where no single bureau dominates but many have influence. Finally, there is the "exterior zone," which is simply another bureau's interior zone, and where the first bureau has either little or no influence. Downs suggests that one of the most important "properties of each bureau's territory is the ambiguity of its boundaries."[23] This ambiguity leads to "an incessant jockeying for position in policy space, as each bureau (or other social agent) struggles to defend or extend the existing borders of its various territorial zones."[24] Bureaux must try to resist even minor territorial invasions, since these may have major effects in the future. These observations lead Downs to conclude that every large organization is in partial conflict with every other social agent.

The most useful weapon in such struggles is organizational cohesion and a sense of mission or goal consensus. Bureaux achieve this through selective recruitment of new personnel, indoctrination of existing personnel, and maintenance of bureaucratic ideologies. These ideologies are developed by senior officials as means of communicating with groups inside and outside the bureau. Bureaucratic ideologies have greater detail, consistency, and depth than traditional political ideologies, principally because they can afford to be narrower, because "consumers" of these ideologies have a higher average intensity of interest in their content, and because the ideologies tend to identify "problems" requiring bureaucratic attention. According to Downs, bureaucratic ideologies are most functional for bureaux that are large, recruiting new personnel, engaged in controversial activities, having overlapping functions, or attempting to expand.

The approach outlined by Downs, Niskanen, and Tullock combines the individualist perspective with the structural approach in a semi-deductive framework. Bureaux have specific autonomy with respect both to other government bureaux and particularly to outside groups. This autonomy may be rooted either in individual officials' desires to further their own interests – which they can do best by establishing the bureau on firm ground – or in the bureau's command of information and expertise, carefully woven into a bureaucratic ideology. Incorporating Nordlinger and Krasner, we can also suggest that bureaucratic actions, indeed the formation of policy itself, will frequently reflect the internal needs of the organization more than pressures put on it by outside groups. Bureaux will be in constant conflict with one another over the contours of the "policy space" and their role in it.[25]

For purposes of this chapter, two key conclusions follow from this description of bureaucratic politics. They are, first, the internal logic of bureaucratic action and, second, inter-bureaucratic rivalry.[26] The internal logic of the organization itself has at least three aspects. First, there is what Downs has identified as bureaucratic ideology, or the organization's vision of itself, its role, and its posture towards the problems it or others have defined for it. It will emphasize the organization's efficiency and success and also serve to define its policy space distinctly enough to protect it from the incursions of other organizations.

Second, there is the bureau's monopoly of information or skill. This expertise should not be confused with the training of any one official or functionary; rather it is assumed to be a general characteristic of the organization in question. Thus, all who work in a direct way with the organization's policy functions are assumed, through practice and exposure, to have special knowledge. As well, the organization becomes a repository for data and other information not easily available to outside groups. This intimacy with policy and information is strongly buttressed by some special skill, which, while not always widely spread in the bureau, helps to define the bureau's special ability to deal with its problems. Thus treasury officials not only possess an intimate knowledge of budgets and financial information but are also familiar with economic science. The bureau's monopoly of information or skill becomes infused with organizational meaning through the bureau's ideology.

Third, there is the importance of intra-organizational goals and needs. These pertain to the organization as an organization and involve primarily its ability to fulfil its functions with some modicum of efficiency as well as maintaining stable growth. Efficiency might involve viable delivery strategies and technologies, while stable growth would include protection from hostile organizations. Thus a particular service might be denied to a given group not out of narrow political motives but because efficient delivery techniques do not exist, while in some cases services will be extended less out of a political mandate than to forestall incursions into the bureau's policy space.

The importance of the internal logic of bureaux is that it provides a basis for understanding how policy may be formed or how governments behave independently from powerful groups. Naturally, this independence is limited, since all bureaux are affected by their environment, but it is substantial enough that we may speak of separate agendas, motives, and goals. While government policies may indeed meet the demands of powerful groups from time to time, this does not necessarily mean that those interests compel the policies. They may be generated autonomously within the organization rather than from outside pressures.

Inter-bureaucratic conflict is important as well, since it suggests the critical environment within which most organizations must function. The conflict may involve only skirmishes, or it may be outright war. It may be about budgets, personnel, co-ordination, centralization, data, or philosophy. Personalities are less important than structure, since the reason officials, as individuals, are in conflict has to do with organizational mandates – without them and the official's perception of how personal interests are served by this mandate, there would be no basis for conflict. Thus, because of organizational needs for prestige and budgets, and because of the ambiguities of policy space, most bureaux have clear rivals and competitors. This is true even of more hierarchically organized forms of government, such as the parliamentary form, though it may be expected that the conflict there might be muted.[27]

Does all inter-bureaucratic conflict lead to policy change? It depends upon one's view of public policy, but if policy means long-term frameworks within which smaller decisions are made and guided, then the answer must be no. Some conflicts, such as those over incremental budgetary or personnel allocations, usually have no effect on broad policy, whatever the outcome. Sometimes conflict is localized to a single decision (e.g. whether or not to close a school) that has no bearing on policy. Policy conflict is at once broader than these examples and more rare. By definition (ours, at any rate) policy is a stable framework for decision-making; it defines problems, goals, preferred solutions, and means of effecting solutions. To be true policy conflicts, the struggle among bureaux must be about these bigger questions. Such conflict will be a small subset of the larger number of frequent interactions among bureaux. Moreover, policy conflict may sometimes be camouflaged, since bureaux often prefer to uphold the myth of fraternity in enacting the public will. Thus vicious territorial battles may be fought through genteel memoranda purporting to clarify minor matters of "co-ordination."

The previous chapter, by taking a society-centred approach emphasizing the role of economic interests, looked *outside* the state for an explanation of major changes to UI. The bureaucratic politics model suggests that an internal, semi-autonomous logic of state organizations is a better explanation. UI provides good ground for exploring the strengths of this approach. First, it is a prominent and sensitive area of public policy combining both income security and economic goals. This makes UI of interest to various departments of government. If inter-bureaucratic conflict affects public policy, then it should be visible in the UI policy area.

Second, UI traditionally has been administered by a commission, which permits maximum independence from departmental or cabinet authority. Thus the commission, in theory at least, has the autonomy to engage in conflict with other agencies if it feels it must, but it also stands as a threat to those agencies and hence presents an incentive for them to emasculate the commission. Moreover, the commission, in the 1940s and 1950s, was one of the largest government agencies, dealing with the most varied and extensive clientele of any government program. UI preceded the Family Allowances program by four years and was considerably more complex to administer because of the various eligibility tests that had to be applied before benefits were payable and because of the detailed worker and employer files that had to be maintained. Size and complexity encourage, as Downs has argued, bureaucratic inertia, intra-organizational interests, and bureaucratic ideology.

Third, UI is an extremely complex program, in operation as well as in philosophy. There are rules about contributions, benefits, and penalties; rules about what constitutes availability, suitable work, and just cause; and all of these general rules are woven together by a program rationale that has income security as well as labour market goals. Putting these rules into practice has in turn generated a body of regulations and routines. Appeals of the legal guidelines and regulations to the umpire have created a body of administrative case law. More than in most other programs, mastery of practical rules and regulations is a high art and requires substantial expertise and skill. As we noted earlier, many observers credit these types of resources as the foundation of bureaucratic power and autonomy. They are resources held in abundant supply by UI officials.

Explaining public policy in terms of bureaucratic politics means looking for the effects of intra-organizational logic (bureaucratic ideology; monopoly of information and expertise; organizational goals and needs) and inter-bureaucratic conflict. Not only should policy reflect these forces, but it should also be shown that these forces are distinct in origin, detail, and sometimes direction from pressures being exerted by outside groups.

The following pages will demonstrate that these two forces to some degree worked at cross purposes but together help explain a substantial proportion of UI policy development. The intra-organizational logic of the commission was crystallized in an actuarial ideology that defined the program narrowly and discouraged large increases in benefits or coverage. Some increases, as we shall see, were permitted by this ideology, but only in carefully defined circumstances. Those times when the program was changed in dramatically "non-actuarially sound" ways – as with supplementary and fishing benefits in the 1950s and with the 1971 act – the commission and hence its ideology were not in control.

INTRA-ORGANIZATIONAL LOGIC

The first two aspects of intra-organizational logic – bureaucratic ideology and monopoly of information and expertise – are intimately related, each sustaining the other. The ideology gives a sense of purpose and distinction and helps to stake out the policy space, thereby implying the information and skills wielded by those in charge of the policy. For purposes of this discussion, these two aspects will be treated as one.

What set of ideas defined the bureaucratic ideology of UI and the commission, and what effects did it have on program and policy development? While it may seem odd to speak of such an ideology existing prior to the bureau implementing it, this was indeed the case with UI because of its long gestation period, from 1928 to 1940. As the program was designed and studied, choices and contrasts had to be made. As we noted in the previous chapter, there could be wide agreement on the need for UI and common allegiance to the principle of insurance against lost wages even while there was substantial debate over program design and implementation. The latter issues should not be mistaken for mere technical detail, since a program's philosophical basis is revealed in the way it is supposed to work. Debates over the contributory principle, for example, were not simply about the most efficient funding mechanisms but about the responsibilities and obligations of workers, employers, and the state regarding unemployment.

The previous chapter showed the paucity of policy advice coming from employers and employee groups in the 1930s and afterwards. Trade unions and employee associations repeatedly focused on only a few features of the policy field, such as coverage and the contributory principle. The ideological framework as well as the detail of UI came from elsewhere, from within the state. Admittedly, UI's place on the political agenda was a consequence – at least before 1940 – of broad political forces, primarily industrial unrest and the success of labour MPs in bringing the issue forward for scrutiny by parliamentary committee. But the substance of policy had to be supplied by experts or technicians of some sort.

This need arose from simple ignorance and uncertainty. The promising beginning made with the Employment Service after the First World War was discontinued once the immediate postwar employment crisis subsided, thus making the collection of accurate information impossible.[28] In its 1928 report, the Select Standing Committee on Industrial and International Relations, though favouring federal funding of provincial UI schemes along shared-cost lines, confessed that on "the very important subject of the cost of unemployment insurance your Committee has experienced great difficulty in arriving at any definite conclusion owing to the lack of data as to the amount of unemployment, either constant or occasional in character. There appears to be no definite method of ascertaining the unemployment at any given point for any length of time."[29] In these circumstances, it is not surprising that Canadian authorities were casting about for a viable program model and that they should study the British system with particular interest. Britain's plan, like many plans being established at the time, was national, compulsory, and contributory. At the end of the 1920s, most informed observers of UI assumed that any Canadian plan would have the same features and be closely modelled on Britain's scheme. The British, however, had had the advantage of large, well-organized sets of data gathered by the trade unions and friendly societies; Canada would have to start virtually from scratch.

The information problem continued through the first half of Prime Minister Bennett's government. UI was not the immediate problem that relief expenditures were, but the lack of clear data made moves on UI untenable. The 1931 census data were to be ready in January 1933, and so Bennett called a federal-provincial conference for that month to discuss the possibility of a transfer of provincial jurisdiction over UI to Ottawa. According to Struthers, Ottawa had no "concrete information or plan" to offer the provinces, and this, despite tepid support from senior advisers such as W.C. Clark (deputy minister of finance) and R.K. Finlayson (Bennett's executive assistant), made federal-provincial agreement unlikely.[30] No agreement was reached, perhaps by design, and political attention shifted once more to relief matters and impending provincial bankruptcy.

While the UI issue was submerged for another year, it did not disappear, and certain crucial assumptions were already being formulated and accepted before detailed program design was undertaken. For example, in a memorandum advising Bennett on the January 1933 federal-provincial conference, Finlayson doubted the usefulness of any UI scheme to combat economic depression, noting that the degree of alleviation would depend upon how much of the work-force "on an actuarial basis" would be covered and the extent of UI reserves.[31] Finlayson seemed worried about program costs, arguing that the "problem is of such magnitude and fraught with such dangers to a country whose continued credit abroad is the life blood of its economic well being" that it must be thoroughly studied by a commission of experts. Not surprisingly, he urged minimal state funding and responsibility for UI, claiming that prevailing expert opinion suggested "that any scheme adopted in Canada should aim to limit the State's financial responsibility to the task of administration, labour and industry sharing the responsibility for premium payments." Nonetheless, joint or divided jurisdiction had to be avoided in favour of Dominion responsibility for the administration of the program and employment offices, if the plan were to "function on a sound actuarial basis" and be kept "free from exploitation." This last reference was doubtless to Britain, where the UI program, because of its administration by the Ministry of Labour, had been subject to political pressures for expansion and increased benefits. Finlayson recommended the German system of an independent commission to administer and insulate the program.

These ideas were not Finlayson's alone but drew upon a December 1932 memorandum on UI written by the superintendent of insurance, G.D. Finlayson (no relation). This is a revealing document, which, when combined with the more detailed elaborations of a UI plan drafted in 1934, forms the basis of what we shall term the "actuarial ideology" underpinning UI at its inception and influencing it throughout its history. The term reflects the importance of actuarial considerations in designing and evaluating UI, though the ideology also incorporates administrative and political aspects. It became the dominant way of understanding UI, at least for the commission. Employers, trade unions, and other experts suggested different visions, perhaps equally valid, but to little avail. The actuarial ideology became the administrative touchstone of UI and remained so for years.

The superintendent of insurance supplied a succinct definition of the insurance character of UI, from which most of its other features flowed: "The word 'insurance' means a provision, by means of single or periodical payments, for protection against an event likely or certain to happen *in the future* and a system of insurance is one set up by which an insurer receives the payments from the insured *before the occurrence of the event insured against*."[32] UI could therefore be expected to deal not with existing unemployment, only with unemployment in the future. If benefits were to be currently paid, then the scheme would simply "amount to the payment of unemployment relief under the guise of payment of insurance benefits." Finlayson thus drew a sharp line between relief and insurance, by a logic that focused on the insurance character of this type of social program. Once one assumes that benefits are to be paid as part of an insurance scheme, one naturally thinks in terms of specific, ear-marked contributions. The contributory principle was a corollary of a program conceived as insurance and did not have its roots in a conscious desire to oppress the working classes.

Finlayson went on to derive another important concept from the insurance principle: "It has long been recognized that every system of insurance involves what is known as moral hazard, by which is meant the bringing about of the event, or the prolongation of a condition, by the action, collusive or otherwise, of the insured, for the purpose of hastening the payment of, or increasing, the indemnity provided."[33] Finlayson argued that in UI there was an "overwhelming moral hazard arising from the indisposition of a minority of people to work." The minority could, unless "rigidly guarded against," undermine the system. This problem led naturally to a discussion of the importance of a sound actuarial basis to the plan, since only in this way could it remain stable and solvent. Moreover, actuarial review and evaluation had to be a constant and consistent feature of the plan, not merely a preliminary precaution. Both the emphasis on moral hazard and the call for expert review were corollaries of a perspective grounded in insurance principles. A sociological perspective – if not to say a socialist one – might have rejected the notion of moral hazard, assuming instead that people work for a variety of reasons that include money, self-esteem, and a desire to be active and useful. A plan funded by general taxation would not have been as concerned about actuarial issues, which involve the determination of categories of risk, contributions, and benefits, as well as the probabilities of incurring certain risks. But, given the notion of insurance, the other concepts came easily.[34]

The notion of actuarial soundness, especially in light of the British experience, led Canadian authorities to want to insulate the plan from political interference. The superintendent of insurance feared that the government might wish to tamper with the scientific basis of the program. In a letter to W.C. Clark early in 1933, Bryce Stewart, responsible for establishing the Employment Service and by then an industrial relations consultant in the United States, urged "the desirability of keeping government out of the financing of unemployment insurance, and, further, keeping the administration of unemployment insurance as far away from government departments as possible."[35] This advice was absorbed by Clark, who passed it on to the prime minister, in the form of a recommendation that UI be kept clearly distinct from other forms of unemployment relief payments, so that "the insurance scheme can be allowed to continue to stand on its own feet, doing what it was actuarially calculated that it could do and not being asked or expected to do more."[36] To Clark's mind, this also had the advantage of permitting a clear division of responsibilities between the provinces and Ottawa, the former managing relief, the latter UI.

Thus, despite little analytical work, some key assumptions about the Canadian program were being forged in 1932-3. These assumptions were reinforced in the summer of 1933, when R.K. Finlayson and Bennett attended the Imperial Economic Conference in London. Finlayson consulted British officials about UI, and a draft of the new British legislation circulated in Ottawa later that year. Convinced now that a UI scheme might work, Finlayson kept in close contact with British officials.[37] A team was soon assembled in Ottawa to work on the UI scheme: R.K. Finlayson, F.G. Price (a British official brought over for advice), A.D. Watson (chief actuary, Department of Insurance), Hugh Wolfenden (a consulting actuary), and Leonard Marsh (head of McGill University's School of Social Research). The key figures were Watson and Wolfenden, who, as actuaries, possessed the expertise to develop a sound financial basis for the plan. They laboured through the latter part of 1933 and had a draft proposal ready by April 1934. The draft underwent only modest revision on its way to becoming the 1935 Employment and Social Insurance Act.

Both Watson and Wolfenden wanted to devise a financially secure insurance program. Indeed, as actuaries, they admitted that financial stability was their primary goal. To some degree this reflected the sober lessons of the British scheme, which had recently gone bankrupt and was being revised, but it also reflected the professional actuarial ethos. Leonard Marsh was to supply the team with unemployment data, but it was up to Watson and

Wolfenden to determine how the level and pattern of unemployment would affect the level of contributions and benefits, along with ancillary administrative rules. Throughout the design process, Watson in particular emphasized the importance of what he called "safeguards" against erosion of the program, so much so that in an April 1934 memorandum to Finlayson he felt it necessary to defend his emphasis of "the importance from the point of view of the actuarial report of including in the scheme appropriate safeguards against improper claims, and of provisions intended to facilitate and induce the return of men to work, and of maintaining benefits on a low scale, to keep down unwarranted claims."[38]

The problem of safeguards was particularly vexing because of the imperfect nature of Canadian unemployment data. In 1934, in Watson's view, the only reliable unemployment data came from the last two censuses. These were too crude for confident calculations, but the problem was compounded by the moral hazard effect of an implemented UI program. Relying on British sickness insurance data, which suggested an increase in alleged disabilities due to the availability of benefits, Watson argued that, as a result of UI, future Canadian unemployment rates would be higher than they might otherwise be: "Unemployment insurance in itself increases in a marked manner the unemployment which will be recorded for benefit purposes."[39] Watson judged that with UI employers would be more willing to lay off workers, some small firms might collapse under the burden of premiums, sick workers might try to claim UI benefits, and more workers might be drawn into insured employment, thus swelling the ranks of the unemployed when laid off. The key problem, however, was that "many workers once on benefit are not so zealous in their search for work as they would be if they had no income at all. The increase in claims due to this cause is very substantial."[40] This was a critical part of the actuarial ideology and was given more elaborate formulation by Wolfenden:

It is essential for any actuary, in undertaking the calculations for such a scheme as this, to emphasize the great importance of providing and maintaining safeguards which will secure in the future both a legislative outlook and an administrative procedure which will not depart either in principle or in any significant detail from the provisions originally laid down. The costs of any plan for providing financial relief in respect of any of the contingencies of human life, and especially the costs of plans in respect of the contingency of unemployment, are virtually dependent upon the extent to which they recognize and deal with those frailties of human nature which, if uncontrolled, may easily produce, through the self-seeking ingenuity of the individual, or opportunist legislation, or unduly sympathetic or even lax administration, a rate of claim for benefits far beyond anything which the actuary can reasonably contemplate.[41]

This actuarial perspective explains many features of the 1935 legislation. As mentioned earlier, the establishment of an independent commission to administer the act reflected fears, among the actuaries but also Finlayson and Bennett himself, of political manipulation and eventual destruction of the plan. The commission's prime responsibility would be to assess the claimant's "willingness to work," an essential test if illegitimate claims were to be avoided. The test itself is of less interest than the fact that, from an actuarial perspective, this could be the program's Achilles heel. A psychology of vigilance was thus imbedded in the program from its start.

Seasonal workers were considered especially prone to abuse the program, since to a large degree their periods of employment and unemployment were predictable and as such a normal and accepted part of their industries. The plan, as a strict insurance plan, was to cover only unanticipated and unwanted wage loss. For this reason, most seasonal industries were not covered by the 1935 act.[42] Other features of the plan were intended to reflect specific Canadian conditions, and so, for example, benefits were substantially higher than in Britain because the Canadian cost-of-living was higher.

Despite the failure of the 1935 act to be fully implemented, the long process of planning begun in 1933 was continued forward, to bear fruit eventually in the 1940 act. It also created a group of officials in the departments of Insurance and Labour who could now comfortably wield an arcane expertise regarding UI. Compared to the long and detailed calculations of Watson's numerous memoranda on UI, private-sector submissions and briefs seemed pathetically inept. It was this expertise that allowed Watson to dismiss easily, almost contemptuously, the request of the Canadian Bankers' Association to be exempted under the act.[43]

The importance of expertise was clear in the changes made to the 1940 version of Canadian UI. While this version was similar in most respects to the 1935 scheme, it had some significant differences, such as the shift to graded from flat-rate benefits. This issue had never been addressed by private-sector groups, but the policy was changed because of internal considerations related to growing expertise as well as the actuarial ideology. Eric Stangroom (chief clerk, Department of Labour) explained the reasons for the change before the Commons Special Committee in 1940. He pointed out that the 1935 act had relied heavily on British experience but that in the interim the United States, Norway, Germany, Italy, and South Africa had implemented plans with graded benefits and this had permitted Canadian officials to assess their experiences. Stangroom also noted that the 1935 act, with its flat-rate benefit system, had not been as easy to administer as one might suppose, since it had had eight different classes of recipients depending on age and sex.

The most telling reason in favour of graded benefits, however, was the problem of "overinsurance": "Any flat benefit must be fixed at the low earnings of any worker in any part of the country; otherwise the benefits would exceed wages. If the benefit exceeds wages you get a tendency to malingering; men will prefer unemployment benefits to a job."[44] This logic simply extended the precepts of Watson's and Wolfenden's actuarial perspective on the program. There also was a political motive involved, since the new system paid higher benefits to higher-wage-earning groups and thus would be "more acceptable to the better educated and more vocal parts of the population."[45]

The influence of the actuarial ideology and expertise may also be seen in the "ratio rule" devised for the 1940 act and part of the program until 1971. Claimants could receive one day of benefits for each five daily contributions made in the preceding five years but lost a day of benefits for each three days of benefits received in the preceding three years. As Stangroom put it: "By relating the period of benefit available directly to the employment history many abuses are removed and advantages given to the worker with good employment records."[46] In other words, this was another safeguard to protect the actuarial soundness of the plan, particularly from seasonal workers and other "bad risks" who might make a habit of drawing UI benefits. There was no evidence of intentional class bias, or, as some writers have termed it, a deliberate attempt to drive a wedge between skilled and unskilled workers. The legislation may indeed have had this result, but more because of the application of cold administrative reason than because of hidden class motives.

It has been suggested that the 1940 act's restricted coverage – approximately 42 per cent of the work-force – was politically motivated, either in a niggardly desire to keep costs down or, once again, to reward "good workers" with an insurance plan and drive "bad workers" onto relief. In fact, the best explanation is much more prosaic and rooted in administrative and actuarial logic. In testimony before the Commons Committee, A.D. Watson pointed out that the plan would centre around the employment offices at which claimants would submit claims, pick up benefits, and receive advice on employment opportunities. Watson argued that "it would be rather useless to bring under the Act particular classes of people who have no prespects [sic] whatsoever of getting employment at an employment office."[47] Policemen, teachers, and civil servants could not be "inspected" in the appropriate way, and neither could those people in occupations such as fishing or logging: "There is a certain amount of logging going on up the Gatineau. People could claim they are employed by so and so and nobody in the world could do the inspection. It would be too expensive."[48]

The control of abuse was vital to actuarial soundness, and this depended, in UI's case, on regular inspection of claimants:

The fact that unemployment may be heavy in an industry does not say that it ought to be under insurance. If it can be subjected to inspection, to control of insurance, there is no reason why it should not be under. The fact that unemployment may be heavy does not say it should be excluded. It might be quite properly under; but, unless that particular industry can, as it were, be gripped by the administrative machinery of the Act you might have too much difficulty in the administration of it; it just cannot be handled.[49]

As the administrative machinery became more sophisticated, the program was gradually extended to industries like logging.

Thus, in its formative years, UI became grounded in an actuarial ideology and administrative logic. Contributions, benefits, duration, coverage, and administrative autonomy all had roots in this bureaucratic perspective on the program. Whereas employee groups tended to view UI in terms of rights, and employers saw it in terms of costs and economic effect, officials were preoccupied with administrative feasibility, actuarial soundness, and strict insurance principles. It is true that in many respects this led to a similarity of views between employers and officials, particularly on the abuse question, but this similarity was coincidental in that officials' views were arrived at independently. They were not the result of "pressure."

The purest form of the actuarial ideology was cultivated and defended by the commission, which had the prime responsibility of administering the UI act.[50] "Actuarial soundness" was, nonetheless, a shibboleth for all politicians and departments that came in touch with UI, though their allegiance to the concept was usually diluted by their own interests and agendas. In practice, this meant that the commission was prepared to extend UI only if such extensions accorded with the inner logic of the program. This inner logic – defined by the actuarial ideology – was often incomprehensible to other policy-makers, who were consequently prepared to use UI to accommodate new unemployment problems. It is thus important to understand that the actuarial ideology in itself did not prevent program enrichment; it simply demanded that such enrichment be consistent with UI principles and not prejudice the program's financial base. When other agencies pressed for UI extensions that violated these principles, the commission was usually forced into a rearguard action to minimize damage.

The best examples of this are the supplementary and fishing benefits of the 1950s and ultimately the dramatic program enrichment contained in the 1971 act. Each of these changes represented significant breaks with actuarial ideology; each was pressed by outside agencies; and each was greeted critically by the commission. The full details of these initiatives are provided in the next section; the interest here is in the commission's response in terms of its actuarial ideology.

The 1940 act had empowered the commission to make special regulations for seasonal workers, whereby they would be ineligible for benefits in the normal off-season.[51] Unemployment during the on-season was compensable, and this accorded with good insurance principles. From another perspective, however, the commission was deliberately denying benefits during the winter months for many workers who might need support. Fortunately, annual unemployment rates between 1946 and 1949 averaged only 2.7 per cent. There were signs of trouble, however, as the winter of 1949 approached, and the newly elected government of Louis St Laurent promised to do something, especially for affected regions. On 18 November 1949 the Economic Policy Committee of cabinet directed the Interdepartmental Committee on Social Security to establish three working committees, one of which was on unemployment and relief, chaired by the deputy minister of labour.[52] The Department of Labour subsequently submitted a proposal for temporary extension of UI benefits to cover winter unemployment, and the Interdepartmental Committee agreed on 30 December 1949 to recommend this scheme to the Economic Policy Committee of cabinet.[53] Cabinet considered the Interdepartmental committee's report on 17 February 1950, and supplementary UI benefits were implemented that winter.[54]

Supplementary benefits were payable at the rate of 80 per cent of regular benefits during the period from 1 January to 31 March (later extended to April), to those who had exhausted benefit rights since the preceding 31 March, or had made at least 90 daily contributions since then. These benefits may have helped the unemployed, but they also created certain problems for the act:

The introduction of supplementary benefits was, however, in direct conflict with the seasonal regulations and the ratio rule. For example, people eligible for supplementary benefits were exempted from seasonal regulations while they were in force. This severely limited the effectiveness of the seasonal regulations. The fact that supplementary benefits were also paid to those who exhausted entitlement and to newly-covered employees, regardless of their contributions, was an enrichment of the program which represented a departure from the principles underlying the original legislation.[55]

The commission was well aware of this and in a report to the minister of labour argued that to "provide assistance under the Act to people who have not contributed, or to people who have committed some act which justifies disqualification, would destroy all the insurance principles provided in the Act, and once they are destroyed then the whole fabric of the scheme would break down."[56] The commission persisted in this view and later in 1954 used the example of supplementary benefits to caution against ill-considered extensions of the program:

Because unemployment insurance is at present the only federal measure dealing with the unemployed, there is a tendency to distort it to meet situations which are properly the function of unemployment assistance. It is not possible to combine insurance and assistance without endangering the insurance plan. The provision of supplementary benefits in 1950 was a step in that direction. Any extension of the supplementary provisions should be most carefully considered to ensure that we do not go further along the wrong road and bring the insurance plan into disrepute.[57]

The commission was in almost precisely the same losing position with regard to the extension of UI to fishermen in 1956. Newfoundland's entry into Confederation in 1949 stimulated a review of the issue. Fishing was Newfoundland's most important industry, but while UI coverage was extended to fishplant workers, to other seasonal industries (under seasonal regulations), and even to fishermen when they worked in insured employment, it did not include fishermen per se. The Department of fisheries was interested in extending some sort of aid and provided information for the commission's 1950 investigation of the industry.[58]

The commission completed its report in April 1951, noting that only 7 per cent of the total fishing work-force was wage labour, with the rest as either lone operators or share workers. Nonetheless, since all fishermen did similar work regardless of employment status, the entire industry would have to be covered. As well, unemployment during the fishing season would be difficult to prove because of inspection problems, and most fishermen did something related to their employment (e.g. repair nets or boats) during the off-season. The report concluded:

The administrative difficulties, although considerable, can be overcome. The main difficulty is not administrative but lies in the fact that the fishing industry in Canada is not suitable to unemployment insurance ... If it is necessary to augment the income derived by fishermen from fishing, subsistence farming and other employment, some form of unemployment assistance should be provided by the proper authorities rather than attempting to strain the framework of unemployment insurance to take care of a situation that is not properly an insurance function.[59]

The matter rested there until March 1953, when an ad hoc committee chaired by the minister of labour was formed to look once again at extending UI to fishermen and agriculture. The commission reiterated its opposition to the idea, but at this stage a cabinet-level decision had been made to include fishermen.[60] The commission's response was to design plans with severely restricted coverage, but the scheme eventually adopted was proposed by an interdepartmental committee of officials.[61] Thus, in this case as with supplementary benefits, the commission's attempt to curtail program enrichments that in its view violated actuarial soundness was overridden by external agencies.

These liberalizations, along with other more modest ones contained in the 1955 act, contributed to the program's insolvency in the face of high unemployment rates between 1957 and 1963. Whereas in the mid-1950s the problem in one sense had been a large surplus in the UI fund, by 1960 the problem was imminent bankruptcy. The actuarial ideology, which had been previously discounted by some departments, once again became a watchword. The Gill Committee's report relied heavily on the idea and roundly criticized those aspects of UI that contradicted insurance principles.

As we noted in the previous chapter, the Gill Committee recommended against certain types of benefits or features of UI that would detract from the program's insurance character. In making these and other recommendations, it stood firmly on the foundations first laid by Watson and Wolfenden in 1935. The cabinet, the Department of Labour, and the commission (though with some reservations discussed in the next section) generally favoured this perspective and approach.

There had been an interdepartmental committee reviewing the UI fund in 1961 and a cabinet committee in the same year as well. Both of these bodies, well before the Gill Committee's report, had called for correction of abuses and better handling of seasonal benefits. This clearly reflected the same general concern with actuarial soundness that was a feature of the Gill Committee's report.[62] A more detailed response to the Gill Committee's recommendation for a more actuarially sound UI program came from G.V. Haythorne, deputy minister of labour, in 1963:

This proposal recognizes that there are different kinds of unemployment requiring different types of action. Short-term or frictional unemployment ... would be provided for by unemployment insurance ... Seasonal, cyclical, and other types of longer-run unemployment result from basic economic and social conditions requiring positive government action as well as extended financial assistance to the workers affected. Such extended financial assistance appears to be beyond the capacity of a sound unemployment insurance system.[63]

The Department of Labour also approved of an extension of coverage because this would meet the "equity principle" that everyone in an employee/employer relationship be covered and also because "it pools the costs of providing for the risks of short-term unemployment." More generally, Haythorne noted that the Gill Committee had devised an integrated package of reform "designed to restore certain principles, lessen the possibility of abuse, and assist the functioning of the labour market in a positive manner." Despite the likely result of "some people losing their present eligibility for benefits or having their benefit duration reduced,"

Haythorne advised acceptance of the proposals as a package, since that would help defuse negative reactions.[64]

The interdepartmental committee on the Gill Committee's report, comprised of the departments of Finance, Justice, Labour, and Insurance and the commission, also commented favourably on what it understood to be the report's finding "that there had been a gradual dissipation of the sound actuarial basis on which the original plan was founded."[65] The interdepartmental committee supported most of the Gill recommendations, and its own report fed into the six-year process of UI study that culminated in the 1968 Comprehensive Review undertaken by the commission and the 1970 White Paper.

The 1970 White Paper, and the 1971 UI act that followed it, might be considered untouched by actuarial ideology and administrative logic. Certainly at the time, employer groups and some politicians were deeply suspicious about the new framework, and the program's subsequent insolvency seemed to bear them out. However, while the White Paper and legislation were indeed strongly affected by new ideas about social services and income security, they also showed the hold that actuarial ideology and bureaucratic hubris had on the program. Without these, sceptics never would have been as effectively silenced as they were.

As we noted earlier, the White Paper, entitled *Unemployment Insurance in the 70's*, was couched in a rhetoric of progress, modern social policy, and compassion. While these elements were indeed evident, the plan was still framed as insurance and so was influenced by the actuarial ideology. One feature of the new act that echoed some of the devices of the 1935 and 1940 acts was the distinction between long-term (over 20 weeks) and short-term (less than 20 weeks) attachment to the labour force. Reminiscent of the venerable distinction between seasonal and non-seasonal workers, or "bad risks" and "good risks," this program feature permitted restriction of the range and duration of benefits, so that, for example, only workers with more than 20 weeks of employment in the last 52 were eligible for maternity or sickness benefits.

Another feature of the act intended to reduce "abuse" was the requirement that all claimants have at least two personal interviews with the commission. While the interviews would permit more careful counselling for re-employment and training, the White Paper acknowledged that "they will also serve to identify people who should not be receiving benefits. The effect will be to reduce to a minimum abuses in the present plan due to the lack of personal contact."[66] The abuse issue arose regularly in debates on the new act, and the minister, Bryce Mackasey, though he did not believe that abuse was rampant, did see the mandatory interviews as a counterweight to the relative generosity of the program. As Mackasey put it before the Standing Committee on Labour, Manpower and Immigration, "In all probability conditions will be a little more rigid under the future plan because we will see these people at least twice."[67]

The most important feature of any insurance plan, from the actuarial perspective, is the balance between contributions and benefits and thus the financial stability of the plan. The Canadian program had already come close to insolvency in 1962, and, though the ledgers looked healthy in 1970, the issue of financial balance could scarely be avoided. Benefits were being increased simultaneous with relaxation of entrance requirements, and so one would have expected careful probing of the new plan's financial forecasts. In fact, there was far less debate about the financial side of the new program in 1971 than one might have expected. Why? The answer has to do with, first, the manner in which actuarial information was provided by the commission and the Department of Labour and, second, the logic or rationale of the new program.

On the first point, the public and politicians were given very little hard data on how the program was expected to operate. To some degree this had to do with the commission's reliance on the Department of Finance for unemployment data, but it had to do also with the sensitivity of those data. The plan called for government funding of selected benefits for unemployment rates over 4 per cent, and any firm numbers of expected financial balances might have permitted deductions about government unemployment forecasts. So, when asked about unemployment projections, a commission official responded: "We have not forecast unemployment rates for the nineteen seventies except insofar as we supposed a certain pattern of unemployment would prevail."[68] The officials claimed that the pattern of unemployment was more important for UI than the overall rate and admitted only to a number of projections about such "mixes" of unemployment, none of which showed UI in any financial trouble.

On the second point, this paucity of data might have been more frustrating in the absence of one important argument made repeatedly by the commission and the Department of Labour. They argued that as complex as the new act would be, and as generous as the new provisions were compared to the old, the new scheme would not require any net increases in government expenditure. Abuse, for example, was to be controlled through the mandatory interview program. More important, extension of coverage would bring into the program thousands of employees who would be paying contributions but who were unlikely to draw UI benefits. Mackasey made the point during his debates on the bill in the Commons, and it was also strongly implied in the White Paper, which noted that universal coverage "in some respects calls upon the good will and responsibility of more fortunate, better-placed Canadians toward those who through lack of education and opportunity are in less secure occupations."[69] Though never exactly quantified, improvements under the new plan, officials implied, would be paid for largely by net contributions made by newly included occupations such as teachers and provincial public servants.

It must be admitted, however, that the traces of the actuarial ideology in the 1971 act were overshadowed by other ideas that together helped give Canada one of the world's most generous UI programs. As in the supplementary/seasonal and fishing benefits episodes, the commission was outflanked by the Department of Labour. As early as 1963, the latter had been developing alternative proposals for a new UI program, all of them stressing a positive manpower or labour market approach, all of them discounting the idea of strict actuarial soundness, and all of them at odds with the commission's approach. It was Bryce Mackasey, as minister of labour, who guided the drafting of the White Paper and the legislation, and senior commission officials were deliberately bypassed in the policy process because their advice, often critical, did not fit the new thrust.[70] This conflict is described in detail in the next section.

The difficulties the program encountered after 1971 engendered a series of legislative and regulatory responses, most of which addressed the flexibility – some would say laxness – of certain provisions in the act. There was a consistent theme running through these changes, however, closely attuned to the key precepts of the actuarial ideology that guided the design of UI in the 1930s. The emphasis in these changes on costs, program abuse, excessive generosity, and slack administration reflected the growing perception that, as an insurance program, UI was being dragged down by the weight of numerous "bad risks." As we have noted before, insurance *as insurance* assumes a pooling of risks but also the existence of some insurable interest, something to lose. It assumes also that benefits, while naturally having some relationship to needs or to the magnitude of the insured loss, depend ultimately on the balance of contributions to pay-outs. In the case of UI, this means that only those with real attachment to the labour force should be covered and that benefits should be determined by actuarial balance, not the social needs of recipients. The major legislative changes in 1975, 1977, and 1978 showed that the government, and many others, felt that UI benefits were being received by people with at best marginal attachment to the labour force and that benefits were too generous, certainly generous enough to dampen work incentives. From an income security or social policy point of view, this logic makes little sense, since it dictates cutbacks among the young, women, unskilled seasonal workers, or those in low-paying volatile industries. Those who need assistance most, in short, are penalized. From the perspective of actuarial ideology, however, this makes perfect sense.

Some examples will show the influence of this type of thinking in the changes of 1975, 1977, and 1978. The resurgence of actuarial ideology in this period reflected several factors. First, the commission was back in charge of administering its program, and its views necessarily carried more weight. Second, as in the early 1960s, insolvency concentrated attention on ways to reduce spending, all of which could conveniently be subsumed under the rubric of "actuarial soundness." Third, as the next section demonstrates, the rhetoric of actuarial soundness was suddenly convenient for manpower officials who wished to mount programs in the face of austerity. By championing UI cuts, they could use the program as a milch cow for job creation schemes.

The 1975 changes (most important, the doubling of the maximum disqualification period for voluntary quits, job refusals, and misconduct firings and elimination of the dependants' benefit) were couched in rhetoric very different from the 1971 White Paper. The social policy aspects of the program were played down, and the limited, short-term nature of UI assistance was emphasized. "The basic act provides short-term income support to unemployed workers while facilitating their quick re-employment."[71] Robert Andras, the minister responsible for the 1975 amendments, defended the increased disqualification period by arguing that "we intend to make certain that Canadians who are working hard to maintain self-sufficiency, to maintain the momentum of this country's economy, and who are contributing to the unemployment insurance program, do not have to carry the added burden of supporting able-bodied people who do not want to work."[72] Andras noted that elimination of dependants' benefits was due to substantial increases in the amount paid by Family Allowances since 1971. He suggested that it was appropriate to support family needs through Family Allowances "rather than through the unemployment insurance plan under which benefits are – and, I strongly believe, should be – essentially wage-related."[73]

An important amendment in 1975 was the change in the formula determining the government's contribution to the program. Under the 1971 formula, most program costs due to unemployment above a national rate of 4 per cent were assumed by Ottawa. The new formula proposed that the threshold be converted to a moving average of monthly unemployment rates over the preceding eight years. This formula would produce a threshold of 5.6 per cent in 1976, thereby reducing the government's obligations. While fiscal restraint was undoubtedly a factor behind this amendment, it should be remembered that originally, when UI was being designed in Canada, it was by no means clear that a government contribution was required or preferred at all. Andras enunciated the principle behind this modest role: "Nevertheless, under social insurance principles, normal cost under the unemployment insurance program should be financed as much as possible through contributions from employers and employees."[74]

The major changes to UI included in Bill C-27, passed in 1977, were increased entrance requirements (what became the variable entrance requirement), a three-phrase rather than five-phase benefit structure, and developmental uses of UI funds. The rationale for these changes closely paralleled that of 1975: "An examination of the characteristics and behaviour of claimants with eight to eleven weeks of insured employment – the so-called 'eight to eleven weekers' – strongly suggests that an increase in the entrance requirement would constitute for many of them an incentive to work longer ... Basically, they have what might best be described as an intermittent or unstable attachment to the active work-force."[75] The new benefit structure was "designed to curtail benefit entitlement to those with a relatively short labour force attachment living in regions of low unemployment."[76] The savings generated through this return to more strict insurance principles were to be used for new programs, essentially job creation, to assist the chronically unemployed.

The 1978 amendments were the most extensive of the 1970s and, though triggered by a prime ministerial initiative to reduce government expenditures, had been planned for some time. They flowed from the long process of internal policy review begun in 1972 and would likely have been implemented in any case, though more gradually. The major 1978 amendments included higher entrance requirements for repeaters, new entrants, and re-entrants and reduction in the benefit rate from 66.6 per cent of insurable earnings to 60 per cent. The purpose of these changes was two-fold: "First, we want to reduce some of the disincentives to work which are present in the program. Second, we want to encourage workers to establish more stable work patterns and develop longer attachments to the active work force, thereby reducing their dependency on unemployment insurance."[77]

The minister added that the "new emphasis will be on encouraging all Canadian workers to look for, accept and remain at work."[78] Though the term *actuarial soundness* was not used in defending these amendments, its underlying precepts were clearly evident. Once again, "bad risks" were being disciplined under the program, and various changes were intended to reduce disincentive effects. Though the language differed, the arguments underscoring the changes made in the 1970s echoed those made by A.D. Watson in 1935.

I have argued that this complex of ideas and logic is an ideology in the sense of being a reconstruction of the world that pretends to, but cannot be, factual. As noted above, the actuarial ideology at the core of UI has defined the nature of the program, its goals, and its problems. As an insurance program, it runs a major risk with moral hazard or, more colloquially, abuse. The problem of abuse is an empirical issue of how many and how much, but beyond this the facts and numbers must be judged to be "big" or "little," heading up or down. It is in the act of judgment that the bias or ideology crystallized in a program and a bureau comes to the surface.

Some flashes of the actuarial ideology may be seen in recent commission documents reviewing UI. The report of the 1981 Task Force on Unemployment Insurance addressed, for example, the issue of UI's impact on unemployment, specifically through its work disincentive effect. While acknowledging the measurement difficulties this question involves, as well as the lack of general agreement in the literature on the extent of the upward shift in unemployment rates, the report concluded that "the above evidence suggests that UI may increase measured unemployment either by lengthening its duration or increasing the number of people on claim."[79] Yet a careful, independent review of the literature on this subject found that no confident conclusions could be drawn from these studies.[80] The task force was applying judgment to the data, and its judgment reflected an ideological disposition to confirm the disincentive effect of UI. As we noted in the previous chapter, this justified heightened emphasis in the task force recommendations on what was called "labour market incentives."

Abuse is thus a main concern for the commission, since abuse is the nodal point of an ideological understanding of the program's raison d'être. As one would expect, the commission has periodically surveyed its benefit population to assess the magnitude of the problem. Surveys were performed in 1973, 1974, and 1977; a random sample of active claimants was drawn for benefit control investigation, supplemented by additional socioeconomic information. The studies defined misuse as disqualifications or disentitlements imposed as a result of the investigation carried out by the benefit control officer.[81] Thousands of claims were investigated, though the 1973 and 1974 samples were larger (14,778 and 19,259 respectively) than the 1978 survey (5,149). The misuse rate for 1973 was estimated to be between 39 per cent and 41 per cent of claims, while for 1974 it was 37-39 per cent, a small but statistically significant decrease.

The 1977 survey suggested a sharp drop in the misuse rate to 19.8 per cent. Of interest is the way in which this shift was explained by the commission. The 1977 survey reviewed various hypotheses extending from the nature of administrative changes to slackness in the economy, as well as the possibility that claimant behaviour had changed so that claimants were now fulfilling their obligations under the act. The report concluded:

There is, unfortunately, also reason to suspect that the drop in the D/D [disqualification/disentitlement] rate may result less from a change in claimant behaviour than from an increase in claimant awareness of, and ability to cope with, our control procedures. Most of the claimants investigated admitted to previous claimant experience. However, in contrast to 1973 and 1974, most of those investigated – even those on their first claim – would have received a personal briefing on their "rights and obligations" – a process often referred to by our staff as "the tip-off interview". In other words, the claimants may not be any better behaved, simply better informed.[82]

The report concluded that while increased control was unnecessary, the current level of controls be maintained in order to demonstrate to the public and claimants "that we are not getting soft."

It is unlikely that commission officials would ever "get soft," because they operate in terms of an understanding of the program deeply rooted in actuarial ideology. As we noted in the previous chapter, officials also have a thinly disguised disdain for lay opinions on UI. Understandably, this arises from the officials' closeness to the day-to-day mechanics of administering the program, their possession of special "factual knowledge," and the ideological framework they share, which sets out the assumptions, limits, and goals of the program.

INTER-BUREAUCRATIC CONFLICT

In the previous section I considered the role of bureaucratic intra-organizational logic in shaping public policy. This section looks at a complementary explanation: inter-bureaucratic conflict. This conflict is semi-autonomous insofar as the stakes and the interests involved are internal to the state and its organizational routines. They have to do with internal conflict over resources, prestige, and responsibility. The preceding section focused on unifying ideological principles that the commission used to define the program; this section examines differences among bureaucratic actors and tries to trace certain program features to the interests of winners and losers.

As mentioned earlier, UI presents a good case study for this approach, since it was administered by an independent commission. This independence was originally granted to ensure protection from political meddling that might undermine the actuarial basis of the plan. As well, since UI funds consisted of employer/employee contributions, it seemed reasonable to give these interests substantial administrative influence. The government would have the right to amend or replace the UI act but would presumably do so upon the commission's advice. In practice, the commission never achieved this high degree of institutional autonomy.

Not all conflicts are worth examining – only those that represented fundamental attempts to subordinate the commission and the program. The most important adversary the commission faced over the years was the Department of Labour, and later the Department of Manpower and Immigration, though other agencies also entered the fray from time to time. The conflict between the two agencies rested more on policy and mandate than on personality.[83] This was because of the tension at the heart of UI between income security and labour market goals. The more secure a claimant's income, the less incentive to seek employment. Thus, in terms of day-to-day administration, a UI program must do more than offer benefits: it must ensure that claimants are available for work and are seeking employment, and, more important, it should provide positive assistance in the form of employment referral services to help claimants in finding stable employment. These latter functions amount to a labour market or manpower policy.

While UI as a benefit program is clearly of primary interest only to the commission, UI as a labour market or manpower policy is of interest to any department of government with major economic, but especially labour market, responsibilities. The Department of Labour was responsible for the National Employment Service in the 1930s but had to turn it over to the newly created commission in 1940. There was little resentment at the time, but once the war effort got under way and the Department of Labour was given control over the National Selective Service regulations – a sort of conscription of civilian labour for war industries – intense rivalry ensued, wherein the department tried and partly succeeded in having the commission subordinated to its mandate.

The commission's autonomy was compromised even earlier, however, in its brief life under the 1935 Employment and Social Insurance Act. Under that legislation a commission was actually established and staffed before the election victory of Mackenzie King's Liberals and the program's reference to the courts. The commission thus led a shadowy and impotent existence, seeking but not receiving instructions from the new prime minister. Gordon S. Harrington had been appointed chief commissioner of the Employment and Social Insurance Commission in July 1935, with Tom Moore and Nazaire R. Beaudet representing employee and employer interests respectively. Harrington wrote to King in November 1935 to acquaint the prime minister with the commission and its responsibilities and also to ask that staffing, which had been in limbo for some time because of the change of government, be undertaken.[84] King deferred a reply, forcing Harrington to write again in January 1936. Harrington claimed that since assuming office the government had not "communicated with this Commission concerning the matters confided to us by the Statute ... In short, there has been a complete absence of intercourse between the Government and this Commission."[85] Harrington tendered his resignation, but the other two commissioners remained.

Despite the commission's impotence, the legislation that had created it retained the force of law even while undergoing judicial review. The act, for example, stipulated that within one month of 31 March of each year the commission would have to submit its annual report, which would have to be tabled in Parliament within 15 days. As things dragged on and the March date approached, the government used section 43 of the act to extend the deadline by three months. This would avoid "questions regarding the Government's intentions with respect to continuing the Commission, etc."[86] Later, in May, Tom Moore reminded the government that the act set a four-month limit on the time taken to replace the chief commissioner. With the legislation still under judicial review, a serious appointment was out of the question. King was advised to appoint an outstanding civil servant to the post, in part to avoid any implications of a permanent sinecure that a "civilian" might suggest.[87] Accordingly, O.D. Skelton, the under-secretary of state for external affairs, was appointed chief commissioner. The decision of the Judicial Committee of the Privy Council was handed down on 28 January 1937, and by 1 March the commission was disbanded.

The significance of these events is proportionate to the widespread concern in 1935 about a "political" UI program. The commission's legal independence was to guarantee that UI, at that time unquestionably the most ambitious, expensive, and administratively complex social program ever contemplated in Canada, would be insulated from political interference. While Skelton's appointment had little practical effect because the commission was moribund, it was a dramatic symbol of how cavalierly the government treated the notion of neutrality and autonomy. Within three years, with a new commission under a new act, the government's respect for the commission's autonomy would be tested once again.

The newly appointed commission in 1940 was given much of the responsibility over employment services previously exercised by the federal Department of Labour and also by provincial employment offices. As part of the war effort, however, came the National Selective Service regulations, administered by the Department of Labour, enabling it to move labour in and out of war-related industries. Completely new machinery to accomplish this would duplicate and interfere with the commission's national system of offices. Co-ordination was required, but this was a delicate matter because the commission form of administration had been originally adopted precisely to forestall departmental interference. Humphrey Mitchell, the minister of labour, wanted to turn the commission into an agency of his department. Tensions between the two agencies ran so high that the prime minister himself was compelled to intervene and mediate the conflict.

In August 1942 King had a series of meetings with Mitchell, his senior officials, and the commission to reach a mutually agreeable solution. The cabinet had already decided that the Department of Labour should be given control over the commission's employment offices, since the National Selective Service regulations involved direct intervention into employer/employee relations, a mandate not given to the commission.[88] King was at some pains to acknowledge that the "Commission itself would have to preserve its autonomy and could not, except by Act of Parliament, be placed under the jurisdiction of any government department"[89] and suggested ways in which the commission's and the department's responsibilities might be co-ordinated without compromising the UI program. According to King, the commissioners would agree to such arrangements, as would Department of Labour representatives, and an order-in-council was to be drafted to formulate the consensus. The prime minister also noted, however:

A view was expressed that the Commission's entire work should be made a part of the Department of Labour. It was explained, however, that this could not be done except by Act of Parliament. It was also pointed out a preferable way of proceeding in any event would be to take, for the present, as a war-time measure, the step which was being proposed. Experience later on would show how far it might be advisable to have a further transfer of functions and duties made.[90]

This view was undoubtedly presented by the Department of Labour, probably by Mitchell himself. One week after the prime minister's meetings, Mitchell submitted a draft order-in-council to the Privy Council Office for discussion in cabinet. He was impatient to have it reviewed, but the Privy Council Office, on King's orders, withheld the draft from that day's cabinet meeting. Mitchell's draft departed significantly from King's understanding of the arrangements. It called, for example, for the entire commission to be placed "under the direction and control of the Minister of Labour for the duration of the present war" and for the UI act to be "administered by the Minister."[91] The draft assigned duties to the three commissioners that paralleled those outlined by King but added "such functions and duties as the Minister of Labour may from time to time assign."[92] The final clause served to remove any doubts as to how Labour wished to proceed: "The officers and employees of the Unemployment Insurance Commission, together with its premises, equipment, files and all other property and records, are hereby transferred to the Department of Labour and shall constitute the Employment Service and Unemployment Insurance Branch of that Department."[93]

The National Selective Service regulations came into effect 1 September 1942, and PC 7994 was passed on 4 September. This order-in-council tried to strike a more conciliatory tone but contained some serious ambiguities that were to cause confusion later. Rather than "transferring" the employees and facilities of the commission to the department, PC 7994 placed them "at the disposal of the Minister of Labour," who could use them to administer the National Selective Service regulations "without prejudice to the autonomy and continuity" of the commission.[94] The minister would, "in co-operation with the Unemployment Insurance Commissioners," administer the UI act, but would nonetheless "exercise the rights, powers, duties and functions of the Unemployment Insurance Commission, which rights, powers, duties and functions are hereby extended to the Minister of Labour" for the duration of the war.[95] The chief commissioner was enjoined to make representations to the minister from time to time to ensure that the UI act was properly administered.

PC 7994 thus sought to protect some part of the commission's autonomy, while granting Labour the authority it needed to administer the National Selective Service regulations. By March 1943, however, the commission felt that the co-operative intent underlying PC 7994 was not being fulfilled. The commissioners finally approached the Department of Justice for clarification of PC 7994, particularly on the scope of powers to be exercised by Labour and the obligation to consult with or receive approval from the commission in the administration of the UI act and the National Selective Service regulations.[96] Justice's reply indicated that the commission had no powers with respect to the National Selective Service.[97] In commenting on this opinion, one commissioner noted the "total lack of the co-operation which we were lead [sic] to expect,"[98] while the chief commissioner, in a letter to the minister, admitted that the situation between the two agencies had been far from satisfactory.[99] Mitchell ignored these complaints, arguing to the contrary that it was up to the commission to work out the administrative details regarding UI, while Labour had met its obligations in informing the commission on the National Selective Service Program.[100] Mitchell clearly had the whip hand in this matter and continued to overshadow and dominate the commission. With the end of the war new challenges arose.

The wartime National Selective Service regulations had been Canada's first real manpower, as opposed to simply labour market, policy. They had looked beyond simple questions of supply and demand or supporting the unemployed; existing skills had been matched to specific needs. This approach had been necessary in wartime because of the imperatives of speed and reliability in war industry production. The need for some sort of manpower policy would not disappear with peace, however, for two reasons. First, there would be large adjustments to be made in a transitional period from a wartime to a peacetime economy. Labour and capital would have to flow, and be encouraged to flow, from one set of industries to another. The speed and smoothness of the transition would depend on government policies. Second, the federal government wished to avoid a postwar recession. While some, like C.D. Howe, were of the opinion that Canada would enjoy a postwar boom, most observers in 1945 feared that with war's end the country would rapidly plunge back into depression. Accordingly, various government committees met in the last years of the war to plan for postwar reconstruction.[101]

The Cabinet Committee on Reconstruction thus was naturally concerned with peacetime labour markets and general economic adjustment and in August 1945 considered aspects of the UI act in this connection. It was concerned with the "question of suitability of employment under the Unemployment Insurance Act as it may affect mobility of labour in the transition and postwar periods."[102] The committee had agreed that stricter interpretation of "suitable employment" and "reasonable period of time" was desirable because of the overall scarcity of labour, the fact that wartime occupations had been exceptional and thus could not count as usual occupations, and the need to keep a reserve of UI funds.[103] In short, the committee was suggesting that UI regulations be interpreted in a manner to encourage the mobility of labour and the husbanding of UI funds.

The commission's reply was a classic defence of bureaucratic territoriality. It was determined to maintain control over the UI program and, while recognizing the imperatives of labour market mobility, was not prepared to sacrifice its key program on the altar of manpower policy: "The Commission feels that its primary duty is to administer the Unemployment Insurance Act of 1940 in accordance with the spirit and letter of that Statute and while it agrees that the factors mentioned in ... your letter are matters which must be taken into consideration in any directions which it gives to its officers, its primary consideration of this question must be whether or not the interpretation is fair and reasonable."[104] The chief commissioner disagreed with the cabinet committee's assessment of severe labour shortages and so did not "agree that a stricter interpretation is necessary on the grounds set out, nor that the principles enumerated are the deciding factors in issuing these instructions."[105] The rest of the reply outlined the means whereby the commissioners would gear the UI program to transitional conditions.

PC 7994 was to expire on 31 March 1946, disengaging the commission and the Department of Labour. At a cabinet meeting in December 1945, Mitchell had proposed that the wartime arrangements be continued through the "transitional period," however long that might be, effectively leaving the commission under departmental control. A complicating factor was that recent employer/employee commissioner vacancies had not been filled, since the UI program and employment offices were being run by Labour. The impending expiry of PC 7994 called for immediate appointments.

The UI advisory committee had already protested to the government on its slowness at filling the posts, but the prime minister faced pressure from Mitchell to keep the commission weak.[106] As King noted in his diary:

I talked first with Mitchell about the Unemployment Insurance Commission. He wanted to have it carried on under the transitional powers act. I told him this was out of the question. He must now appoint the additional commissioners, so as to have the commission carry on under the statute, as originally planned. It appears that he and McNamara [sic] want to keep control in their own hands. I told him I saw no objection to an arrangement under the commissioners, whereby McNamara might give some managerial direction. Later he might definitely be made a manager.[107]

The "managerial" function to which King referred was embodied in an October 1946 amendment to the UI act that made the commissioners responsible to the minister of labour for the administration of the National Employment Service. This device established a link between department and commission not originally contained in the 1940 legislation. The arrangement was extended in the 1955 act, which stated: "The Commission shall administer this Act and shall assume and carry out such other duties and responsibilities as the Governor in Council, on the recommendation of the Minister, requires and, in respect of such other duties and responsibilities, is responsible to the Minister."[108] Under the terms of the 1940 act, the commission had not been responsible to anyone in this way. In addition, the minister of labour placed his deputy minister (A. MacNamara) on the UI advisory committee as alternate chairman to enhance further his department's control.[109]

The de jure reduction of the commission's autonomy only reflected the de facto attenuation over the years. From its earliest beginnings in 1935 and then through the war, the commission, for the reasons outlined, never had the opportunity to build a solid foundation of independence. No department or agency of government can ever be wholly independent, of course, but the commission had deliberately been given an extraordinary degree of formal autonomy in its founding legislation. Moreover, as in the cases of supplementary and fishing benefits in the 1950s, it lost important battles, not mere skirmishes.

As noted earlier, the cabinet instructed the Interdepartmental Committee on Social Security to review unemployment and relief issues in November 1949, as evidence of winter unemployment mounted. The government estimated that the winter rate might be as high as 7 per cent, more than double the annual average rate. The initiative for supplementary benefits came from Labour, which drafted the scheme and submitted it to the interdepartmental committee on 29 December 1949.[110] The department clearly knew that the commission was a reluctant partner, however, for the deputy minister was urged by his assistant a month earlier that the "important thing is to express clearly to the UIC what we desire them to do."[111] The department was also using the occasion of supplementary benefits to propose, yet again, that the commission come "under the direction of the Minister." Mitchell drafted a memorandum to cabinet to this effect dated 24 January 1950,[112] which was then submitted to cabinet on 1 February.[113] At that meeting and the next, on 8 February, the cabinet deferred consideration of shifting control over the commission to the minister, and the issue died.

Meanwhile, the interdepartmental committee continued to consider supplementary benefits. At its 31 January 1950 meeting, at which members of the commission were present, the committee considered 11 changes to UI. Ten of these, all minor, were presented by commission officials; the eleventh, dealing with supplementary benefits, was introduced and described by the deputy minister of labour.[114] At a subsequent meeting on 6 February, the funding issue was raised by Mitchell Sharp, representing the Department of Finance, since A.D. Watson's December 1949 actuarial report on the program had raised doubts about the fundamental health of the UI fund. With additional prodding from W.A. Mackintosh, chairman of the UI advisory committee, Labour agreed to amend the proposal so that it contained a provision whereby the government would pay for those claimants without previous contributions and make up any shortfall in the fund resulting from these special benefits.[115] It is evident from these proceedings that the decision on supplementary UI benefits arose at the cabinet level, impelled by Labour. Unemployment was high, the department saw itself as responsible for dealing with the situation, and it decided to force the UI program to carry the burden.

The same array of bureaucratic and political forces defeated the commission over UI benefits to fishermen. In its April 1951 report, the commission cogently argued that fishermen, as self-employed workers, could not be embraced by the logic of the act. In this, the commission was seeing the problem through the lens of its actuarial ideology. The Department of Fisheries, in contrast, faced diffuse but clear pressure to do something for indigent fishermen, particularly in Newfoundland.[116] The commission's suggestion that poor fishermen be given means-tested relief did not sit well with the department, which wanted a more "positive" form of assistance.[117]

The idea of fishing benefits was revived in 1953, and a confidential Fisheries memorandum nearly a decade later to the Gill Committee explained the reason: "While there is no formal comprehensive statement on the matter, public and private discussions leading up to the inclusion of fishermen under the unemployment insurance scheme strongly suggest that the real objective underlying their inclusion was to bolster the incomes of these fishermen in areas of chronic under-employment rather than to provide an 'insurance' scheme."[118]

The commission opposed UI benefits for fishermen in 1954 as it had done in 1951,[119] but by 1954 the cabinet had decided. Milton Gregg, minister of labour, attended the first meeting of the Ad Hoc Committee on Unemployment Insurance on 5 April 1954 to indicate that the cabinet wished an extension of UI to fishing and agriculture.[120] The ad hoc committee floundered for several meetings over two years, until by a 9 August 1956 directive the cabinet designed a decision process that would neutralize the commission's influence. The cabinet directive established an interdepartmental committee, chaired by a representative of the commission, with representation from Finance, Labour, Insurance, and Fisheries, the Dominion Bureau of Statistics, and the Privy Council, to advise the commission on a scheme. The commission was then to report to a senior committee of officials chaired by the secretary to the cabinet.[121]

Two plans were eventually submitted to the senior committee in January 1957. Plan 1 was a commission product, while plan 2 had been designed by the interdepartmental committee. The commission's scheme was clearly a rearguard action designed to minimize the damage to actuarial principles. It proposed flat-rate benefits, for instance, and the use of special insurance stamps so that fishermen could never collect regular benefits.[122] A senior Fisheries official attacked the commission's scheme: "In fact Plan 1 is in no way a scheme of Unemployment Insurance but simply a relief scheme administered by the Unemployment Insurance Commission."[123] A comparison of the plans with the eventual UI fishing benefit regulations of 1957 shows that plan 2 was accepted instead of plan 1.

The commission had been convinced that supplementary and fishing benefits were steps along the "wrong road," and so, as internal reviews of UI began in 1960 in the face of growing insolvency, its natural reaction was to press for restrictions and reductions. Its old foe, Labour, also wanted a revised UI program, but one that could be fitted into its wider vision of a national employment or manpower strategy.

Manpower and employment policies came to prominence at the beginning of the 1960s,[124] as the result of a number of factors. Canada, along with most of the rest of the world, experienced a sharp, deep recession at the end of the 1950s. The recession lasted in Canada from 1957 to 1963, longer than in most other advanced economies. This stimulated a search for new solutions. It came to be widely accepted that the recession signified a fundamental shift away from traditional industries to more technologically based ones. A large portion of Canada's unemployment problem, it was thought, was "structural" in nature, the result of the inability of workers in old industries, or with old or no skills, to find work in the new areas of manufacturing. If this diagnosis were correct, then government economic policy would have to focus on labour markets, assisting and enhancing them through training programs and better placement services. This argument certainly suited the Department of Labour.

Interdepartmental consultations on UI amendments began in 1960, shortly before the Gill Committee was established. In January 1960 the commission proposed separation of seasonal (supplementary benefits from 1950 to 1955), fishing, and logging benefits from UI. Comments by the deputy minister of labour reveal the department's view that the commission was something of a dinosaur on the social and economic policy landscape:

Personally I think the proposals contained in this memorandum are entirely outdated and relate back to the thinking of the late 1930's at the time this Act was first being drafted. It is quite useless to think of the unemployment insurance scheme in terms of an insurance scheme per se. It must be thought of in terms of a social security scheme today. The overall proposals and concept of the Commission are, I believe, both politically and socially unacceptable.[125]

Another senior official, in the department's Economics and Research

Branch, described the commission's proposals as "a rather muddled and unrealistic attempt to move history back several years."[126] The difference in views between department and commission surfaced once again in the context of the Gill Committee, specifically in regard to an improved labour market policy.

The Gill Committee addressed the issue in its 1962 report. One of its most controversial recommendations was transfer of the National Employment Service (NES) to Labour. In the committee's view, the NES had a vital role to play in providing referral and job placement services across the entire economy. As part of the commission, however, the NES was bogged down in the details of administering the UI act. Its broader purpose was distracted through having to police claims, and it tended to be restricted to a particular clientele, those on or seeking UI benefits. In the committee's view, severing the commission from the NES would permit a wider range of manpower services to be offered to a broader spectrum of the Canadian labour force.

Predictably, Labour and the commission disagreed over this recommendation. The department shared the Gill Committee's view that the NES's primary function should be employment and that therefore it should become an integral part of the department. The NES would continue to deliver UI benefits, but as a contracted service for the commission.

The commission took the opposite view in a lengthy memorandum to the minister in January 1963.[127] It argued that it would be impossible to run the UI program without the NES or something like it, since UI required work tests. The only way to apply a work test was to refer a claimant to a job. The commission had already taken steps to improve the NES, but there could never be, nor should there be, a complete divorce of UI from the NES.

To suggest then that the transferring of the employment function to another jurisdiction would cure what seems to be a main problem is a snare and a delusion. It is submitted that the complete reverse would be more true, i.e. this problem would be underlined. The position stemming from a transfer, in so far as the UIC is concerned, is that it will have responsibility without authority. That is, it will be responsible for the taking of claims, for the payment (or non-payment) of claims and yet will have to depend almost entirely on a staff over which it has no jurisdiction to carry this out.[128]

The commission suggested that, instead of the NES and the department being merged, the NES, within the UIC, be given more resources and responsibility. Moving to the offensive, the commission argued for its bureaucratic territoriality, suggesting that the real problems underlying the issue were inadequate government recognition of the NES's value, inadequate staffing and salary levels, "the practice by other federal agencies of developing parallel services," "lack of definition of jurisdiction and terms of reference between the UIC and the Department of Labour," and "failure of Department of Labour to give proper credit to the initiative of NES and the tendency of that department to appropriate to itself and develop policies initiated or practised by NES."[129] Indicating that the tension between the department and the commission stemming from the 1940s had persisted, the commission suggested that "it would appear therefore preferable and more appropriate to select the status quo and solve once and for all the matters of jurisdiction, the functions and terms of reference of the UIC and the Department of Labour."[130]

For the commission this was an important battle, since one-third of its staff was attached to the NES. A transfer of the NES would seriously diminish the commission as a bureaucratic entity. Significantly, when the Interdepartmental Committee on the Gill Committee Report submitted its recommendations to cabinet, the only issue that it had not considered was the transfer of the NES. The commission and the department were so opposed in their positions that the interdepartmental committee, upon which both were represented, would have been unable to function had this issue been addressed.

The commission lost its battle nonetheless, and in 1964 the NES was transferred to Labour, effective in 1965. Ironically, the Economic Council of Canada's 1965 report suggested even greater steps to co-ordinate and focus employment policies through the creation of a distinct department. In 1966 the government created the Department of Manpower and Immigration, which then took over the NES from Labour. It proceeded to change the old NES offices to "Canada Manpower Centres." Labour retained responsibility for UI, though this as well was transferred to Manpower and Immigration in 1972.

The transfer of the NES was the only concrete outcome of the Gill Committee. Its report launched an eight-year, intermittent review of the program, punctuated by three federal elections and hobbled by internecine struggles between the commission and Labour. The Interdepartmental Committee on the Gill Committee Report met frequently in January and February 1963 but then suffered a hiatus because of the federal election that spring. It began to meet again in August and submitted its report in October. Allan MacEachen, as the new minister of labour, pursued the transfer of the NES in 1964, leaving further changes to UI for later consideration. It was clear, however, that even by 1963 Labour had ideas for an alternate UI plan quite distinct from the commission's or the Gill Committee's.

In December 1963 the department, after some months of discussion, had produced an outline of "a new approach to unemployment insurance."[131] The department disagreed with the Gill Committee's rejection of seasonal UI benefits (though it too proposed a less generous extended benefits scheme as a replacement); its special restrictions on female workers; its treatment of special income such as bonuses, gratuities, severance, and holiday pay; and its approach to industrial disputes. In the department's view, the Gill Committee had been preoccupied with "the insurability of certain types of unemployment, the true insurable interest of claimants, and the possibilities of abuse of the plan." Gill's preferred UI scheme was designed to "conform as closely as possible to certain enunciated insurance principles." Labour felt that this design would "have harmful effects on labour force development, on labour market functioning, or on industrial relations. At the same time, it was felt that a good deal more could be done in a positive way both to fit benefits to needs, and to make the system of Unemployment Compensation more coherent with federal government activities in the field of manpower development."[132]

The deputy minister of labour, in forwarding these proposals to Allan MacEachen in February 1964, noted: "With respect to the differences, it drops the insurance concept but retains a regular benefit program. It also develops much more fully a positive employment adjustment program for unemployed workers who require adjustment measures through retaining [sic], counselling, rehabilitation, etc., before they are in a position to secure employment."[133] On 21 July 1965 MacEachen directed the chief commissioner to establish an Interdepartmental Committee on Changes to the Unemployment Insurance Programme, suggesting that it not feel tied to the Gill report: "I should like to think that the Committee will start afresh."[134] The committee's report was unsatisfactory, at least to key officials in Labour,[135] and so the minister established yet another committee, the Interdepartmental Committee of Officials on Unemployment Insurance.[136]

Throughout this period Labour continued to elaborate a UI scheme that emphasized a positive labour market approach. This was the corpus of ideas that eventually dominated the design of the 1971 act. MacEachen had consistently forestalled revisions to UI along the lines of Gill (with the exception of the NES transfer) through the simple device of ordering fresh reviews of old reports by new committees. Bryce Mackasey simply continued this strategy by having the White Paper and legislation designed largely by his department, without much commission assistance.[137]

As described in the preceding section, post-1971 UI amendments tightened the program and returned it to more of an insurance basis. Many of these changes derived directly from the actuarial ideology that gripped the commission and other policy-makers. UI had to be "sound," and this meant ensuring that "bad risks" did not overburden the program. Put another way, this implied increasing the incentives for people to return to or remain in the labour market. The commission therefore could be said to have been concerned with the labour market implications of UI, but only in a limited way. An increased entrance requirement, for example, would succeed in reducing the number of young UI claimants without work experience, thus reducing a "bad risk," but it would leave them to search for work unaided. This amounts to little more than a negative labour market policy; a positive policy seeks to employ workers either directly through what are essentially public works or indirectly through training to provide marketable skills. The distinction is important, since the actuarial paradigm left the commission indisposed to pursuing more positive manpower policies. These came from "outside," especially from Manpower and Immigration. The latter, however, had little to say about the UI program itself, and so the two sides of Canadian manpower policy in the early 1970s developed separately with only a tenuous connection.

The commission was at first overwhelmed with the implementation of the 1971 act. New offices, processing technologies, and staff compounded the organizational and logistical problems inherent in the legislation itself. But the commission soon was pressuring cabinet to make changes in the act that would reintroduce firmer insurance principles. In fact, many of the major changes made in 1975 were proposed in 1974 or earlier. Some of these included the increased maximum period of disqualification, the closer relation between benefit duration and number of weeks worked, the redesign of the extended benefit period to make it depend more on regional rather than national unemployment rates, and more flexible maternity benefits.[138] The commission's preference, one official surmised, "could involve a program with few 'welfare' aspects. Marginal workers, fishermen, those on extended benefits, etc., would be shifted to 'support/supplementation' programs, leaving a U.I. program which could be financed more readily on an insurance basis."[139] The 1975 budget changes were essentially financing provisions dealing with the benefit rate, a revised threshold for government contributions, and increased premiums. The budget had originally contained changes to the benefit structure, but cost uncertainties forced their withdrawal and postponement. One of these changes was the three-phase benefit structure, not introduced until 1977 in Bill C-27.

Meanwhile, for most practical purposes Manpower and Immigration was slowly and informally integrating with the commission. In 1972 the commission sought to improve liaison with Canada Manpower Centres to improve services provided to claimants.[140] By 1974-5 co-ordination had become a "top priority" for the commission. It established a Joint Policy Coordinating Committee to assess proposed co-operative programs with the department. Indeed, 1974 saw the first acknowledged "developmental" use of UI funds, in a Newfoundland pilot project wherein UI-eligible manpower trainees were wholly supported by UI benefits rather than traditional training grants.[141] Also in 1974-5, the commission and the department co-operated in the Special Job Finding and Placement Drive, which made Canada Manpower interviews mandatory for claimants in occupations with strong labour market demand. In 1975, the two agencies began to house their operations in adjacent offices or buildings. It was becoming clear that a positive manpower policy pursued by the department had to deal with UI claimants, and a more negative approach of "tightening up" the UI program needed to be able to apply employment tests. Reamalgamation was inevitable, but on whose terms, the commission's or the department's?

Amalgamation was to be on the department's terms, with its officials and its approach striking the dominant chord in the new organization. A new department and commission were established, the Department of Employment and Immigration and the Canada Employment and Immigration Commission (CEIC). Amalgamation was effected by making the deputy and associate deputy ministers of the department the chairman and vice-chairman of the commission, which would still retain commissioners for employers and employees. The commission would have expanded responsibilities for immigration as well as UI.

Senior officials in the ministry recognized that the commission was "one of the most autonomous Crown corporations":

It seems that in the performance of its responsibilities and duties in this area it was intended that it be completely free of ministerial direction and control. However, during the past few years the Government and responsible Minister have been held so accountable and responsible by Parliament, the press and public with respect to the administration of unemployment insurance that they have been obliged to become concerned with the manner in which unemployment insurance is administered and to assume an active interest and role in its administration.[142]

The proposed amendments were thus intended to "give the Minister the authority to exercise the desired management and control."[143]

This change was of historic importance to the Canadian UI program because it finally buried the 1940 principles that UI should be "insulated" from political pressure through management by an autonomous commission and that employers and employees had a propietary right to the program and should therefore be represented on the commission. The first principle was eroded in the 1946 amendment, which made the commission "responsible" to the minister of labour, and again in 1966, when the NES was taken from the commission. The 1977 amalgamation went much further, however, in placing the deputy minister in the chair and reducing private-sector representation on the commission from two out of three to two out of four (though the vice-chairman has no vote except when acting as chairman). The government in effect "expropriated" the UI program.[144]

The announcements of the amalgamation made it clear that the UI program was to become a feature of a broad employment strategy and thus subordinate to the positive manpower policy approach that animated the former Department of Manpower and Immigration. UI was now perceived as just another labour market program:

The new integrated organization will consist of both a commission and a small support department. The new Canadian employment and immigration commission will be responsible for the administration of labour market programs and the policies underlying those programs. These will include the payment of benefits under the unemployment insurance program, immigration, recruitment, selection, settlement, enforcement and control, placement, counselling and training, and the administration of other employment programs such as direct job-creation.[145]

The Canada Employment and Immigration Advisory Council (CEIAC) was also established, but its powers and responsibilities differed significantly from previous legislation. The Unemployment Insurance Advisory Committee established under the 1940 legislation, for example, had access to any commission information that it "reasonably" required to fulfil its functions, but the CEIAC can receive only information that "in the Minister's opinion" is so needed. The 1940 committee had the specific duty of reporting on the state of the UI fund, while the CEIAC had no list of specific responsibilities; moreover, the 1940 committee was enjoined to make recommendations to the commission, while the CEIAC only submits annual reports. Finally, the CEIAC has no independent power to mount inquiries or hold hearings; the 1940 committee did. Ministerial control over the council, and thus the commission, is substantial and firm.

The government's rationale for the amalgamation clearly demonstrated the ascendancy of employment and manpower considerations over UI, narrowly conceived. "Amendments will also allow us to take a more positive approach to unemployment problems through resource allocation ... The changes to the Unemployment Insurance Act will result in a government saving of about $110 million next fiscal year ... The purpose of the amendments is not to save money; it is to let us and the unemployed utilize some of the funds now required for income maintenance to held [sic] provide jobs, incomes, and training."[146] The minister added that much of the incremental funding for the employment strategy would come from reductions in UI expenditure.[147] The UI account had achieved a surplus in 1976, and it was clear by the time Bill C-27 was introduced that it would produce another surplus in 1978. This, in addition to monies saved by pruning the program, presented an opportunity to fund new employment programs without raiding other programs or raising taxes.[148]

The 1978 Bill C-14 amendments were also in part linked to a desire by the minister and senior officials to reduce the government share of UI funding in order to free resources for further employment policies. The "positive" use of UI for developmental purposes (training, work sharing, and job creation) flowed from this perspective as well. By 1978 the UI account's surpluses were becoming a problem, since they were creating pressures for premium reductions. As one Department of Finance memorandum put it:

Another factor which might be borne in mind is that senior CEIC officials are acutely aware of the impending $720 million surplus in the U.I. premium account. It is perhaps not surprising, therefore, that they have advanced proposals to implement wage supplements for youths, the costs of which could be borne by the U.I. program. Similarly, T.B.S. [Treasury Board Secretariat] advises that consideration is being given to major administrative improvements at CEIC, the costs of which might also be charged to the premium account. Finally, the current legislation provides for charge of certain training and job creation costs to the UI account in the context of what is called the "developmental use of U.I. funds". These various initiatives could well change the future outlook of the U.I. account to an unknown, but substantial, degree.[149]

The memorandum noted that though technically there might be an opportunity for premium reductions in 1979, the "CEIC may wish to propose using portions of this surplus to finance new initiatives."[150]

As we noted in the previous chapter, these moves to make UI a funding source as well as an instrument of direct state intervention in the labour market have not been welcomed by either employers or employees. Their respective commissioners made their opposition felt with regard to developmental UI uses, for example, but the department went ahead with these programs.[151] The 1981 report of the Task Force on Unemployment Insurance, while not wholeheartedly supporting developmental UI programs, did support an increased labour market orientation for UI as a whole, particularly for women in the labour force and workers shifting occupations or regions. Firmly embedded in an organization largely focused on labour market development, the UI program by 1981 had been absorbed into an employment perspective, measured against and considered with other programs in that category. The bureaucratic battle over UI was ended.

CONCLUSION

The previous chapter tried to explain changes to UI policy in terms of society-centred approaches that concentrate upon the opposing interests of employer and employee organizations. According to at least some variants of this approach, political pressure from employers – who are presumed to be more powerful – is critical. The evidence did not support this conclusion. This chapter has turned the hypothesis on its head and explored the possibility that policy may be determined largely within the state itself, in relatively autonomous bureaucratic organizations.

The internal logic of bureaux, for example, rests on the need for organizational ideologies, the possession of scarce information, and technical goals. This chapter developed the concept of an "actuarial ideology" to help bring these aspects into focus. Much more about the Canadian UI program, both about how it was designed and how it evolved, can be learned by observing the consequences of this ideology. The initially restricted coverage, the type of benefits, the nature of the rules about duration and disqualifications, and even some of the later expansions of the program may be understood in terms of this ideology. The ideology, while shared by other interests and individuals, did not float, disembodied, above the policy-making arena. It was crystallized in an organization, the commission, and became an instrument for defining its policy space. It helped organize perspectives on problems and solutions in the 1970s, particularly "abuse" and "bad risks." While it is true that employers were pressing for the same types of changes in that period, this was coincidental. Many of their specific suggestions were ignored; others were simply noted as the standard employer position on UI. Much more important were analyses and assumptions within the commission and the department, suggesting that the program had abandoned the actuarial soundness that even the 1971 act was to have upheld.

Another aspect of bureaucratic generation of policy is inter-bureaucratic conflict. This chapter has traced the most important conflict surrounding UI, that between the commission and the Department of Labour (and later Manpower and Immigration). Superficially, this conflict was over control of the NES, but it involved the independence and autonomy of the commission and the nature of UI itself, with regard to manpower policy. The commission's actuarial ideology led it to consider UI's effects on the labour market, but in a primarily negative or passive way. With the perception in the 1960s and increasingly in the 1970s that a concerted, positive manpower policy was needed came the view that UI had to be integrated with such a policy. The commission's traditional autonomy was thereby reduced, with the consequences for UI described earlier. The Forget Commission in 1986 recommended re-establishment of a separate, autonomous Unemployment Insurance Commission without government representation. This is quite logical in terms of the argument presented in this chapter. Insofar as the commission wished to redefine UI as an insurance program, it echoed the actuarial ideology. For example, the report rejected active labour market aspects of UI such as job creation and the variable entrance requirement. An actuarial perspective on UI leads logically to demands that the program be run as insurance, without political interference.[152]

The conflict and eventual triumph of the department over the commission are useful in explaining only some UI policy developments in the 1970s but, combined with the effects of actuarial ideology, provide a rich, nuanced understanding of the program's history since 1940.

CHAPTER SIX

The Role of Federalism

Chapters four and five have explored two society-centred (neo-pluralist and neo-Marxist) and one state-centred (bureaucratic politics) explanations of Canadian UI. Another influential framework in the policy literature, also state-centred, is the institutional approach, which may include political party conflict, electoral systems, parliamentary procedures, or degree of centralization. An examination of all of these would be difficult, and so this chapter focuses on only the last one, the degree of centralization, or, in a word, federalism.

Federalism has long been a preoccupation with students of Canadian public policy but has gained even greater prominence recently with the growing visibility of federal-provincial interaction and the adoption of a new constitution. Keith Banting, for example, has noted that Canadian political scientists "are prone to assume that these structures are somehow critical to the major social programs that we take for granted today, and that constitutional change would usher in a new policy world."[1] Garth Stevenson notes the "obsession with federalism" that marks both Canadian political affairs and political inquiry. Canadians always ask the fundamental questions of politics – who gets what, when, and how – in jurisdictional or interprovincial terms.[2] Doern and Phidd, in a recent textbook on Canadian public policy, argue that federal-provincial relations "are a dominant element of Ottawa's policy process both because of the interdependent effect of each level of government's decisions and because of the competition, partisan and otherwise, for citizen loyalty and the acquisition of political credit."[3] While the influence of legislatures and political parties on policy outcomes has apparently declined recently, that of federalism seems to grow.

There is wide agreement that federalism is important in explaining and understanding Canadian public policy, but there is no clear definition of precisely what "federalism" is, how it exercises this influence over policy, and whether we may expect any particular pattern of consequences. As

Stevenson notes, almost any possible definition of federalism has its problems and its opponents. One tendency is to define federalism in legal or institutional terms. Federalism, to use Smiley's definition, is "a division of law-making powers between the central and regional governments."[4] Wheare's classic definition of the federal principle is more rigid: "What is necessary for the federal principle is not merely that the general government, like the regional governments, should operate directly upon the people, but, further, that each government should be limited to its own sphere and, within that sphere, should be independent of the other."[5] Thus, not only should there be separate and distinct jurisdictions, but these should be relatively well-protected, at least to the degree that one level of government may not abolish another.

In this view, the essence of federalism – as an institutional variable that affects and may determine public policy – is its structural assignment of powers and responsibilities between two levels of government. Federalism makes a difference insofar as it establishes certain channels along which political activity and influence will flow. For example, since Ottawa is solely responsible for defence under the constitution, defence issues will tend to be organized on a national rather than a provincial plane. At any given time in a federal state there is an understanding of who is to do what, an appreciation of the jurisdictional boundaries dividing the policy terrain. In specific circumstances, this division of powers may either accelerate or impede the pace of policy-making. More highly centralized federations, for example, may permit swift and bold initiatives from a strong central government; highly decentralized federations, however, permit numerous points of political access for those demanding change.

Federalism as structure, as action channels for political conflict, is a static concept. A more dynamic view of federalism understands it as a political process, characterized by bargaining. This occurs largely because the structure of federalism creates levels of government that, juridically at least, are roughly equal. But the simple existence of two or more actors is only a necessary condition for intergovernmental bargaining, not a sufficient one. While a federal structure encourages intergovernmental processes, other conditions are also important. Any constitution will be silent on some issues, for example, and thus create a need for clarification that is met partly through intergovernmental negotiation. Social, economic, and political pressures may force intergovernmental bargaining where none before might have been contemplated. The Depression, for example, crippled provincial finances while it simultaneously increased provincial expenditures on social services. In a unitary state the bargaining might have been between the central government and affected groups; in a federal state the axis of bargaining was intergovernmental. The constitution, or federalism as structure, did not dictate that there be negotiation and bargaining; federalism as process arose from a perceived need to co-ordinate because of external circumstances. A final and increasingly important reason for federalism as process is the interdependence of the levels of government. No constitution can be so airtight that the jurisdictions and powers listed in it will not "bump" into each other. Since the Second World War, as governments at both levels have become more active, there has been a growing need to co-ordinate policies to avoid duplication and contradiction.

As a variable explaining public policy or politics, then, federalism may be seen statically as the division of powers itself, or more dynamically as the process of intergovernmental bargaining that inevitably accompanies this division. Federalism may be seen as structure or as process, or both. A more difficult issue is the impact that either of these is likely to have on public policy. Banting, in his excellent study of social policy and Canadian federalism, isolates a number of general and specific connections.[6] He argues that political institutions such as federalism "influence the basic economic and cultural patterns of a nation's life, and thereby exercise an important *indirect* influence on the social policies that it chooses to adopt."[7] Stable political arrangements, national boundaries, and state economic policies have affected economic as well as cultural developments. In the Canadian case, federal institutions appear to accentuate regional conflict.

Federalism also may have three more direct consequences, according to Banting. First, as structure and process it fragments the political system and thus impedes "the capacity of government to introduce and coordinate a large public sector."[8] It is, in short, a conservative force. Second, federalism may emphasize regional claims as against redistributive claims made by categories of persons such as the old or the unemployed, irrespective of where they might live. Banting finds this not to be the case, since the postwar expansion and centralization of the Canadian welfare state has been effected through income security programs based almost exclusively on personal rather than regional or residential characteristics. UI, however, "stands out as a regionalized federal income-security program."[9] Banting offers no explanation for UI's distinctiveness. Finally, federalism "influences the opportunities available to different political interests to shape policy decisions."[10] In particular, it "ensures that the interests of governments, as governments, assume an unusual importance in decision-making."[11] The federal system may insulate decision-makers from public wishes.

Banting finds that Canadian federalism has been a conservative force in income security development and that it has insulated decision-makers and elevated the interests of governments. However, federalism has not heightened regional concerns against redistributional ones across classes of individuals. Moreover, Banting is careful to suggest that the connections he does find are by no means overpowering; federalism does influence Canadian public policy but probably less than economic, demographic, or cultural variables.[12]

Banting's findings suggest the importance of federalism as structure and as process. The conservative influence of federalism in social policy development derives from the impediments to decision-making that a federal structure erects. The insulation of decision-making reflects federalism as a process that involves time-consuming bargaining among political and administrative actors to the exclusion of other types of political influence, arising for example from interest groups or public opinion.

At first glance, UI might appear an inappropriate or weak case in which to explore these conservative and restrictive implications of federalism. It has been, since 1940, completely within Ottawa's jurisdiction and so would seem beyond provincial influence. In fact, UI presents a revealing case for weighing the effects of federalism on Canadian public policy. Between the wars, as we have already seen, UI was discussed and advocated and even implemented briefly at the federal level. Did federalism as structure or process impede the adoption of UI? Was it a more conservative force than business resistance to the program? Even after the constitutional amendment, however, UI remained an intergovernmental issue because of its substantial effect on provincial economies and provincial government budgets. Moreover, while UI was clearly within federal jurisdiction, it was only one of many programs aimed at manpower or the labour market. Jurisdictional divisions within this broader field are not so clear, and so provinces retain some interest in UI not only as a major spending program but as one of a range of programs that may affect their own labour market priorities.

Finally, as I argued in chapter four, UI should be strongly influenced by business and labour interests. It is not, partly because of the weight of intragovernmental interests that spring from the actuarial ideology and interbureaucratic conflict. Another reason might be what Banting sees as the insulation that federalism provides for intergovernmental decision-makers. By accentuating regional interests and the importance of regional effects, and by institutionalizing provinces as spokesmen for the regions, federalism may contribute to the relative weakness of business and labour in this field.

In short, UI may be a good case in which to probe the effect of federalism precisely because it seems at first blush the least likely to be affected. If federalism as structure and process has the anticipated effects on UI, then it is likely to be even more salient for other areas of Canadian public policy, which are less clearly defined jurisdictionally.

BEFORE 1940:
THE JURISDICTIONAL QUESTION

In the inter-war period the debate over unemployment was as much about what should be done as "who should do it."[13] Growing out of Britain's Poor Law tradition, Canadian practice had given the major responsibilities for "relief" to local authorities. Under Canadian constitutional law, the municipalities were creatures of the provinces, the latter also being responsible under the BNA Act of 1867 for charitable organizations and hospitals. In the nineteenth century most local relief was organized by voluntary, usually religious, organizations, with sporadic help from municipal authorities in cases such as local boards of health. Ontario took a lead in developing provincial programs in health, as well as workers' compensation and mothers' allowances.[14]

The federal government was nonetheless linked to employment issues in various ways. First, it was considered responsible for a major part of Canadian economic growth through encouraging railway and canal construction and settlement of the west.[15] Second, its power over immigration gave it substantial influence over labour supply, and by the early twentieth century unions routinely demanded that Ottawa halt immigration when unemployment was high. Third, Ottawa had financial resources unavailable to local and provincial governments during the Depression. When times were good, with provincial coffers filled and unemployment low, local authorities could manage relief services easily. The Depression, however, dried up funds while simultaneously increasing the burden of relief.[16] This was a partial key to Ottawa's fourth claim on employment policy, the perception that the issues of employment and unemployment had a national character or dimension that demanded and justified national policies.

The immediate catalyst for federal action in employment after the turn of the century was the First World War. In contrast to the studied indifference of both federal and provincial governments before 1914, there "was a flurry of government activity on unemployment once war was declared."[17] Ottawa was responsible for the war effort, which stimulated an unparalleled degree of state intervention. As well, patriotic duty in the service of country could not be forgotten once veterans returned home. The issue would be whether Ottawa's responsibility extended beyond veterans to the unemployed as a whole.

The confusion of jurisdictions was evident at the very outset of the war. In the fall of 1914, after the outbreak of war, Ottawa made plans for a national system of employment offices along with national standards and a national fund for relief. The latter two were intended to standardize relief, to reduce the flow of transients from one city to the next seeking help. The natural logic of local relief was that some cities (and groups within cities) provided it, in varying quality and quantity, while others did not. In these circumstances, the destitute tended to be drawn to municipalities offering relief, usually overburdening a system designed for local needs. Residency requirements were only a partial defence against such migrations.

That federal authorities recognized what has come to be termed externalities suggests that they had stumbled across what is sometimes seen as a major drawback to federalism in the provision of social services. As Banting puts it:

Any provincial or state government that establishes new social programs, especially those involving direct employer contributions, places its regions at an economic disadvantage compared to those whose governments do not; established industries are likely to protest vigorously and perhaps transfer some of their operations out of the region, and new investment is less inclined to locate there. On the other hand, provinces or states with superior programs are likely to attract a growing proportion of the nation's indigent, as resident indigents refuse to migrate and new ones arrive from other regions to take advantage of the richer benefit levels.[18]

At the same time that Ottawa was admitting a national dimension to unemployment, provincial authorities were replying that they were "able to deal adequately with their own unemployment problem."[19] Ontario established a Royal Commission on Unemployment, which as noted earlier called in its 1916 report for provincial policies to deal with these problems: a provincial Department of Labour, vocational training, and labour exchanges. These were well within Ontario's jurisdiction but illustrate the potential clash of policies coming from two levels of government attacking the same problems.

Co-ordination was needed, and the first evidence of it was the federal Employment Offices Co-ordination Act of 1918. Ottawa, faced with the prospect of demobilization as well as rising unemployment due to the drop in war production, agreed by this legislation to help fund and administer a national network of labour exchanges. It agreed to a permanent subsidy along with transitional matched funding for any province establishing a provincial network. In Struthers's view, "the creation of a permanent Employment Service was the most tangible evidence of a new federal commitment to tackling unemployment as an industrial, not merely as a reconstruction, problem."[20]

The next three years, however, saw a cautious retreat from this first, bold move on unemployment. The momentum built up during the war and with the Employment Service carried forward in 1920 to produce a draft UI scheme, but one that rested on shaky constitutional grounds. As a signatory of the 1919 Washington agreement that included a commitment to UI, Ottawa might have claimed jurisdiction as part of its treaty powers under section 132 of the BNA Act. Alternatively, it might have tried the peace, order, and good government clause.[21] Neither was persuasive, however, because of the absence of political support at the cabinet level. Prime Minister Meighen, staring at a postwar recession of unprecedented magnitude in 1920-1, desperately wanted to withdraw Ottawa from unemployment relief, not extend it further. The federal government had made financial contributions for the relief of unemployed veterans in the winter of 1919-20. It feared, however, that this might be considered a permanent commitment insofar as some veterans were always likely to be among the ranks of the unemployed.

Meighen's way out of this potentially dangerous responsibility was the offer in December 1920 to share one-third of the costs of municipal relief for all unemployed persons, because, as the government argued, the winter unemployment crisis was a direct consequence of the war. According to Struthers, while this was the first time that a national government in North America had acknowledged some responsibility for the unemployed, it was cleverly limited to a war-induced recession.[22] Once this recession abated, Ottawa's responsibility would too. In the spring of 1921 the assistance was ended. The federal government then drafted a policy that dissociated it from relief at least to the extent that it was a local and provincial responsibility.

Even though Meighen's government was defeated shortly thereafter, this redefinition of the proper role for the three levels of government remained the organizing framework for policy over the next decade. PC 3831, dated 7 October 1921, contained the new policy:

1. Unemployment relief always has been, and must continue to be, primarily a municipal responsibility, and in the second instance the responsibility of the Province.
2. That because of the present situation being due to causes beyond the power of local, or even national control, Provincial and Federal Governments should co-operate with municipal authorities in:
    (a) helping to create and provide employment.
    (b) where employment cannot be furnished to workmen who are willing to work, to aid in providing food and shelter for themselves and dependents until the present emergency period is past.
3. That Federal funds used for unemployment relief or for relief work must be disbursed only through responsible municipal authorities, who in each case shall bear at least one-third of the total or extra cost.[23]

The newly elected government of Mackenzie King lost no time in announcing a national conference on unemployment for the fall of 1922. King wished, however, "to dismantle, not to extend Ottawa's responsibility for the jobless."[24] The conference was open only to the federal and provincial governments, even though it had long been acknowledged that the municipalities had the first responsibility. Labour, business, and farmers were not invited: the conference was entirely intergovernmental. Even at this early stage, federal-provincial bargaining succeeded in freezing out other legitimate interests. This may be because both federal and provincial politicians were concerned to avoid major, ongoing commitments to assist in what hitherto had been a local issue.

The assembled governments were comfortably able to conclude that the unemployment crisis was temporary and that therefore only temporary relief was needed, relief that could be offered at the local level. Ottawa, for example, announced in February 1923 that in the past unemployment relief had "properly emphasized the principle" that such relief was "fundamentally a responsibility of the local authorities, and that the Federal authorities are justified in undertaking any share of the obligation arising only under abnormal conditions."[25] A 1924 conference on unemployment, this time including municipalities, labour, and business, saw Ottawa reaffirm its view that it had no fundamental obligations in the unemployment area.[26] By the end of the decade the Employment Service had been emasculated, and Ottawa had succeeded in avoiding financial commitments to aid provinces or municipalities in their relief work.

The issue of responsibility, for both relief and unemployment insurance, hinged on the constitutional jurisdiction and obligation of the various levels of government. As mentioned earlier, the Poor Law tradition had given municipalities the leading role in local relief, but this assignment of responsibility had presumed that the problem was indeed local and that local resources were sufficient to deal with it. Claims that either the provincial or federal governments also bore some responsibility for the problem were thus inevitably entwined with the view that the problem could not be merely local but was a feature of modern industrialism or regional labour markets. Certainly the evidence of strained municipal resources demonstrated that local authorities could not easily deal with the problem, however they might muddle through from winter to winter. Federal and provincial resistance to more permanent participation in relief policy was partly due to parsimony and a desire to reduce or stabilize expenditures but was also a consequence of honest confusion over constitutional jurisdiction. This issue did not arise in as pointed a fashion in the relief question – which could be addressed through periodic grants-in-aid – as it did in the case of UI.

As noted earlier, the federal Department of Justice had originally advised in 1920 that federal jurisdiction over UI could be claimed on the basis of section 132 of the BNA Act, dealing with treaties, since Ottawa had signed the 1919 Washington Treaty. Another view at the time was that jurisdiction over UI could be claimed under the peace, order, and good government preamble to section 91, which lists federal powers. This was, in light of legal precedents, not unreasonable. The leading judicial decisions on this residual clause at the time were *Russell* v. *The Queen* (1882) and the *Local Prohibition* case (1896). In *Russell* v. *The Queen* the Judicial Committee of the Privy Council, acting as Canada's final court of appeal, had decided that Dominion temperance legislation fell into the residual clause because such legislation affected public order and safety.[27]

In the *Local Prohibition* case the Judicial Committee reversed its 1882 decision and ruled that provinces did have the power to enact local prohibition laws. Its ruling argued that the residual clause did not give Ottawa a general writ to override provincial legislation. While this was a "serious diminution of the general power,"[28] the text of the decision did admit that "some matters, in their origin local and provincial, might attain such dimensions as to affect the body politic of the Dominion, and to justify the Canadian Parliament in passing laws for their regulation or abolition in the interest of the Dominion."[29] Though the Judicial Committee urged "great caution" in this more liberal interpretation of the residual power, there was at least the presumption that a major initiative, such as UI, would be considered by the court as a reasonable matter for federal jurisdiction.

A 1922 decision of the Judicial Committee of the Privy Council, the *Board of Commerce* case, took a further step, however, in attenuating the residual clause and cast doubts on Ottawa's ability to claim UI as federal jurisdiction. In brief, the court held that the residual clause could be invoked by the federal government only in the case of emergency, such as a "great war." Otherwise, interference with the property and civil rights of inhabitants of the provinces could not be condoned. Another decision the following year extended this emergency doctrine and, though upholding Ottawa's use of the power, affirmed its emergency or crisis character. From the legal and constitutional perspective, then, it seemed highly unlikely by 1923 that Ottawa could claim jurisdiction over UI under peace, order, and good government.[30]

By 1928 the Department of Justice was of the opinion that UI, if introduced as a compulsory plan, came under provincial jurisdiction over property and civil rights.[31] The 1928 Select Standing Committee on Industrial and International Relations concluded, as a result of Justice Department testimony, that it was "clear that the responsibility for such legislation rests on the Provincial authorities."[32] The committee went on to note, however: "It would be within the power of Parliament to contribute, by grant, to such Provinces as adopted such legislation, following the precedent set in the matter of Technical Education, Highway Construction and, more recently, the Old Age Pension Act."[33] The Old Age Pension Act provided grants-in-aid to the provinces to mount provincial, means-tested pensions for persons over 70 years of age.[34] The pension field was clearly a provincial jurisdiction, as UI now was understood to be, but Mackenzie King had agreed to extend assistance to the provinces on a 50-50 basis, at provincial discretion, in exchange for the parliamentary support of the two labour members in 1927. This recent piece of legislation showed that it was possible for Ottawa to use its spending power in a field normally reserved for the provinces, as long as it left the acceptance of such assistance up to the voluntary decision of provincial authorities.

The 1928 Commons committee noted a problem that distinguished UI from retirement pensions. It could be assumed that the distribution of elderly people across the country was more or less uniform and stable; unemployment, however, varied considerably from province to province and could swing unpredictably within a province. Thus the committee, in its 1928 report, recommended that "it would be very desirable, for the success of any plan of unemployment insurance that several of the Provinces should be willing to act simultaneously."[35] The municipal relief experience had shown that the unemployed were prepared to move to find assistance or jobs and that without uniform administration and services those areas offering help simply became magnets drawing the destitute.

The Department of Labour followed the standing committee's recommendations and sought provincial reactions to a scheme paralleling Old Age Pensions. The Justice Department remained "very definite" on the point that UI was within provincial jurisdiction, and the provinces took this view as well.[36] The provinces were not prepared to take immediate action, but the Department of Labour did not press the issue, in view of Mackenzie King's well-known hesitance to embark on such a program. From the provincial perspective, aside from the long-standing reluctance to assume resonsibility for all the unemployed, it was too soon after the 1927 retirement program to embark on a new and expensive UI scheme.

At the threshold of the Depression, therefore, federalism as structure had thrown up a barrier to establishment of a UI program. This barrier was not insurmountable, since it did give the provinces legal jurisdiction in the field. The nature of UI, and of the unemployment problem, however, made some national participation almost mandatory were UI ever to be implemented. Britain, France, and even Germany enjoyed highly centralized forms of government that allowed unemployment to be addressed through national policies. Because UI was expensive, any single sub-national jurisdiction adopting it would place its economy at a competitive disadvantage with respect to those who did not and would also possibly attract large numbers of the unemployed seeking assistance.

This problem was acutely felt in the United States, another federal system, and was appreciated in Canada. The conditional grant instrument was available, but, unlike in Old Age Pensions, most if not all provinces would have to adopt UI simultaneously, it was thought, to make it workable. Thus the structural constraints of constitutional jurisdiction combined with the specific nature of the unemployment problem and UI to create a real legal impediment to reform. It is impossible to say whether Canada might have had a UI scheme earlier had this not been the case, but it is clear that had UI been considered after 1923 to be, beyond question, within the federal domain, the balance of forces would have been more favourable to its adoption.

The structural impediment thrown up by the constitution stimulated the other dimension of federalism, federalism as process. The standing committee's report recommended further consultations between the provinces and Ottawa, with business and labour representation, to work out a compromise that would permit implementation of the program. No such conference was called immediately, largely because Mackenzie King had no interest in embarking on UI.[37] In the Commons he expressed quite clearly that any moves on UI would have to be made by the provinces; federal actions would be purely secondary:

I think I expressed the view yesterday that in my opinion a system of unemployment insurance would be a constructive way to deal with the unemployment problem, to which system not only the employer and the governments concerned would contribute but the worker also. If the provinces make a move in this matter and it appears that the federal government can be of assistance in helping to bring about uniformity as between the provinces of any plan proposed, or can cooperate in other ways in any discussion on the subject, we shall be glad upon invitation to take the matter under consideration.[38]

King had no immediate chance to display his willingness to consider UI because he lost the 1930 federal election to R.B. Bennett and the Conservatives. Bennett immediately proposed a Relief Act, the first of an annual series, in the unprecedented amount of $20 million. The monies were grants-in-aid to local authorities to meet the costs of unemployment relief. The act was passed during a special session of Parliament called to deal with "exceptional economic conditions with the resultant unemployment."[39] In introducing the bill, the prime minister closely associated himself with the views of his predecessor in saying that the legislation did not propose "that this Dominion government should in any sense deal with these problems directly. These are primarily problems of provinces or municipalities, and apart from national undertakings."[40]

Bennett was to argue, in terms strikingly similar to those used in the 1922 decision by the Judicial Committee of the Privy Council, that "a problem, local and provincial in its nature, may become a national problem."[41] Later, in the second reading introduction to the bill, Bennett once again alluded to the fact that the unemployment problem had developed a national character, requiring co-operation among the levels of government. In Bennett's mind, and in the preamble to the 1930 Relief Act, unemployment remained primarily a provincial and local responsibility, and so in constitutional terms the act represented only a temporary commitment of funds to deal with what Bennett thought a temporary, though serious problem. The problem was not temporary and indeed was exacerbated by the severe drought that hit the western prairie provinces in 1931. So crushing was this blow that Ottawa was forced to pass yet another Relief Act, again lamely affirming that the care of the unemployed was primarily a provincial and municipal responsibility. This principle was followed to the point of simply turning monies over to provincial and municipal authorities to spend largely as they saw fit; Bennett was trying to avoid the establishment of a costly and extensive federal bureaucratic apparatus.[42]

When pressed in the House in April 1931 to embark immediately upon establishment of "unemployment, sickness, and invalidity" insurance, Bennett gave a comprehensive answer that stressed the complications of constitutional jurisdiction and the process of reaching agreement with nine provinces. Bennett argued that such insurance "can never be successful if each province has a different system or if one province has a system and another has not."[43] This obviously implied negotiation, though Bennett hedged on this point by stressing the paucity of data and the complexity of any consultations with the provinces on these matters.

Consultations there were, though initially they addressed only the relief problem. There were two meetings, the first, in April 1932, to rearrange relief payments and the second, in January 1933, on UI. The first meeting had no real constitutional content, because the issue was simply the technique of providing relief. The western provinces at this stage were virtually incapable of meeting any of their responsibilities and were dependent on federal financial assistance. The January meeting, however, was called expressly to consider jurisdictional issues pertaining to UI that had impeded action over the last decade.

Neither Bennett nor his principal advisers, R.K. Finlayson and W.C. Clark, were under any illusions that UI could deal with the current employment crisis. This was largely because they were without concrete data or even a plan to offer the provinces, and all of them believed that any constitutional division of powers had to take a back seat to dealing with the crisis of relief. But Bennett had promised steps on UI, and so the January conference was called. Finlayson advised Bennett to exercise "the utmost caution in any statement made as to the form the proposed scheme is to take, and the extent to which it may be expected to alleviate unusual unemployment problems in the future."[44]

Finlayson pointed out that the federal government had every right to establish a royal commission on the subject of UI and to collect and digest data relevant to such a scheme, so that the real issue at the conference would be jurisdictional. He dismissed any notion of cost-sharing or joint administration of UI, as had been done in the case of Old Age Pensions and, earlier, in the 1918 act establishing the Employment Service of Canada. It appears once again that the program peculiarities of UI made joint federal-provincial control impossible. First, there was the need to have employment and unemployment offices in the same agency and under one administration. Second, in view of the financial magnitude of the program, the actuarial problems, and the perception that there would be incentives to collect benefits dishonestly, the program would have to be entrusted to one, single governmental authority.[45] Two years of irregular municipal administration of relief monies had clearly influenced Finlayson's judgments.

In view of these considerations, Finlayson suggested that a constitutional amendment would be necessary to give Ottawa jurisdiction over UI. However, since Ottawa had no detailed plan in mind, he suggested that Bennett simply ask for general permission from the provinces to amend the constitution, in keeping with the details of a future plan. This was unlikely to be accepted. The question is whether Finlayson and Bennett had deliberately designed the conference agenda to ensure its failure.[46] It appears that they were sincere, if naive, about addressing UI. Their naiveté arose from lack of information and a desire to "trade" UI for clear provincial assumption of direct relief. As it turned out, the provinces were not prepared to give Ottawa exclusive jurisdiction over UI without knowing the plan's details.

From the provincial, and especially western provincial, point of view, Ottawa seemed to want a new area of jurisdiction without continuing its responsibilities in supporting relief. The problem intensified over the next year, as the western provinces found themselves borrowing heavily from a reluctant Ottawa to avoid bankruptcy. Another Dominion-provincial conference was held to address the relief problem in January 1934, and it was after this meeting that Bennett allowed UI planning to go forward in the federal government.

The scheme was largely drafted by mid-summer 1934, and Bennett was advised to proceed immediately with a bill. At this point he still believed that a constitutional amendment was necessary and that unanimous provincial agreement was politically, if not legally, required for such an amendment. Provincial good-will had, however, evaporated as a result of Bennett's moves that summer to reduce unilaterally federal relief expenditures. Again, the provinces could hardly be expected to accept UI if it implied that Ottawa would leave the very costly area of relief entirely to them.

In introducing the bill in 1935, Bennett adopted the new position that UI was in fact within federal jurisdiction. The basis of the claim was Ottawa's responsibility for peace, order, and good government. Mackenzie King maintained, as he had for years, that UI was within the provincial power but agreed to vote for the legislation nonetheless. In November 1935, after winning the federal election, King had the Employment and Social Insurance Act, along with the rest of Bennett's "New Deal" legislation, referred to the courts. Provincial governments entered the cases as well, in most cases rejecting federal jurisdictional claims, but in some cases supporting such claims. Ontario, for example, supported the Employment and Social Insurance Act.

Both the Supreme Court and the Judicial Committee on appeal saw the legislation as ultra vires the federal power. The government argued that the legislation, dealing with a problem unforeseen in 1867 and hence not specifically mentioned in the BNA Act, fell within the residual powers of section 91. Unemployment was a national problem that required a national solution. The Judicial Committee concluded that insurance of this kind fell within the area of property and civil rights and thus was an exclusive provincial domain. The argument that unemployment was a special emergency found no favour with the court, since UI was to be a permanent program. Further, the court denied the argument that Ottawa could implement a UI program based on its spending power, that is the control over public debt and property (section 91.1), and the raising of money by any mode or system of taxation (section 91.3). These powers could not be permitted to become a basis of federal invasions of provincial jurisdiction.

The Judicial Committee's decision was not handed down until 1937. Virtually nothing had been done with UI during the intervening years, but once the constitutional air was cleared, King moved swiftly. Almost immediately upon release of the decision, the federal cabinet dismantled the Employment and Social Insurance Commission established under the legislation, and the Department of Labour set about drafting a new, but similar UI bill. On 5 November 1937 King sent a letter to the nine provincial premiers proposing a constitutional amendment to give Ottawa exclusive jurisdiction over UI. At this stage, King was merely sounding out the general position of his counterparts, all of whom replied by the end of the month. Three of the nine, Duplessis of Quebec, Dysart of New Brunswick, and Aberhart of Alberta, refused to endorse such an amendment without a specific proposal to consider; the other six provinces agreed in principle.[47]

King's next step was to circulate a draft amendment for reaction. Once again the same six provinces agreed to the inclusion of UI under section 91, which lists federal powers. Quebec, New Brunswick, and Alberta refused, however. Duplessis was unprepared to grant any aspect of provincial jurisdiction to Ottawa, though he publicly argued in favour of a jointly funded scheme modelled on the Old Age Pension. Alberta and New Brunswick demanded a review of the entire range of federal-provincial problems before tackling a specific issue like UI.[48]

King was advised of three alternative reactions to this provincial balance of opinion. First, the government could simply enact the legislation and wait for a constitutional amendment before proclaiming it in force. This would have the advantage of pressing the three recalcitrant provinces but might appear contemptuous of constitutional propriety because the legislation, while not proclaimed, would be admittedly ultra vires. Second, the federal government could unilaterally proceed with a constitutional amendment. This would have the virtue of finally enacting a national UI scheme but could prejudice federal-provincial relations in connection with a broader constitutional settlement after the issuing of the report of the

Rowell-Sirois Commission. Finally, Ottawa could postpone the matter until such a general constitutional agreement were secured and then pursue UI within a new framework of federal-provincial relations.[49]

King decided to postpone UI until the Rowell-Sirois Report was submitted. In a speech in the Commons, he declared that unanimous provincial agreement was necessary.[50] He did not actively press the issue, though it did arise occasionally in the House. It appeared that UI would have to await the Rowell-Sirois recommendations, now delayed until the next year at the earliest.

A new opportunity for UI was created with the outbreak of war in September 1939. According to Struthers, the advent of war led to a "turning-point in federal policy."[51] From a reluctant advocate of UI, King changed to a firm supporter, largely because of the connection between a sound, well-established UI program and demobilization. UI would provide a cushion during any economic decline after the end of the war, and the time to establish the program was now, while the pace of economic activity increased. As well, the war effort itself would be furthered by UI. The contributions made by employers and employees would be a form of national saving which, apart from a small portion reserved for administration, could be immediately invested in the country's war effort. UI contributions would reduce the amount of money spent on consumer goods and thus free resources for war production.[52]

The importance of UI for the war effort made continued provincial opposition seem unpatriotic. King had further luck, however: by January 1940, Quebec's Duplessis had been replaced by Premier Godbout, thus removing the most adamant opposition. On 15 January, King wrote to the premiers of Quebec, New Brunswick, and Alberta to suggest once again a constitutional amendment, and this time he received affirmative replies. Additional information had to be provided to Quebec and Alberta, and so they did not give their full agreement until May 1940. Britain amended the BNA Act by July 1940, and UI was passed a month later.

With passage of the constitutional amendment, the impact of federalism as structure on policy development in UI was almost completely erased. Ottawa was given exclusive jurisdiction over UI, but only UI, so that this new clause in the constitution could never be used as a basis for extensions of federal power in the income security field. By the same token, however, provincial policy on unemployment was not completely constrained. An issue that was to take on some prominence in the 1970s illustrates the scope of remaining provincial opportunities: what causes of unemployment would be admitted within the UI program? Unemployment may arise because, for example, a person is pregnant, has retired, or is retraining. The current UI program insures wages lost due to these causes, but they remain areas within which the provinces may legislate. Indeed, to anticipate the argument made at the end of this chapter, the jurisdictional issue of UI may once again take on prominence as the program evolves into more of a labour market, as opposed to an income security, instrument.

How did federalism affect UI development to 1940? Until recently, the conventional view was that federalism and the ambiguities of the BNA Act had retarded development of the Canadian welfare state in general and UI in particular. Banting has argued, for example, that in the pre-Second World War era, federalism was "a conservative force in welfare politics."[53] As we saw, in 1928 and 1929 Ottawa approached the provinces about a constitutional amendment or at very least some cost-sharing scheme for UI but was met with indifference. Unanimity was the major stumbling block, and even when Bennett tried again in 1933, the provinces were understandably reluctant to give their approval to a program the details of which remained secret. The Employment and Social Insurance Act, 1935, was referred by King to the courts, though it is likely that one or another of the provinces would have challenged it sooner or later. When the legislation was struck down, the prime minister tried unsuccessfully to get unanimous provincial agreement to a constitutional amendment; rebuffed, he let the issue sit until wartime circumstances created an opportune moment for change. In short, one could conclude that while other forces may have impeded or delayed the introduction of UI to Canada, it might have been possible to have a program as early as 1922 – had jurisdiction been clearly in Ottawa's hands – or 1928 – had the provinces been more responsive to federal overtures.

Struthers, in his excellent history of unemployment relief to the passage of UI in 1940, has put forward another interpretation, which argues that constitutional barriers were merely convenient excuses for inaction, at both federal and provincial levels:

No legal barriers barred Bennett or King from providing work for the jobless. Nothing in the constitution stopped Ottawa from defining a national minimum standard of relief and making provincial compliance a condition of federal aid. No province ever took the dominion government to court for assuming responsibility for the relief of unemployed single men ... Even with unemployment insurance, the constitution in the 1930s, as in the 1920s, provided more of a convenient excuse for delay than a barrier to action for both Bennett and King ... Clearly, neither man during the 1930s was anxious to accept the costs or the risks of an unemployment insurance scheme launched in a time of heavy unemployment. The constitution provided a useful justification for delay.[54]

Struthers is undoubtedly correct on the relief question: Ottawa's role in the 1920s and 1930s was based on its spending power, which is virtually unlimited as long as the recipients have a choice to refuse or accept federal aid. To say that the constitution provided only an excuse for inaction on

UI, and not a real barrier, is wrong. First, while there can be no doubt about Bennett's and King's reservations on UI, even the most willing proponent of the program would have had to address the constitutional issue. The weight of legal opinion was that UI was within provincial jurisdiction, even though it would be most efficiently administered by federal authorities. Some constitutional amendment was needed, most experts agreed, because UI could not be administered very well by sub-national authorities.

Second, the 1940 constitutional amendment was the first one that transferred powers from one level of government to another. It is anachronistic to say that such a transfer should have been treated more lightly. Third, the constitution as excuse and the constitution as barrier are not mutually exclusive categories. Politics, after all, is a process of bargaining, and the outcomes depend as much on the resources that each player may bring to the process as on the skill with which the resources are manoeuvred. Both federal and provincial governments were reluctant to deal with UI, but their reluctance might have been more effectively challenged had they not been able to argue the jurisdictional point.

It is impossible to tell whether UI might have been introduced earlier to Canada had it been clearly and always in the federal domain. The best that might be said is that federalism weighed in on the side of a set of forces that together acted to delay implementation.

AFTER 1940: FEDERALISM AND POLICY CO-ORDINATION

Though the constitutional issue may have been resolved in 1940, the effect of federalism in the sense of a fairly continuous process of co-ordination did not wane. In some respects it increased. This was because of the way that UI, once implemented, encroached upon two other broad policy areas, both largely within provincial jurisdiction. The first was social policy, or, more specifically, income security programs for all but the able-bodied unemployed. UI as a program quite deliberately sliced off a segment of Canada's needy population, comprised of regular members of the labour force who were temporarily unemployed. Since they had worked at one time, they were presumably physically fit and perhaps not without savings. They could collect benefits while looking for work but would eventually – except for the chronically unemployed – return to a job. In this regard, then, Ottawa was responsible under UI for the least troubled part of the population requiring help.

The provinces, in contrast, were left with single mothers, the elderly, the handicapped, the young, and generally all those who were unlikely to earn a livelihood through the labour market. Since UI had been designed largely to be self-financing, there were inevitable pressures on Ottawa to help the provinces. A further connection also induced this pressure: UI recipients, once their benefits were exhausted and they were still without work, were "transferred" from the federal UI jurisdiction to the provincial social assistance system. The transfer was informal and effected by the recipient in seeking help, but it created a human bridge between a federal program and provincial ones, thereby establishing a strong if undefined federal obligation to help the provinces. Ottawa could meet this obligation indirectly by making UI benefit provisions more generous, or directly by providing grants to the provinces for their social assistance programs. The 1955 and 1971 UI acts largely accomplished the first; the 1956 Unemployment Assistance Act and the 1966 Canada Assistance Plan accomplished the second.

The second provincial area that UI affected was labour market policy. As we noted, UI deliberately absorbed the pre-existing provincial employment offices. UI was thus intended to have a labour market dimension, and this was given increasing weight through the 1960s and 1970s. Provincial responsibilities usually encompass at least the following: enforcement of collective bargaining legislation, minimum wage laws, minimum standards, and vocational training. The last has created the most serious conflicts, but even then largely between Quebec and Ottawa. By the end of the 1970s, however, UI was being altered to enhance its effects on labour mobility (by lowering benefits and thereby inducing people to move to regions of low unemployment). This point of friction between federal and provincial authorities has been less noticeable in UI than in social policy, but it may flare up in the future as provinces become more serious about managing their own economies and directing provincial labour force development.

The Rowell-Sirois Commission finally submitted its report in 1940, too late to influence significantly the UI debate but well timed to influence the debate over unemployment relief, or social assistance. The royal commission argued that Ottawa should receive the main sources of tax revenue in the country – principally personal and corporate income tax and succession duties – in return for the payment to provincial governments of national adjustment grants that would equalize standards of public services across the country. The commission also recommended that Ottawa take over full responsibility for unemployment relief, even if it were not given the sole control of lucrative tax fields. From the commission's perspective, federal responsibility for relief would remove one of the worst features of provincial/municipal relief administration during the 1930s: the variation of levels of service and benefits between rich and poor areas of the country. At a federal-provincial conference in 1941 the premiers of Ontario, Alberta, and British Columbia refused to swap jurisdiction over relief for jurisdiction over taxes, and so the issue went into limbo as Canada undertook its war effort. Ottawa occupied the tax fields anyway, but because of wartime production there was virtually no unemployment and hence no significant relief expenditures.

Despite this abeyance in federal-provincial negotiations over social policy during the war, Ottawa did not ignore these issues entirely. Canada's experience in the First World War had persuaded many in government that this time there had to be planning for the period immediately following the cessation of hostilities. It was also widely agreed that Canadians, after sacrificing for the war effort, would not support a return to prewar economic conditions. Planning for "reconstruction" thus began almost immediately in 1939-40, as part of the general machinery of wartime planning.

With the declaration of war, the federal cabinet underwent significant reorganization. In August and again in December 1939 the cabinet committee system was developed and revised until 10 separate committees were in charge of different aspects of wartime planning.[55] The most important committee, from the point of view of social policy, was Demobilization and Re-establishment. This committee in turn created an interdepartmental committee called the Advisory Committee on Demobilization and Rehabilitation. As their titles suggest, these committees were primarily concerned with problems stemming from the demobilization of returning soldiers. At first these and other committees focused exclusively on immediate defence issues, but by 1941, with Canada's defence commitment and war policy in place, they turned to reconstruction questions. Demobilization and Re-establishment expanded its terms of reference in 1941, and the government also established the Committee on Reconstruction, headed by Principal F. Cyril James of McGill University.[56] Both the Senate and the House of Commons appointed committees to address reconstruction issues, and in 1944 the federal government established a Department of Reconstruction under C.D. Howe. By this point, the Department of Finance had also turned its attention to reconstruction, because of its financial and intergovernmental implications.

In preparation for the postwar era, Ottawa released its White Paper on Employment and Income[57] in 1945, shortly before the federal election that year. The Liberals hung on to power, with a platform promising substantial social reform and an extensive net of social programs to ensure, in the White Paper's words, a "high and stable level" of employment.[58] With the Canadian election won, the war in Europe over, and public expectation high, Ottawa called a Dominion-provincial conference for August 1945. The 1941 Wartime Tax Agreements were due to expire in any case, and so this conference was an ideal opportunity to carry forward the proposals of Rowell-Sirois as well as those developed by Ottawa itself in the process of reconstruction planning. At the opening of the conference, federal representatives tabled a thick package of proposals, later known as the Green Book proposals, in effect part 2 of the more general posture developed in the White Paper.[59]

Ottawa's plan was in effect to continue the Wartime Tax Agreements, but under a new guise, whereby Ottawa would have exclusive claim to succession duties and personal and corporate income tax in exchange for grants and assistance to the provinces. These grants fell into two categories: unconditional transfers tied to GNP but never less than $12 per capita based on the 1941 census, and a host of cost-sharing schemes in the social security and economic fields. The shared-cost schemes included pensions, unemployment assistance, health insurance, and public works.

Ottawa's proposals were far-reaching and if successful would have redrawn the jurisdictional map at one stroke. It was also a highly centralized vision, reflecting the habit of control and federal dominance developed during the war.[60] The August 1945 conference ended without agreement, at least partly because of the tone of the federal proposals. But other factors were also important. The provinces, for example, had no warning of what was coming and so were incapable of responding in anything but rhetorical terms. Moreover, premiers Drew of Ontario and Duplessis of Quebec were fresh from election victories and sensed a mandate to reassert provincial prerogatives now that the war was over. The August meeting lasted four acrimonious days, after which committees of ministers and officials were struck to study the proposals in detail. Study continued until April 1946, when the governments met again. Ottawa had by this time increased its original offer of $12 per capita to $15 but could not persuade the provinces to agree to its package of proposals. Ottawa needed the tax fields to fund the grants, and so without provincial release of major revenue sources the whole package of proposals collapsed.

Part of the original package concerned unemployment assistance. The federal government made the following offer:

In addition to unemployment insurance, the Dominion will set up a system of unemployment assistance under which it will pay benefits equal to 85 per cent of unemployment insurance benefits, to unemployed persons able and willing to work who are not entitled, or who have ceased to be entitled, to unemployment insurance benefits. This assistance will be limited to two years of continuous assistance, but a person will again become eligible for this assistance following an approved period of employment.[61]

The original 1945 proposal to the provinces acknowledged that both the National Employment Commission and the Rowell-Sirois Commission had called for Ottawa to assume responsibility for the "employable unemployed" as part of "any general settlement with the provinces."[62] Ottawa's offer echoed the concerns raised by both earlier commissions about the "problems of administration being separated from financial responsibility" and the "make-shift arrangements and controversy with provincial governments which otherwise would be almost certain to recur under the old methods of providing relief."[63]

The federal plan would not have relied on a means test, which it saw as more suitable to provincial and municipal administration, but would have applied some sort of test to ensure that benefits would not go to persons who, "by reasons of independent income or family status, are not dependent on employment for a livelihood."[64] It would have been a national plan, with national standards, and would have been closely allied with the UI system, using its administrative machinery and relying on its basic tests, such as the ability to get and hold a job. The government noted that at the time UI did not extend to certain categories of employment such as farm employees, domestic servants, and certain government employees and office employees earning $2,400 or more per year; insured persons who did not qualify for or had exhausted UI benefits; young persons without any employment experience; and previously self-employed persons (farmers, tradesmen, trappers, etc.) who gave up their businesses to seek wage employment.[65]

Accordingly, Ottawa promised that "as rapidly as possible the Unemployment Insurance Act will be widened to embrace all employed persons," with modest exceptions. Unemployment assistance would be particularly valuable as a transitional measure while UI was being thus extended, and the federal government even permitted itself to hope that if "ultimately unemployment insurance can cover all possible cases, it would be possible to dispense with unemployment assistance, and in any event its scope would diminish to the extent that unemployment insurance is broadened."[66]

The financial terms of Ottawa's offer were to pay those claimants who were insured or who had been previously employed 85 per cent of the UI benefit rate to which they would have normally been entitled. Persons without a previous employment record would receive flat-rate benefits. These benefits were to be paid out of the Consolidated Revenue Fund and the Unemployment Insurance Fund.[67]

This was a sweeping proposal, and for the first time Ottawa showed itself prepared to accept entire responsibility for the employable unemployed. Under this scheme, the provinces would have remained responsible for the unemployable categories of the population: the disabled, single mothers, orphans, and the elderly poor.

The problem with the proposal was that it remained part of a package that the provinces saw as highly centralizing, so much so that Premier Macdonald of Nova Scotia, on hearing the federal proposals in 1945, replied: "Provincial autonomy will be gone. Provincial independence will vanish. Provincial dignity will disappear. Provincial governments will become mere annuitants of Ottawa. Provincial public life ... will be debased and degraded."[68] The main opposition to the federal proposals came from Drew and Duplessis. Quebec maintained a strong provincial rights position, while Ontario responded to Ottawa's proposals with one of its own, the costs of which were considered too high by federal negotiators to make it acceptable.[69]

The end of the August 1945 conference was not the end of the federal proposals, however. Instead of being implemented at one time, within a general framework, the components of Ottawa's original Green Book proposals were passed piece by piece through the 1950s and 1960s, until, with the Medical Care Act of 1968, the 1945 design was virtually in place. This was achieved through postwar tax agreements that allowed Ottawa to monopolize the income tax field.[70] With these revenues in hand, and with generally favourable economic conditions until the mid-1950s, Ottawa made a series of offers concerning health grants, hospital insurance, medical insurance, assistance to the blind and disabled, pensions, and unemployment assistance.

By the time the Unemployment Assistance Act, 1956, was passed, conditions had changed sufficiently to alter the program's design. Stimulated to action by growing unemployment rates in the mid-1950s, largely a consequence of the post-Korean War recession, Ottawa and the provinces agreed at the 1955 federal-provincial conference to embark on a cost-shared program to assist those who had exhausted or were ineligible for UI benefits. This was the first target group for the program, as it had been in 1945. But this time, Ottawa was more receptive to concerns of provincial autonomy. The 1945 proposal would have established a federal program under federal administrative control, linked directly to the UI program. The Unemployment Assistance Act of 1956 left administration of the program to provincial authorities and thereby raised a crucial problem: how to distinguish between employables and unemployables. With administration in provincial hands, there might be strong temptations to shift the program clientele onto federal shoulders by simply labelling applicants employable. Ottawa therefore devised, with provincial agreement, a formula that effectively disregarded the distinction (in practice it was hard to apply, anyway) between unemployables and employables and set federal contributions as a fixed portion of the total caseload.

The formula agreed to in 1955 and embodied in legislation a year later was that Ottawa would pay one-half of the average cost of assistance for that portion of caseload in excess of 0.45 per cent of the provincial population. Some expenditures, such as medical, hospital, and dental care, were excluded from cost-sharing, as were cases in public or private institutions and those persons receiving benefits under provincial mothers' allowances programs.[71] Recently passed legislation providing old age security and pensions for the blind and disabled effectively excluded these groups as well. There can be no doubt therefore that the Unemployment Assistance program was meant to be, at least in federal eyes, an adjunct to the UI program. In 1966 it was incorporated, along with various other federal-provincial cost-shared social assistance programs, into the Canada Assistance Plan. Much broader in scope, the plan saw Ottawa contributing one-half of the costs of general social assistance administered by provinces and municipalities.[72]

With passage of the Canada Assistance Plan the federal and provincial levels became fused into a virtually seamless authority in the social policy field. In sharp contrast to the 1930s, when each level seemed determined to avoid as much responsibility as possible, within 10 years of war's end the distinction between employables and unemployables was rejected in favour of federal-provincial co-operation in social assistance, and 10 years after that the distinction was not used at all and the definition of need was broadened. Close co-operation between Ottawa and the provinces made the Canada Assistance Plan an extremely flexible instrument. At the same time, however, it implied increased responsibility on Ottawa's part to calculate the effects of any changes of UI on provincial social assistance payments. With co-operation came responsibility. At first, up to 1975, this did not present a problem because as UI was enriched it reduced provincial welfare expenditures. After 1975, however, precisely because UI was so critical to some provincial economies, cuts were strongly resisted by provinces that felt that Ottawa was simply shifting the burden of unemployment from UI on to provincial social assistance.

The need for co-ordination between Ottawa and the provinces thus remained even after UI was made a clear federal jurisdiction. But the co-ordination described above, federalism as a process, did not have a direct effect on UI itself. Indeed, provincial pressure to change UI was modest in this period before 1971, largely for three reasons. The first was the expansionist dynamic already imbedded in UI. The federal government had committed itself in 1945 to expanding the UI program as rapidly as possible, in accord with the original program design. When implemented in 1941, UI coverage was restricted largely for technical reasons. It had been assumed that when administrative mechanisms became available, more occupations could be included in the program. As economic circumstances improved in the 1950s, there seemed little risk in widening the program. This expansion came from within Ottawa itself, not from provincial pressures.

The second reason had to do with the way the program began to recognize regional differences in employment. The original act had had several negatively couched regional provisions, which excluded certain occupations that by their nature were concentrated in particular areas of the country: fishing, forestry, hunting, and trapping. The key aspect of employment in the poorer regions of the country such as the Atlantic provinces is its seasonality. The original benefit provisions also were designed to minimize the use of UI by seasonal workers. Indeed, as coverage was extended immediately after the war to some seasonal industries, the commission passed seasonal regulations that served to restrict benefits. In 1950 the government amended the act to provide supplementary benefits for the winter months for those who had exhausted normal benefits. Amendments in 1956 brought fishermen under the act, thereby extending UI to a major category of workers in the Atlantic provinces, even though, strictly speaking, many fishermen were self-employed. The 1955 act had established seasonal benefits payable between January and April, and this also dramatically increased the regional incidence of UI benefits.

The final reason for the absence of strong provincial pressure to change UI was that the gains of such endeavours would have been modest. The program was in place and seemed to be expanding, and so provincial attention was more profitably directed at persuading Ottawa to contribute to provincial social assistance programs.

The 1960s saw immense upheavals in Canadian federalism that in part reflected growing confidence among provincial authorities as well as a growing desire to manage and build provincial economies.[73] Another important development was the federal government's realization of the importance of more regionally specific and regionally targeted programs.[74] This was evident in reports at the time that stressed issues such as structural unemployment[75] and indeed in the Diefenbaker government's general policy posture favouring regional (originally rural) development.[76] The Economic Council of Canada's first annual report also addressed the question of manpower policy and regional development, and the new Trudeau government of 1968 embarked immediately on a consolidation of federal regional programs under the newly created Department of Regional Economic Expansion.

This new concern with regions and regional differences represented an important change in federal policy. Immediately after the war, Ottawa assumed that its responsibility as the national government was to establish national standards in social programs. This had a powerful redistributive effect insofar as provinces well below the standard were raised up more than those close to the standard. This was the case with hospital insurance, for example, and even with Unemployment Assistance and later the Canada Assistance Plan. Social assistance programs or cost-sharing programs are normally regionally sensitive because the agreement covers costs that themselves vary regionally. UI, as an insurance program geared to individual contributions, reflected regional differences in a perverse way. The higher the long-term unemployment in an area, the less likely that UI could act as a cushion for unemployed individuals. To receive benefits, one must have worked and worked regularly. Supplementary and later seasonal benefits partly addressed this problem, as did extension of coverage to occupations such as forestry and fishing. But the program logic and structure of UI require rather specific devices to ensure a positive regional effect.

Through the 1960s the federal government wrestled with the problem of whether to include such devices in the UI program or make UI strictly an individually based insurance program without intended regional impact. The Gill Committee, as we noted earlier, had recommended a return to a more actuarially sound UI program that addressed temporary unemployment for regular members of the labour force.[77] Accordingly, it suggested a shorter duration for regular benefits (with expanded coverage, however), coupled with an extended unemployment benefit phase. Regular benefits would be supported by premiums, while extended benefits under UI would be financed by government alone. Under this proposal, regular benefits would respond to frictional unemployment, and extended benefits would respond to seasonal unemployment; Unemployment Assistance would address chronic unemployment. The latter two programs would have had the largest regional impact. The Gill Committee also suggested that fishermen no longer be covered under UI, though they could come under extended benefits. The committee recommended against experience or merit rating, since this would have, in its view, negative economic consequences.[78]

The Gill Committee had wanted extended benefits to be distinct from insurance, even while they were delivered by the UIC. The other choice was to keep extended benefits within a restructured UI program, labelled as insurance benefits. This was the option suggested by the 1968 review committee and the proposal that eventually won support from the government in its White Paper and subsequent legislation.

As described in previous chapters, the 1970 White Paper proposals amounted to substantial extension of benefits and an increase in the generosity of UI. At the time, officials were convinced that the new program would not cost very much more than the old one, for four reasons. First, new employment categories were to be brought under the plan that typically did not have high rates of unemployment, and so it was thought that these groups would subsidize, through contributions, the benefits paid to high-risk claimants. Second, future national unemployment rates had been underestimated. Third, new control measures such as mandatory interviews were proposed to ensure that the new program was not abused. Finally, experience or merit rating was included in the scheme so that high-risk industries would pay premiums reflecting their industry-specific unemployment patterns. In these terms, the 1971 act was a complex balance of countervailing components. The balance did not occur, and so costs went up dramatically. The confidence in these components, however, persuaded officials that there was no need to develop a new and separate program for extended benefits – these could simply be part of the grand design.

Extended benefits became part of a five-phase benefit structure. Phase 1 was available to those with 20 weeks of insurable employment in the last 52 and paid a lump sum three-week benefit that could be kept regardless of when the claimant became re-employed. Phase 2 was for those ineligible for phase 1 or who had exhausted their phase 1 benefits and lasted a maximum of 12 weeks. Phase 3 was calibrated against the national unemployment rate and was available to claimants completing phase 2. If the national unemployment rate were 4 per cent or less, phase 3 provided 10 weeks of benefits; if the rate were between 4 and 5 per cent, then 15 weeks of benefits; if it were over 5, then 18 weeks. Phase 4 was calibrated against the claimant's labour force attachment, so that claimants with over 20 weeks of insurable employment were eligible for up to an additional 18 weeks of benefit. Phase 5 was the regionally calibrated benefit phase, with an additional 18 weeks of benefit available to claimants living in regions where the regional unemployment rate was over 4 per cent and exceeded the national level by more than 1 per cent. No claimant, however, could receive more than 51 weeks of benefit from all phases.[79] Table 7 outlines the phases as described in the 1970 White Paper.

An extended benefit system for claimants facing difficulties in getting re-employed and more specifically for high-unemployment regions was therefore part of the 1971 UI scheme. Another component that would necessarily have a regional effect was continued coverage of self-employed fishermen in the program. It was clear from the White Paper, however, that this was to be no more than a temporary expedient until a new, separate income security program could be devised.[80]

As we noted above, these features of the plan represented the federal government's own policy priorities in regional development. They were not pressed upon Ottawa by provinces desiring that a federal program be changed to suit their interests.

In the early 1970s, the provinces were not preoccupied with UI. The 1971 revisions did not raise serious problems, for three reasons. First, since the intent was to make UI payments sufficient on their own to sustain an unemployed person, provincial welfare expenditures would be reduced.[81] Second, provincial governments were not compelled to bring their own employees into the program.[82] If they did decide to, however, then all employees would have to be covered. This last provision prevented provinces from placing only "bad risks" (e.g. seasonal employees) under the federal plan. Third, Quebec's objection that sickness and maternity benefits were within provincial jurisdiction led to the legislation providing an "opting out" clause, whereby UI special benefits would be reduced or eliminated upon the implementation of provincial plans.[83]

Expenditure reductions of course create different political dynamics from expenditure increases. UI expenditures are vital to the economies of the high-unemployment provinces, principally the Atlantic region and Quebec. Table 8 shows the interprovincial transfers of UI monies and demonstrates their importance to the eastern provinces. Bill C-14 reduced UI expenditures in the eastern provinces by 9.6 per cent in 1979.[84] Predictably, therefore, the greatest resistance to the 1975-8 changes came from these regions.

TABLE 7
Benefit Structure, 1971 Act

Type	Identification	Eligibility	Duration	Rate	Financing
Regular Unemployment Benefit	Phase 1	20 or more employment weeks in past 52	3 weeks paid in advance after two-week waiting period. Maximum 3 weeks	66 ⅔% of earnings with maximum of $100 per week	Employees: flat rate. Employers: experience rate. Government pays extra cost when national unemp. rate exceeds 4%[1]
	Phase 2 8-15 wks - 8 ben. wks 16 wks - 9 ben. wks 17 wks - 10 ben. wks 18 wks - 11 ben. wks 19 wks - 12 ben. wks (2 calendar weeks allowed to draw each benefit week)	8-19 employment weeks in past 52. Available after phase 1 or as an entrance to the system	8-12 weeks in bi-weekly payments after two-weeks waiting period if entering system. Maximum 12 weeks	Same as phase 1	Same as phase 1
	Phase 3	National unemp. rate: 0-4%[2] Predetermined at time claimant emerges from phase 2	10 weeks	Same as phase 1, although 75% provided after 10th week with dependants	Shared by employee and employer up to 4%, and full cost borne by government over 4%[1]
		Over 4-up to 5% Over 5% Predetermined after 10th week	4 weeks 8 weeks Maximum 18 weeks		

TABLE 7 (continued)

Type	Identification	Eligibility	Duration	Rate	Financing
	Phase 4	Labour force attachment less than 20 wks 20 wks 21 to 52 wks (one benefit week for each two employment weeks in excess of 20 weeks) Available to claimants emerging from phase 3 who have 20 or more employment weeks in past 52 weeks	0 weeks 2 weeks 3-16 weeks Maximum 18 weeks	66⅔% of earnings if single; 75% of earnings with dependants	Full cost borne by government
	Phase 5	Regional unemp. rate[3] If regional rate is over 4% and exceeds national rate by: up to 1% over 1 up to 2% over 2 up to 3% over 3%	0 weeks 6 weeks 12 weeks 18 weeks Maximum 18 weeks	Same as phase 4	Same as phase 4

TABLE 7 (continued)

Type	Identification	Eligibility	Duration	Rate	Financing
		Not predetermined, but available on monthly basis for claimants who are not eligible for phase 4 or who have exhausted phase 4	Note: Maximum entitlement, from all phases is limited to 51 weeks.		
Special Unemployment Benefits	Sickness	Same as phase 1	15 weeks after two-week waiting period	Same as phase 1	Private sector, but experience rating for employer applicable
	Maternity	Same as phase 1	9 weeks before and 6 weeks after confinement after two-week waiting period	Same as phase 1	Private sector, but experience rating for employer not applicable
	Retirement	Same as phase 1	Same as phase 1 but no waiting period	Same as phase 1	Private sector, but experience rating for employer not applicable

Source: Unemployment Insurance in the 70's, pp. 34-5.

Notes:

Earnings of 25% of benefit rate allowed in phases 2 to 5.

No earnings allowed in waiting periods or in Sickness and Maternity.

Earnings ignored in phase 1 and Retirement.

Maximum benefit is $100 per week in all phases.

1 Based on national annual average.

2 Seasonally adjusted three-month moving average.

3 Seasonally unadjusted twelve-month moving average for the region.

TABLE 8

Unemployment Insurance Benefits/Contributions by Province, 1984

Province	Ratio of benefits to contributions	Excess of benefits over contributions ($ million)
Newfoundland	3.38	348
Prince Edward Island	2.83	60
Nova Scotia	1.40	115
New Brunswick	2.24	266
Quebec	1.24	578
Ontario	0.67	− 1,323
Manitoba	0.78	− 85
Saskatchewan	0.74	− 83
Alberta	0.88	− 122
British Columbia	1.22	248
Yukon	1.80	9
Northwest Territories	0.61	− 10

Source: Commission of Inquiry on Unemployment Insurance, Report, Figure G.12 at p. 388.

This resistance was expressed on a number of levels. The first was cabinet. Bud Cullen tried in 1977, for example, to drop fishermen from the program. As self-employed workers, they should not be eligible for coverage, but they had been left in the 1971 act until the Department of Fisheries could arrive at a plan to help them.[85] Roméo LeBlanc, minister of fisheries and New Brunswick's spokesman in cabinet, rejected the proposal. Consequently, Cullen never took this idea to the public.[86] The second level was the Liberal caucus. Cullen brought Bill C-27 forward without having had extensive caucus discussions and found himself facing strong objections from Atlantic MPs. The variable entrance requirement, originally an Opposition suggestion, provided one way out of the impasse, though Liberal backbench MPs "had a significant impact on the bill."[87]

The third level of resistance came from the provinces themselves, primarily over the greater welfare costs they expected because of tighter UI provisions. Three provinces – Newfoundland, Nova Scotia, and Ontario – took the rare step of appearing before the Standing Committee on Labour, Manpower and Immigration during its examination of Bill C-14.[88] Ottawa agreed that provincial welfare costs would increase. It simply argued that these costs would be small and that in any case they were shared.[89] The provinces disputed these figures, claiming that they would be higher.[90]

It became clear to federal policy-makers by 1978 that substantial program changes reducing costs and emphasizing manpower goals would raise vociferous complaints, not primarily from private interests but from provincial and regional ones. Employers supported most of the changes, usually calling for even tighter restrictions, and the Canadian Labour Congress, perhaps still smarting from the wage controls episode in 1975-8, raised only passive resistance. Despite UI's substantial redistributive effects among income classes,[91] resistance to the retreat from the 1971 legislation was organized not primarily along class lines, but along regional and governmental ones.

The impact of these regional and governmental pressures has been felt primarily in two ways. First, Ottawa's readiness to consult has increased greatly since 1975. Disillusioned somewhat with the fortunes of the Social Security Review of 1973-5, and determined to guard its powers in one of the few social programs over which it has full constitutional control, Ottawa was less than enthusiastic and open in its consultations with the provinces on the 1975-8 UI changes. With the need, towards the end of the controls program, to co-ordinate federal and provincial economic policies, however, the willingness to consult increased.[92] But the specific willingness to deal more openly on UI probably had as much to do with the strong regional representations that had been made previously. The Clark government (1979-80) tried to have discussions with the provinces about proposed UI changes well in advance of legislation. As well, there were intensive intergovernmental consultations over the report of the Task Force on Unemployment Insurance. The Forget Commission recognized in 1986 that federal-provincial consultation was necessary if income supplementation schemes were to replace regionally extended benefits.

This new consultative relationship was illustrated in the November 1978 meeting of first ministers on the economy. This meeting was to "establish mechanisms and processes whereby labour market problems could be jointly resolved."[93] One issue this meeting, and subsequent ones by officials, addressed was harmonization of UI with other social security programs. The UI review was a "major agenda item" at a September 1979 meeting of deputy ministers, which agreed on circulation of simulations and data on all options to the provinces, a vehicle for provincial response, and co-ordination of UI changes with the Canada Assistance Plan.[94]

Second, the way that UI policy changes themselves are designed has altered. In 1975, program changes were made without prolonged consideration of their regional impact. By 1980, as a result partly of the growth in UI expenditures themselves and partly of the 1975-8 regional responses to program changes, policy-makers favoured modifications that have the least detrimental effect in the east.[95] From simply having regional effects, the program has come to have regional intent, even in its most pedestrian features. The government's reaction to the Forget report illustrates this nicely. The report's suggestion to eliminate regionally extended benefits was without doubt the cause of its rejection. By 1986 the incidence of regional benefit provisions was heavily concentrated in Quebec and the Maritimes. Any cut to UI affects these regions disproportionately, but an attack on regionally extended benefits is tantamount to an attack on the economies of eastern Canada. To appear to do this, especially in the latter half of a government's term in office, is political suicide.

CONCLUSION

Federalism traditionally has been assumed to be a major force in Canadian public policy. As we noted at the beginning of this chapter, federalism has been understood to exercise its effect through the structural constraints and opportunities that it establishes or the process of intergovernmental co-ordination that it encourages.

Federalism as structure did affect UI. It has been noted, by Banting among others, that constitutional structures introduce brittleness into policy-making that may impede new proposals and initiatives. In the UI case, the constitutional responsibility for UI remained with the provinces until 1940, but almost everyone agreed that a UI program had to be within federal jurisdiction if it were to be run efficiently. While it is fairly clear that Ottawa was reluctant to accept responsibility for UI in the 1930s, federal authorities were aided by constitutional structures that forced a high degree of consensus before anything could be done. While one cannot be certain, it would appear likely that Canada would have had UI sooner had constitutional complications not stood in the way.

The effect of federalism as process is more difficult to gauge. It is certain that intergovernmental consultations did not end once UI was transferred to federal authority. But it seems that once Ottawa had accepted jurisdiction, it became sensitive to regional effects of the national program so that it was not necessary to have provincial representations to enforce sensitivity. While the program grew in scope and generosity through the 1950s and 1960s, the provinces adopted a posture of benign neglect towards UI – each extension lowered their net social assistance costs, and they could scarcely object. Quebec remained the exception in that it became increasingly interested in a unified, provincially managed social security system that might include UI.[96] However, even Quebec fell in line with the other provinces over the 1971 changes because the new act seemed so clearly beneficial to the provinces.

Since 1975 the picture has changed substantially. First, UI has become an extremely important program to certain sections of the country, especially Atlantic Canada. The long series of UI cuts since 1975 has therefore generated substantial provincial opposition. Second, UI has changed its focus to emphasize its labour market impact rather than its income security goals. Inevitably, UI training and job creation bump up against provincial programs in the same fields. This too creates a new need for consultation and co-ordination. Thus, by the end of the 1970s, even though UI was nominally a program completely within federal jurisdiction, consultations with the provinces over any major changes were an integral part of the policy process.

How important are these consultations? UI is a program that has private-sector interests built into it, and so federalism as process could never completely insulate policy-making from outside interests. But the lessons of the 1977-8 cuts seem clear: major opposition came not from labour groups but from regional interests, both provincial and parliamentary. Ottawa has more to fear from regional than from class-based opposition, perhaps partly because of the way in which federalism organizes political constituencies and interests. By the end of the 1970s, at any rate, provincial and regional concerns had taken on greater direct weight than ever before. Though this can be only a matter of judgment, this weight seems at least equal to that of private-sector interests and may even be greater, depending on the political context of federal-provincial relations.

CHAPTER SEVEN

Conclusion

Chapters four through six have reviewed the history and development of UI in Canada from the vantage point of three major explanations of public policy: neo-pluralism/neo-Marxism (taken together), bureaucratic politics, and institutionalism (in this case, the effect of federalism). The first represents society-centred approaches, the latter two, state-centred. Each theory was defined by its assumptions and expectations and was applied to the available evidence to see how useful it was in explaining why UI developed the way that it did in Canada over this period. As argued in chapter one, UI has many of the characteristics one would want in a case study of this type. UI is relevant for both economic and social policy; it is important to employers and employees; it is organizationally and conceptually complex; and, at least in the 1930s, it was at the centre of some heated intergovernmental debates. A lengthy time period was deliberately chosen so that the full play of the forces described in each chapter could be revealed.

As good a case as UI may be, it does not amount to a "critical test" by which one or the other approach could be decisively rejected. UI presents, at best, a "suitable case" to examine how viable each approach is, both in terms of its own assumptions and in comparison with the other. The modern philosophy of science, while accepting that the positivistic confirmation or falsification of theories is rarely if ever possible, defends the practice of theory comparison and the goal of scientific advancement. In practice, as chapter one noted, students of public policy spend a good deal of time arguing in favour of some theories and against others, with the implicit belief that the function of a community of scholars is to avoid or at least minimize error in the imperfect and halting pursuit of truth. This book has simply tried to apply these principles in a more systematic and rigorous way. Its goal has been to assess which of these theoretical approaches to public policy is the most promising and fruitful – which, in short, is most likely to reward further elaboration and research.

Perhaps the central characteristic of science as a form of knowledge is rational criticism, and so this book's contribution will doubtless be sharpened and measured in subsequent debate. Several key objections to the analysis contained in these pages can be easily anticipated, however, and so in an effort to clarify further the arguments, the closing section of this chapter lists those objections and some preliminary responses. But first, a reprise of the arguments.

REPRISE

The neo-pluralist and neo-Marxist theories trace changes and developments in public policy back to the interests and balance of power among key economic groups. The interests should be opposed, politicians and policy-makers will be aware of this opposition, and they will respond to the interests and views of the most powerful groups, or, in short, business interests. Chapter four found that employers and employees have indeed, with few exceptions, been on opposite sides of almost every UI issue. Employers, before UI was passed, wanted delay and a narrow program; employees pressed for a generous scheme. Later, when UI was in place, employers almost always wanted lower benefits, higher entrance requirements, and shorter benefit duration than employees did. Moreover, politicians and policy-makers were well aware of these different views. However, even though policy-makers knew what business wanted, they rarely followed the business view for this reason alone. In fact, most of the legislative history of UI seems to run counter to business demands, at least as represented by their various associations in the public arena over the last half-century. It might seem that labour was the "winner," but the evidence from the late 1970s, when Ottawa tried to cut UI back severely, suggests that a simple pressure model of public policy formation is not very useful. The strong version of these society-centred approaches, that employers usually get their way, seems flatly contradicted by the evidence.

As noted earlier, UI is a program with direct and substantial effects on the capitalist labour market. It is not peripheral to employers' or employees' basic economic interests, and this has been recognized through the establishment of an administrative structure for UI in which employers and employees are directly represented. If a society-centred explanation is not very useful for UI, then it is unlikely to be very useful in explaining long-term developments in other policy areas.

Admittedly, chapter four's version of neo-pluralist and neo-Marxist explanation was essentially a simple pressure model, wherein the state was supposed to respond directly to the interests and desires of strategic economic groups. More recent and subtle versions of this approach stress the state's autonomy in responding to interests and the ways in which the state serves to manage class and economic conflict over the long term by sometimes contradicting the immediate interests of capital. These versions necessarily focus on the internal calculations made by policy-makers and, indeed, on forces internal to the state that may influence policy.

Chapter five isolated two broad sets of bureaucratic state forces that might have influenced UI: intra-organizational forces such as bureaucratic ideology, monopoly of information and expertise, and organizational goals; and inter-bureaucratic conflict among different state agencies. There was ample evidence for both sets of forces. In the first category, it was clear that detailed ideas on UI had to come from somewhere, since the external advice being given by business and labour on the whole tended to be of little use. The details were hammered out by a small group of experts within the departments of Labour and Insurance and the prime minister's office between 1932 and 1935. They developed an actuarial ideology that strongly influenced the program in its early years and still retained its force in the mid- and late 1970s. Many features of the UI program that have appeared to others as evidence of clear class bias by the state – for example, restricted coverage and graduated benefits – are in fact explained more adequately as corollaries drawn from the program's ideological foundations. The ideology, and the program built upon it, are sufficiently complex that understanding them is a mark of the expert. Lay opinions on UI, whether from business, labour, politicians, the public, or the media, are received with scepticism by officials, who see themselves as possessors of special information and experience. In this respect, intra-bureaucratic forces serve to insulate policy development from external pressures.

The main dimension of inter-bureaucratic conflict examined in chapter five concerned the labour market goals of UI. The actuarial ideology applied to UI as insurance and led the program to consider labour market goals in largely a passive or negative way. But the Department of Labour and later the Department of Manpower and Immigration obviously had a keen interest in labour market policy and the effect of UI on such policy. From its inception, UI has been at the centre of a battle between the commission and these other departments over whether the program should be primarily insurance-oriented and administratively separate from the rest of the government or labour market-oriented and more directly under the control of economic development ministers. From 1940 to the early 1960s, the battle appeared superficially as one about the National Employment Service and special benefits, but by the mid-1970s it was clear that it was about the philosophical goals of UI and its administrative autonomy. The current commission structure makes it less autonomous from ministerial control than was envisaged in 1940, and the program has increasingly taken on a labour market orientation. The balance and combination of these two sets of forces provide a much richer and detailed appreciation of the development of UI policy than simple neo-pluralist or neo-Marxist explanations do. Moreover, viewed from the vantage point of more than 40 years of development, the intra- and inter-bureaucratic forces described in chapter five do not appear to have been directly or intentionally associated with the long-term interests of capital. In other words, the evidence shows little of what some have phrased "the state acting in the long term interests" of capital. Such action may be the result of policy undertaken by the state, but at least in the case of UI the reasons or intentions behind policy are not so straightforward.

Chapter six examined the impact of federalism on UI policy development. In this instance, UI appears as a "least likely" case, because since 1940 it has been exclusively under federal jurisdiction. If federalism did have an effect on policy development in this case, then it would be reasonable to assume that it has an effect on other policy fields that are usually less constitutionally clear-cut. The evidence suggests that federalism as structure, as the formal division of power, probably did delay implementation of UI in the 1930s before a constitutional amendment was made, transferring jurisdiction to Ottawa. Federalism as process, the ongoing consultation made necessary by the simple fact that policy problems do not respect constitutional boundaries, had an effect on program development only in the 1970s, when UI cuts threatened to hurt the poorer regions of the country. By 1980, UI was so entwined with the web of federal-provincial social security programs that any substantial program changes unaccompanied by provincial consultation was unthinkable. Indeed, regional impact is now a primary consideration in policy design.

Of the three theories, bureaucratic politics was the most helpful in understanding detailed policy developments pertaining to the main aspects of the UI program: coverage, eligibility, benefits, financing, and administration. In other words, if we could choose only one theory to help explain policy, we would choose this one. It is markedly superior to neo-pluralism/neo-Marxism and institutional theories of federalism in explaining what happened in the UI field. However, it did not explain everything and in this respect was also a limited approach. Nevertheless, bureaucratic politics is broadly representative of theoretical perspectives that focus on the internal dynamics of state action in policy formation and implementation. Thus it would seem from the evidence presented here that state-centred approaches to public policy are more promising and fruitful than society-centred theories.

CRITICISMS AND RESPONSE

1. It is impossible to see facts "objectively"; they are always interpreted by or filtered through theories. A comparison of theories such as the one attempted in this book is therefore impossible, since each theory contains implicit values that construe some facts and forestall others.

This objection is rooted in a relativistic Weltanschauungen epistemology and expresses the view held widely in the social sciences that facts cannot be divorced from values. The mistake that relativists make is to assume that since all observations are theory-laden, no observations can be presumed to be inter-subjectively valid. It is indeed true that theories inevitably and necessarily structure our empirical perceptions, but the theories discussed in these pages are not incommensurate languages. They are comprehensible to their opponents, and they have discernible logical structures that permit confrontations with evidence.

It is true that these theories each stress a different key factor as determinative in the policy process. That is what makes them different. Neo-pluralism and neo-Marxism, as defined here, focus on organized pressure; bureaucratic politics, on internal state dynamics; and federalism, on inter-governmental dynamics. By stressing one factor, each theory discounts the others. The comparison is inter-subjectively valid, however, because it was conducted in terms of a single standard: the satisfactory explanation of public policy.

This is where the relativist's objection has more bite. What strikes me as satisfying may not be so to someone else. However this may be, I would submit that my criteria are reasonable. "Policy" as the dependent variable in this book was defined in terms of the key features of program design and their development over time. An alternative criterion might be the effect of policy, so that the explanatory challenge would be to arrive at a satisfying explanation of policy impact. I certainly agree that policy impact is a central question in the study of any public policy, but it seems to me to be separate from the content of policy itself. In my view, confusing policy content with policy impact risks confusing subjective and objective factors in the policy process. Policy content must be traced back always to an amalgam of intentions, perhaps not always fully conscious, but intentions nonetheless. Policy impact concerns the complex articulation of policy content with social, political, and economic systems. Without this elementary distinction, it is difficult to grasp the role of unintended consequences in the policy process.

If the preceding is granted, then this book's approach would seem reasonable. Incidentally, the theories were accepted at face value as they were being explored, and to that degree their strengths and weaknesses also reflect their own internal standards of success and failure.

2. UI is not a representative policy, and so it is impossible to generalize any of the findings of this study. It may explain UI, but nothing more.

This objection cannot logically maintain that UI is unique, since UI has come, after all, from the same policy process that has produced other economic and social programs. So, the objection must be that it is not sufficiently representative to permit confident generalization. Assuming for the moment that this objection is logically valid, on what could it be based?

UI does have several distinctive features that set it apart from other policies. It is a social insurance program, and its closest parallel is the Canada/Quebec Pension Plan. It institutionalizes business and labour representation and perhaps in this way provides a unique opportunity for labour to counterbalance business influences that are ubiquitous in other policy areas. It is a federal income security program, whereas the income security field is dominated (at least legally) by the provinces. It is a national program with built-in features that make it sensitive to regional circumstances.

While such features among others certainly make UI distinctive as a program, they do not affect its validity as a case study. As I argued in chapter one, the external validity problem in case studies is different from that encountered in survey research. UI's suitability depends on its susceptibility to the factors identified by each of the theories. In this respect UI is indeed peculiar, but its peculiarity gives it a unique ability usefully to engage each of the three approaches. It is open to organized interests and can be expected to attract them; it invites bureaucratic intervention because of its multiple goals; and it should be largely untouched by provincial pressures. The relative failure of society-centred approaches to cast light on UI policy development does not "falsify" them, but it does cast doubt upon them. The logic of this approach is thus to claim not that UI somehow represents all policies but that it generates certain strong expectations for given theories. The findings are thus generalized to the theory, which itself purports to provide general explanations of all policies. We are therefore entitled to say that if the findings do not accord with reasonable expectations, something is wrong with the theory.

3. The theories examined in this book are artificial constructions. No one uses theories of precisely the type I describe, since I borrowed aspects for each theory from several sources.

This is quite true but irrelevant. My interest has been to indicate which directions might be fruitful for further research. As long as the theories, even as I construed them, can reasonably be taken to represent central tendencies in a given corpus of theory, my general conclusions will be valid.

4. What about studies that show that business pressures, even as I have defined them here, are decisive in the policy process?

The response to this objection is two-fold. First, this study should not be interpreted as concluding that business, or for that matter labour, pressures never have any bearing on public policy. Clearly they do, though I would suggest less than has been traditionally assumed. One important implication of the analysis provided here is that much more work needs to be done to gauge the precise character of the impact of pressure politics.

Second, I am not aware of any major studies of the success of business lobbies that simultaneously try to assess the impact of internal state dynamics. To show that business demands correlate with policy outputs is not the same as demonstrating that they caused them.

5. My definition of neo-pluralism and especially neo-Marxism is too narrow. I ignore the degree to which business or capital enjoys an ideological hegemony that
makes specific political victories unnecessary. Alternatively, the political and
ideological hegemony of capital is organized through the state, and so a broader
neo-Marxist framework can subsume what I have presented as separate theories.

These are, without question, the most fundamental objections to the approach I have taken in this book. The arguments are by now familiar enough to need only a short rehearsal.

The power of business is properly conceived as power exercised through and in a social system defined in terms of relations of production. Thus business organizations are at best fractious and imperfect expressions of the interests of a capitalist class, defined objectively through its position in the social formation. Viewed as a social system, every capitalist society contains institutional means whereby the ideas of the ruling class become the ruling ideas. There is neither conspiracy nor cabal; the hegemony is an objective, systemic result of forces beyond the control or even the understanding of social actors. Schools, media, churches, family: all simultaneously transmit and reproduce domination. Politics in capitalist societies can, of course, produce options that violate the interests of capital, but it normally succumbs to the system's ideological undertow.

With respect to UI, for example, it might be argued that the actuarial ideology in fact reflected the broad interest of capital as a class, irrespective of what specific fractions of capital may have thought. It was, after all, elaborated by actuaries, one of whom (Wolfenden) was recommended by the insurance industry. Indeed, as chapter four showed, business associations frequently demanded a return to "sound insurance," demonstrating the affinity between their views and the actuarial ideology.

There can be no argument with the fact that UI is inconceivable outside capitalism. UI assumes wage labour and the kind of systemic unemployment that is characteristic of capitalism. The issue then is not whether capitalism has no relevance to UI but whether those experts and bureaucrats who designed and administered UI unwittingly reflected the ideological hegemony of the capitalist classes. In my judgment this is implausible. First, unless one believes that international variations in UI policy are of no importance, the argument of ideological hegemony fails to explain why the United States lacks employee UI contributions, or why Britain's plan was originally controlled by a cabinet minister. Second, some of the features of the actuarial ideology were adopted in trade union UI plans at the turn of the century and so would not appear to be uniquely associated with any single class. Third, the actuarial ideology explains only one dimension of UI development, the conservative dimension. The expansionary dynamic expressed in supplementary and fishing benefits, as well as in the 1971 act, was traced back to the defeat of the actuarial ideology by the Department of Labour.

This leads directly to the alternative hypothesis, the most sophisticated and nuanced version of which may be found in Rianne Mahon, *The Politics of Industrial Restructuring: Canadian Textiles* (1984). Mahon's argument consists of claiming that the state in capitalist society acts to organize capitalist class hegemony and disorganize subordinate classes. Moreover, she sees the state as the crystallization of class antagonisms; it is not a separate institution but is more properly conceived as a terrain of class struggle. Departments and agencies represent different class fractions, so the conflict and compromise that take place among bureaux in fact are the mechanism whereby the state invents and enforces compromise among classes.

This is an intriguing argument but rests upon several implausible assumptions. First, it is simply assumed that certain agencies represent certain classes. Second, there are no criteria to distinguish unimportant bureaucratic skirmishes from battles over hegemony. In the case of UI, for example, what class fractions were represented by the commission and the Department of Labour? In what ways did their conflict over the National Employment Service and supplementary and fishing benefits express broader class struggles? As far as I am able to tell, there are no clear, unambiguous answers to these questions that could establish that what I identified as an autonomous state dynamic was in fact expressive of class struggle.

6. What about the influence of other forces and actors, such as cabinet, individual ministers, political parties, and public opinion? Do they have no bearing, and is the state's autonomy absolute?

Throughout this study several alternative factors were shown to affect UI policy development. Cabinet-level decisions were apparently decisive in forcing the issue of fishing benefits, and ministerial manoeuvres were important to the 1971 act. Revolts by backbench MPs on both sides of the House of Commons led to the introduction of the variable entrance requirement. Left-wing MPs kept the UI issue alive through the 1930s, and the NDP forestalled legislative amendments to UI by the minority Liberal government between 1972 and 1974. In specific historical circumstances, all these factors will at one time or another have some effect in the policy process. The historian's art consists of the faithful and intelligible re-creation of past events. The political scientist, however, is interested in general forces over the long term – not single events but the run of events. Inevitably, this compels consideration of general theories that, by their nature, must gloss over the detail so dear to the historian, in favour of the larger canvas. This book addressed widely held theories; its goal was not a history of UI, but UI as a case study in policy theory. As far as I am aware, there are no widely held and well-developed theories of these other forces, and it was for this reason that they were not explicitly addressed.

As for the state's autonomy from these forces, it of course is not absolute. The theoretical challenge is to understand how social and political forces are filtered through, deflected by, and directed by state authorities for their own purposes. There was ample evidence in previous chapters to show that politicians and bureaucrats were aware of and sensitive to such forces as the "public mood" and "organized pressures." But these people did not act simply as ciphers for these forces; they interpreted them, manipulated them, and if necessary rejected them as they saw fit in terms of their own interests.

7. How fruitful in fact are the theories presented in chapters five and six? Are bureaucratic politics and institutionalism (federalism) not too narrow a reed upon which to rest further work?

This objection incorrectly assumes that my purpose in this book was to defend a single middle-range theory. In fact, my intention was to assess the strengths of these specific theories as indicators of fruitful directions for future research and theory. My findings suggest that the most rewarding direction to take is towards state-centred theories of the policy process. This direction might be pursued by neo-Marxist or public choice theorists, each in their own terms. Its clear challenge will be careful articulation of specific intra-state forces, their modes of combination, and their ultimate effects on public policy.

Three examples will show the new terrain opened up by this theoretical reorientation. First, what is the political calculus used by different state actors in the policy process? Chapter five relied on a calculus of bureaucratic self-interest, but there must be separate and distinct versions of this for politicians, and indeed for the judicial branch. Understanding these calculi may help clarify how different state sectors process policy problems.

Second, how does the state's capacity to deal with specific problems vary from time to time, agency to agency, and problem to problem? Assuming that capacity is a structural feature and not merely an accident of personal competence, what factors contribute to resilient regimes? Third, and linked to the first two: what strategies do groups and classes adopt to influence political calculi and state capacity? This is a different question from the older one of how groups influence government, since it begins with the assumption that there are internal state forces to which these groups must accommodate themselves.

It would be foolish to try to chart what by definition is largely unexplored terrain. This book will have succeeded if, like a good compass, it has revealed the opposing poles of policy analysis. It is up to others to choose their way.

APPENDIX

Chronology 1919-87

1919		First International Labour Conference, Washington, DC Canadian officials endorse draft recommendation favouring state-administered UI.
		First Liberal national leadership convention endorses UI.
1928	March-June	House of Commons Standing Committee on Industrial and International Relations investigates UI and recommends national plan and constitutional amendment.
1930	Sept	Unemployment Relief Act
1931	29 April	Bennett makes speech in House of Commons promising UI.
1932	22 Nov	Bennett, in House of Commons, promises UI.
1934	Jan-June	Officials draft a UI plan.
	August	Bennett writes premiers asking for constitutional power over UI.
1935	Jan	Bennett's radio speeches
	June	Employment and Social Insurance Act passed
1936	17 June	Supreme Court rules Employment and Social Insurance Act ultra vires.
1937		Judicial Committee upholds Supreme Court decision.
	summer	Government decides to go ahead with a UI scheme, and King writes to premiers – Dysart (NB), Duplessis (Quebec), and Aberhart (Alberta) refuse.
	Dec	National Employment Commission recommends Ottawa assume full responsibility for unemployed.
1938	June	King delays UI decision until Rowell-Sirois Report.
1940	June	Agreement reached with provinces on constitutional revision
	10 July	Britain passes amendment to BNA Act (sec 91.2.a).
	7 Aug	UI passed (*Statutes of Canada,* 1940, c. 44)

1941	1 July	UI contributions begin.
1942	27 Jan	UI benefit payments begin.
1950	Feb	UI amendment introduces, among other things, "supplementary benefits" for new entrants and exhaustees payable January to March.
1955	2 Oct	1940 act repealed and new UI act passed (*Statutes of Canada*, 1955, c. 50)
1960		For the first time, benefits top $500 million and benefit payments exceed contributions.
1961	17 July	Commission of inquiry on UI appointed, headed by E.C. Gill
1962	Nov	Gill Committee reports.
1963		Interdepartmental Committee formed to review program
1964		To become effective by 1 April 1965, employment services of Unemployment Insurance Commission assumed by Department of Labour (*Statutes of Canada*, 1964-65, c. 35, Schedule B, Department of Labour, Vote 7a)
1966	25 March	Interdepartmental Committee reports to minister of labour.
		Effective 1 October 1966, employment services transferred from minister of labour to minister of manpower and immigration (*Statutes of Canada*, 1966-67, c. 25)
1969		UIC releases *Report of the Study for Updating the Employment Insurance Programme*.
1970	17 June	Bryce Mackasey tables White Paper entitled *Unemployment Insurance in the 70's* in House of Commons; referred to Standing Committee on Labour, Manpower and Immigration
1971	14 June	New UI act passed; to go into effect 27 June
1972	28 Jan	Responsibility for UI act transferred from minister of labour to minister of manpower and immigration
	Aug/Sept	First signs of large, unanticipated increase in benefits payments
1973		Effective 8 February ceiling on government advances to UI account revised (*Statutes of Canada*, 1973-74, c. 2)
	spring/fall	New administrative procedures introduced to prevent misuse of UI
1974	fall	UIC commissions first public opinion survey on UI since 1971 legislation; ⅓ of respondents concerned with abuse.
1975	throughout	Benefit control procedures tightened up further
	20 Dec	Bill C-69 passed (*Statutes of Canada*, 1974-75-76, c. 80)
1977	1 Feb	*Comprehensive Review of the Unemployment Insurance Program in Canada* released

	5 Aug	Royal assent to Bill C-27, which passes House of Commons under closure (*Statutes of Canada*, 1976–77, c. 54)
1978	Aug	Prime Minister Trudeau's restraint message
	22 Dec	Royal assent to Bill C-14, which passes House of Commons under closure
1979	July	*Unemployment Insurance in the 1980's: A Review of Its Appropriate Role and Design* released
1980	July	Task force on UI established
	17 July	Royal assent to Bill C-3 (*Statutes of Canada*, 1980, c. 35)
1981	July	Task force report, *Unemployment Insurance in the 1980's*, released
	22 Dec	Work sharing program funded through UI announced
1982	Feb	Federal-provincial agreement to use UI funds for job creation
1983	June	Maternity benefit provisions relaxed; go into effect January 1984
1984	Nov	New Conservative government announces intention to review UI.
1985	July	Forget Commission of Inquiry on Unemployment Insurance established
1986	Nov	Forget Commission submits report.
	4 Dec	Minister of Employment and Immigration Benoît Bouchard announces that government will take action on UI on 15 May 1987.
1987	19 March	Standing Committee on Labour, Employment and Immigration submits report on UI.
	15 May	Bouchard announces that UI will not be overhauled.

Notes

CHAPTER ONE

1 Popper, *Conjectures and Refutations* and *The Logic of Scientific Discovery*.
2 Employment and Immigration Canada, *Annual Report, 1984-85*, 41.
3 Struthers, *No Fault of Their Own*.
4 Johnson, "A Minister as an Agent of Policy Change."
5 Employment and Immigration Canada, *Labour Market Development in the 1980s* and *Unemployment Insurance in the 1980s*.
6 Published 1962; second edition 1970.
7 Ibid., 94.
8 Ibid., 103.
9 See his "Postscript," ibid., 174-210. Also see Kuhn, "Logic of Discovery or Psychology of Research" and "Second Thoughts on Paradigms."
10 Feyerabend, *Against Method*, 39.
11 Ibid., 43-4.
12 Ibid., 298.
13 While Feyerabend's theoretical framework is ultimately barren, he has tackled real problems, and his observations on the practice of science are not entirely without merit.
14 Suppe, "Afterword," 649.
15 Ibid., 706.
16 Popper applied his philosophy of science to the social sciences, but his model still highlighted the centrality of refutation and falsification. See Popper, "The Logic of the Social Sciences" and *The Povery of Historicism*.
17 See, for example, Zukav, *The Dancing Wu Li Masters*.
18 Doern and Phidd, *Canadian Public Policy*, 41 and chap. 6.
19 Atkinson and Chandler, "Strategies for Policy Analysis," 3-19.
20 Wilson, *Canadian Public Policy and Administration*, 160-3.
21 Aucoin, "Public-Policy Theory and Analysis."

22 Simeon, "Studying Public Policy," 566.

23 Ibid., 573.

24 This approach has been useful, however, in explaining some of the policy differences across countries and is still popular, though it has evolved. The following articles are good examples of the evolution of the genre: Cutright, "Political Structure"; Cameron, "The Expansion of the Public Economy."

25 This is true perhaps of even the leading Canadian work in this genre, Bryden, *Old Age Pensions and Policy-Making in Canada*.

26 Skocpol, "Bringing the State Back In: Stategies of Analysis in Current Research," 4.

27 Poulantzas, *Political Power and Social Classes* and *State, Power, Socialism*, are good introductions to this approach. Also see Wright, *Class, Crisis and the State*, and Laclau, *Politics and Ideology in Marxist Theory*.

28 Miliband, *The State in Capitalist Society* and *Marxism and Politics*. Miliband and Poulantzas aired their differences on the theory of the state in the *New Left Review*, numbers 58, 59, and 82.

29 Habermas, *Legitimation Crisis*, and Offe and Ronge, "Theses on the Theory of the State."

30 Holloway and Picciotto, eds., *State and Capital*.

31 Dahl, *Who Governs?*; see Domhoff, *Who Really Rules?*, for a critique. Dahl develops his theme more fully in *Polyarchy*.

32 Bentley, *The Process of Government*, and Truman, *The Governmental Process*.

33 Nichols, *Three Varieties of Pluralism*.

34 McFarland, *Power and Leadership in Pluralist Systems*, 32-44.

35 The best example, in my view, is the work of Louis Althusser. Ironically, the "structural Marxist" school of which he is principal founder has frequently been criticized as deterministic and procrustean. It is my view that Althusser's concepts such as "levels of a social formation," "relative autonomy," "overdetermination," and "conjuncture" actually contributed to a more supple Marxism that could accommodate the complex causal patterns that had always been the mark of pluralism. See Althusser, *For Marx*, especially chap. 3, and Althusser and Balibar, *Reading Capital*, parts I and II.

36 For early versions of neo-pluralism, see McConnell, *Private Power and American Democracy*, and Lowi, *The End of Liberalism*. Canadian versions of this perspective may be found in Thompson and Stanbury, "The Political Economy," Pross, "Space, Function and Interest," and Paltiel, "The Changing Environment."

37 Schmitter and Lembruch, eds., *Trends towards Corporatist Intermediation*. The theory of "corporatism" is by no means the exclusive intellectual property of non-Marxists; see Panitch, "Trade Unions and the State." For a discussion of corporatism and its relation to both Marxist and non-Marxist theories of the state, see Crouch, "The State, Capital and Liberal Democracy."

38 Lindblom, *Politics and Markets*.

39 Dahl, *Dilemmas of Pluralist Democracy*, chap. 4.

40 Abraham, *The Collapse of the Weimar Republic*.

41 For a fuller discussion of neo-pluralism, with replies by Dahl and Lindblom, see Manley, "Neo-Pluralism." Also see Pross, *Group Politics and Public Policy*, chap. 10.

42 See Mahon, *The Politics of Industrial Restructuring*. For an earlier version of her argument, see Mahon, "Canadian Public Policy."

43 See, for example, Downs, *Inside Bureaucracy*, Tullock, *The Politics of Bureaucracy*, and Niskanen, Jr, *Bureaucracy and Representative Government*. Other approaches to the autonomy of the state apparatus are Krasner, *Defending the National Interest*, and Nordlinger, *On the Autonomy of the Democratic State*.

44 The impotence of legislatures in the Canadian policy process is by now widely recognized, though they can play an influential role from time to time. One textbook forthrightly proclaims that Parliament is merely a "catalyst" in the policy process; see Hockin, *Government in Canada*, chaps. 5 and 6. A more recent textbook notes the constraints on Parliament and political parties in key policy areas; see Jackson et al., *Politics in Canada*, 299, 426, and 633. Another possible candidate is the executive in the form of the prime minister and cabinet, but there are no available theories – as opposed to descriptions – that explain the policy process in these terms.

45 See Pross, "Pressure Groups," 301-6; Lowi, "American Business" and "Four Systems of Policy."

46 Yin, *Case Study Research*, 18.

47 Ibid., 20.

48 The other classic logical tests of the quality of research designs are construct validity (correct operational measures for key concepts), internal validity (establishing clear causal links), and reliability (replicability). See ibid., 36. The first two of these were addressed above, and the study is replicable insofar as anyone can research the cited sources.

49 Ibid., 39.

CHAPTER TWO

1 Flora and Heidenheimer, "The Historical Core and Changing Boundaries of the Welfare State."

2 The classic source for this interpretation of the welfare state is Marshall, *Class, Citizenship and Social Development*.

3 Flora and Heidenheimer, "The Historical Core," 27. Also see Pryor, *Public Expenditures in Communist and Capitalist Nations*, Mishra, *Society and Social Policy*, and Kaim-Caudle, *Comparative Social Policy and Social Security*.

4 Garraty, *Unemployment in History*, 12-13.

5 Ibid., 17. There were, of course, vagabonds and beggars.

6   Rose, "The Crisis of Poor Law Relief," 51.

7   Garraty, *Unemployment*, chap. 6.

8   Mill, *Priniciples of Political Economy*, 346.

9   Keynes, *The General Theory of Employment, Interest, and Money*. Keynes, in introducing his arguments, pointed out that the "classical economists" (by whom he meant both pre- and post-Ricardians) assumed that the supply of available labour was determined by the level of real wages, when in fact it was more closely determined by nominal or money wages. A fall in real wages (or the price paid for labour) led, in classical theory, to a reduced supply of labour, but it was clear that such a fall, induced through a rise in the cost of living relative to money wages, would actually bring forth more labour. Keynes also disputed the classical assumption that real wages were set by the wage bargains struck by employers and workers. This was the most fundamental objection, because if it were true, employees could not increase the demand for labour by lowering real wages, since they could not independently affect real wages.

10 Beveridge, *Unemployment, A Problem of Industry*, 12.

11 Ibid., chap. 5.

12 Though we shall see in chapter 3 that in Canada it took somewhat longer for this conceptual revolution to have its effect in official circles.

13 This is not the place to discuss the problem of UI abuse, but the best available evidence suggests that it is not as widespread as commonly thought. Fraud, by its nature, is difficult to detect, but an early classic on the subject, Becker, *The Problem of Abuse in Unemployment Benefits* (1953), estimated the annual national average of working violators at 1 per cent of benefits. Two good reviews of the abuse and work disincentive questions are Adams, *Public Attitudes Toward Unemployment Insurance*, and Hum, *Unemployment Insurance and Work Effort*.

14 Lanphier et al, *An Analysis of Attitudes toward Unemployment Insurance*, 36. These findings are for the less liberal pre-1971 UI program.

15 The term for this syndrome is *moral hazard*. See Grubel and Walker, "Moral Hazard."

16 Becker, "Twenty-five Years of Unemployment Insurance," 483-4.

17 One of the best catalogues of the early UI programs is Gibbon, *Unemployment Insurance*.

18 Abler, "Government Responses to the Challenge of Unemployment," 152.

19 Wolfenden, *Unemployment Funds*. Union plans were restricted in Europe as well, essentially to craft unions.

20 International Labour Office, *Unemployment Insurance Schemes*, 12. Some unions, principally American ones, joined with their employers to establish company plans. Usually only large companies such as General Electric could afford such schemes, but on occasion, as with the National Electrical Manufacturers' Association in 1932, plans could cover an entire industry.

21 Details on the early history of the British plan may be found in Heclo, *Modern*

Social Politics in Britain and Sweden, chap. 8; Gilbert, *The Evolution of National Insurance in Great Britain*; and Hennock, "The Origins of British National Insurance and the German Precedent, 1880-1914."

22 Ogus, "Great Britain," 189.

23 Haber and Murray, *Unemployment Insurance in the American Economy*, 27-8.

24 Ibid., 65-6. The principal architect of the first Wisconsin bills was Professor J.R. Commons, who had been the state's first administrator of its workers' compensation program. A unique feature of American UI, which goes back to its roots in workers' compensation, is that employees do not make contributions.

25 On the American Federation of Labor position, see Nelson, *Unemployment Insurance*, chap. 4.

26 International Labour Office, *Unemployment Insurance Schemes*, 8-9.

27 Blaustein, *Unemployment Insurance Objectives and Issues*, chap. 1.

28 Some of these issues are discussed in Hauser and Burrows, *The Economics of Unemployment Insurance*, chap. 2.

29 Best, *Work Sharing*.

30 Rea, Jr, "Unemployment Insurance and Labour Supply."

31 Hauser and Burrows, *The Economics of Unemployment Insurance*, chap. 3. For a discussion of this issue in an American context, see Hammermesh, *Jobless Pay and the Economy*, chap. 4.

32 The rest of this chapter relies on the following: International Labour Office, *Unemployment Insurance Schemes*, and Blaustein and Craig, *An International Review of Unemployment Insurance Schemes*.

33 The other countries in the sample were Austria, Belgium, Greece, Ireland, Italy, Japan, the Netherlands, Norway, South Africa, Switzerland, the United Kingdom, the United States, West Germany, and Yugoslavia.

34 The rest of the countries were Austria, Belgium, Denmark, Egypt, Finland, France, Germany, Greece, Iceland, Ireland, Israel, Italy, Japan, the Netherlands, Norway, South Africa, Spain, Sweden, Switzerland, the United Kingdom, and the United States.

35 These contributions, in whole or in part, are, however, "shifted" back to consumers, so that in the United States and elsewhere employer contributions represent only the nominal source. See Hammermesh, *Jobless Pay and the Economy*.

CHAPTER THREE

1 Pentland, *Labour and Capital in Canada, 1650-1860*, 185.

2 For a vivid portrait of working conditions in late-nineteenth-century Canada, see Kealey, ed., *Canada Investigates Industrialism*.

3 Struthers, *No Fault of Their Own*, 15.

4 Ontario, Ontario Commission on Unemployment, *Interim Report*, 5.

5 Ontario, Ontario Commission on Unemployment, *Report of the Ontario*

Commission on Unemployment, 80. Beveridge's influence may be seen in the report's discussion of labour exchanges on pp. 124-39. Struthers, *No Fault of Their Own*, calls the report "ambiguous" and, though mildly progressive, a "jumbling of nineteenth- and twentieth-century ideas." This may be unduly harsh, at least insofar as the report reflected some of the more advanced thinking of the time. The commission might have recommended compulsory UI had better data been available.

6 Struthers, *No Fault of Their Own*, 17.

7 Canada, Royal Commission on Industrial Relations, *Report*, 5; reprinted as a supplement to the *Labour Gazette*, July 1919.

8 Ibid., 8.

9 Ibid., 20-6.

10 As quoted in Dawson, *William Lyon Mackenzie King*, 300.

11 Struthers, *No Fault of Their Own*, 27-33.

12 See for example, Canada, House of Commons, *Debates* 24 April 1922, p. 1073; 20 May 1924, pp. 2344-8; 10 February 1925, p. 60; 29 January 1926, p. 497.

13 Canada, Parliament, House of Commons, Select Standing Committee on Industrial and International Relations, *Final Report*.

14 Ibid.

15 Struthers, *No Fault of Their Own*, 47.

16 Ibid., 87.

17 For details, see McConnell, "Judicial Review."

18 Canada, National Employment Commission, *Interim Report*.

19 Canada, National Employment Commission, *Final Report*, 28.

20 *Unemployment Insurance Act*, SC 1940, c. 44. For a descriptive account of Canadian UI legislation from 1940 to 1980, see Dingledine, *A Chronology of Response*.

21 *Unemployment Insurance Act*, SC 1955, c. 50.

22 Dingledine, *A Chronology of Response*, 37.

23 Canada, Unemployment Insurance Commission, *Annual Report 1964*, 50, Appendix X. One crude measure of the fund's solvency is the ratio of reserves to total benefits paid. This ratio declined from 4.7 in 1954 to 0.0024 in 1964. The recession was not the sole cause of insolvency; according to Kelly the erosion of the fund really began in 1948; see Kelly, "Unemployment Insurance in Canada," 164.

24 Dingledine, *A Chronology of Response*, 45-6.

25 Canada, Unemployment Insurance Commission, *Report of the Study for Updating the Unemployment Insurance Programme*.

26 For discussion of this shift, see Phidd and Doern, *The Politics and Management of Canadian Economic Policy*, chap. 10; and McDonald, "Labour, Manpower and Government Reorganization."

27 On the internal governmental debate over social policy options, and UI's place in the debate, see Johnson, "A Minister as an Agent of Policy Change," 612-33.

28 Canada, Department of Labour, *Unemployment Insurance in the 70's*, 3.

29 Ibid., 6. UI has traditionally been seen as a program that permits people either to search longer for a job commensurate with their abilities or to wait until economic conditions improve enough to supply such jobs. See International Labour Office, *Unemployment Insurance Schemes*, 101-2; Blaustein, *Unemployment Insurance Objectives and Issues*, 8-11; Hauser and Burrows, *The Economics of Unemployment Insurance*.

30 For example, Bryce Mackasey, the minister of labour and the guiding spirit behind the changes, argued that in "all probability conditions [of the program] will be a little more rigid under the future plan because we will see these people at least twice"; Canada, Parliament, House of Commons, Standing Committee on Labour, Manpower and Immigration, *Minutes of Proceedings and Evidence,* 15 September 1970, 19. Later, during committee review of the bill, D. Allen, director of policy analysis and formulation for the Unemployment Insurance Commission, commented that the upper limit on any deficits the scheme might incur was $800 million; ibid., 19 May 1971, 29. Mackasey's main argument was that increased benefits under the new program would be balanced by increased contributions by newly covered occupations such as teachers and government employees.

31 Saywell, ed., *Canadian Annual Review of Politics and Public Affairs 1971*, 358.

32 Saywell, ed., *Canadian Annual Review of Politics and Public Affairs 1972*, 353-5.

33 The program also encountered administrative difficulties at the beginning. Since some parts of the 1955 act remained temporarily in force after 1971, the commission had to deal with two pieces of legislation simultaneously. The changeover to computers was made at the same time, adding to the confusion.

34 Canada, Unemployment Insurance Commission, *Annual Report 1973*, 7. As the report put it: "The Separation Certificate was replaced by the Record of Employment, making it possible to cross-check by computer the validity of the information provided by the claimant and the employer."

35 Ibid., 4. Benefit control costs increased 68 per cent in 1973 over 1972, compared to a 15 per cent increase in total administration costs in the same period.

36 Calculated from Statistics Canada, Cat. 86-201, 1978, Tables 2 and 3 at pages 145 and 148.

37 "The initiatives undertaken in 1975 shifted the emphasis of the system toward preventative measures"; Canada, Unemployment Insurance Commission, *Annual Report 1975*, 2. The experimental Special Job Finding and Placement Drive alone was successful in disqualifying or disentitling over 80,000 claimants.

38 On the developmental uses of UI in the late 1970s, see Pal, "The Fall and Rise of Developmental Uses of UI Funds."

39 Employment and Immigration Canada, *Unemployment Insurance in the 1980s* and *Labour Market Development in the 1980s*.

40 Commission of Inquiry on Unemployment Insurance, *Report*, 299.
41 *Globe and Mail*, 3 December 1986, 1.

CHAPTER FOUR

1   See Wright, *Class, Crisis and the State*, chap. 2, for a review and discussion. A practical application of this sensitivity to class "fractions" may be found in Abraham, *The Collapse of the Weimar Republic*, and also in Mahon, *The Politics of Industrial Restructuring*. This new approach is well captured in William Coleman's description of the relation of business to the state as "privileged and conflictual"; see Coleman, "Canadian Business and the State."
2   Olson, *The Logic of Collective Action*, 143. Olson subsequently applied these ideas to the problem of economic growth; see his *The Rise and Decline of Nations*.
3   Sproule-Jones, "Institutions, Constitutions, and Public Policies," 145.
4   Doern and Phidd, *Canadian Public Policy*, 82.
5   Thompson and Stanbury, "The Political Economy," 227.
6   Schlozman and Verba, *Injury to Insult*, 1.
7   Kincaid, *Poverty and Equality in Britain*, 215-16.
8   Brunelle, *Le Code civil*, 93-114.
9   Polly Hill, *The Unemployment Services*, xii.
10 Cohen, *The Canadian Unemployment Act*, chap. 7. Two further examples of this style of argument, in a British context, may be found in Michael Hill, *Policies for the Unemployed*, and Marsden, *Workless*.
11 Becker, "Twenty-five Years of Unemployment Insurance," 484-5.
12 Blaustein, *Unemployment Insurance Objectives and Issues*, 31.
13 Haber and Murray, *Unemployment Insurance in the American Economy*, 135.
14 Adams, *Public Attitudes toward Unemployment Insurance*, chaps. 3 and 4.
15 Employment and Immigration Canada, *Highlights of An Evaluation*, Highlight paper number 4.
16 Ibid., Highlight paper number 11.
17 Lanphier et al, *An Analysis of Attitudes toward Unemployment Insurance*, 11.
18 Struthers, *No Fault of Their Own*, 25, 64, 88-9, 105, 114, 131.
19 Pelletier, *De la sécurité*, 291-305. He also stresses the bankruptcy of Keynesianism as a tool for managing economic contradictions.
20 Cuneo, "State, Class and Reserve Labour."
21 Ibid., 148.
22 Struthers, *No Fault of Their Own*, 24.
23 Ontario, Ontario Commission on Unemployment, *Report of the Ontario Commission on Unemployment*, 253-4.
24 Struthers, *No Fault of Their Own*, 23.
25 For a fuller discussion of the 1920s, see ibid., chap. 1.
26 For testimony to this effect by William Edwards, deputy minister of justice,

see Canada, House of Commons, Select Standing Committee on Industrial and International Relations, *Minutes of Evidence*, 10 May 1928, No. 7, 113.

27 Ibid., 11 April 1928, No. 2, 23-30.

28 Ibid., 19 April 1928, No. 3, 49.

29 Ibid., 32.

30 Ibid., 11 April 1928, No. 2, 32.

31 Ibid., 19 April 1928, No. 3, 51.

32 Ibid., 52.

33 Ibid.

34 Ibid., 11 April 1928, No. 3, 37.

35 See Cuneo, "State Mediation."

36 Public Archives of Canada (hereafter PAC), R.B. Bennett Papers, MG 26 K, p. 501937.

37 Ibid., pp. 501980-1, 501983.

38 Ibid., p. 501954.

39 Ibid., Bennett to Kyle, 18 August 1930, p. 501852.

40 Canada, House of Commons, *Debates*, 19 April 1931, pp. 1099-1104.

41 For examples of the style of letters and petitions, see PAC, Bennett Papers, pp. 502632-7, 502639-54, 502670-9, 502682-5, and 502943-8.

42 Ibid., pp. 503493-4.

43 Struthers, *No Fault of Their Own*, 90-1.

44 PAC, Bennett Papers, pp. 504014-18.

45 Ibid., Holmes to Finlayson, 17 November 1933, pp. 502991-3036.

46 Struthers, *No Fault of Their Own*, 126.

47 PAC, Bennett Papers, pp. 504138-9.

48 *Employment and Social Insurance Act,* SC 1935, c. 38, secs. 4(2) and 35(1) and (2).

49 Canada, House of Commons, Special Committee on Bill No. 98 Respecting Unemployment Insurance, *Minutes of Proceedings and Evidence* (1940), 109, 150-1, 219-20.

50 Ibid., 151.

51 Select Standing Committee on Industrial and International Relations, *Minutes of Evidence*, 24 April 1928, No. 4, 62.

52 Alvin Finkel, however, argues: "The long list of businessmen who applauded the Bennett proposals in the New Deal radio speeches indicates a fairly widespread business support for some form of social insurance"; *Business and Social Reform in the Thirties*, 90. Cuneo, "State Mediation," 44-5, rightly takes Finkel to task on this issue, because Finkel's own evidence, drawn from public statements by businessmen, shows more ambivalence than he is willing to admit. Cuneo, however, relies entirely on 16 private letters by businessmen to Bennett written between January 1931 and January 1933. There is of course no reason to restrict artificially the sample this way, since Bennett continued to receive communications to 1935, and these letters should indeed be supplemented by the public record.

53 PAC, Bennett Papers, Kyle to Bennett, 15 August 1930, p. 501851.
54 Ibid., Nesbitt to Bennett, 30 April 1931, p. 502056.
55 Ibid., McLean to Bennett, 21 April 1931, p. 502212, also see pp. 501889, 502200, 502618-19, 502727, 502820-2, and 502978-9.
56 Ibid., White to Bennett, 22 August 1934, p. 503201.
57 Ibid., Walsh to Bennett, 10 January 1933, p. 502746. The following discussion of the CMA's position relies on this letter and its attached memorandum, together to be found at pp. 502746-58.
58 Ibid., p. 502794.
59 Ibid., p. 502796.
60 Ibid., Sturgeon to Bennett, 14 May 1932, pp. 502461-2.
61 Ibid., Vancouver Board of Trade to Bennett, 19 November 1932, p. 502581.
62 Ibid., Gordon to Bennett, 6 January 1934, p. 503059.
63 Ibid., Clarke to Bennett, 13 January 1933, p. 502816.
64 Ibid., Reilly to Bennett, 11 January 1933, p. 502788; Reilly to Bennett, 3 February 1934, p. 503124.
65 Ibid., Dawson to Bennett, 11 November 1932, pp. 502567-8.
66 Wolfenden, *The Real Meaning of Social Insurance* and *Unemployment Funds*.
67 PAC, Bennett Papers, p. 502736.
68 Ibid., p. 502737.
69 Ibid., emphasis removed from original.
70 Ibid., pp. 503374-5, 503430-2, 5043463, 503537, 503562-5, and 503570.
71 Ibid., pp. 503562-8.
72 PAC, Department of Insurance Files, RG 40, vol. 24, file 3-25-1-5, memorandum by A.D. Watson to Department of Labour, 5 March 1938.
73 Special Committee on Bill No. 98 Respecting Unemployment Insurance, *Minutes of Proceedings and Evidence*, 96-102.
74 Ibid., 93.
75 PAC, William Lyon Mackenzie King Papers, MG 26, J 4, "The Opposition to Unemployment Insurance," n.d., but in 1940, p. c231930.
76 Ibid., p. c231931.
77 PAC, Unemployment Insurance Commission Files, RG 50, vol. 28, file 1-2-21-1, memorandum from Stangroom to MacNamara, 6 March 1943, pp. 1-2.
78 Special Committee on Bill No. 98, *Minutes*, 134-48.
79 Dingledine, *A Chronology of Response*, 11, 38.
80 This judgment is based on a survey and comparison of pre- and post-1940 government files at the PAC.
81 Kelly, "Unemployment Insurance in Canada," 106, comes to the same conclusion.
82 Committee of Inquiry into Unemployment Insurance, *Report*, 16.
83 Ibid., 1-15.
84 Canadian Manufacturers' Association, Submission to the Committee of Inquiry into the Unemployment Insurance Act, October 1961, 3.
85 Ibid., 4.

86 Ibid., 19.

87 PAC, Department of Labour Files, RG 27, vol. 3390, file 8-4-18, vol. 1, memorandum from G. Schonning to G.V. Haythorne, 18 January 1962.

88 Ibid., 1.

89 Ibid., 1-2; emphasis added.

90 Ibid., 2.

91 PAC, Department of Labour Files, vol. 3390, file 8-4-18, vol. 2, "Unemployment Insurance: Comparison of Recommendations of Gill Committee with Proposals regarding Unemployment Insurance Fund by Interdepartmental Committee on 1 March 1961, and by the Cabinet Committee on 15 May 1961," n.d. but ca. November 1962-February 1963.

92 See Doern and Phidd, *Canadian Public Policy*, chap. 17.

93 Johnson, "A Minister as an Agent of Policy Change," 619-20.

94 Canada, Department of Labour, *Unemployment Insurance in the 70's*, 3.

95 Ibid., 3.

96 Ibid., 4.

97 Ibid., 5.

98 See, for example, Economic Council of Canada, *First Annual Review* and *Second Annual Review*.

99 Johnson, "Political Leadership and the Process of Policy-Making," chap. 3.

100 Ibid.

101 There was apparently a substantial response, but in the form of letters to members of the standing committee, who used them to raise questions with the officials who appeared before them. There is no public record of these communications, however.

102 "Unemployment Insurance in Canada," A Submission to the House of Commons on Labour, Manpower and Immigration by The Canadian Manufacturers' Association; reprinted as Appendix N in Canada, House of Commons, Standing Committee on Labour, Manpower and Immigration, *Minutes of Proceedings and Evidence*.

103 Submission on "Unemployment Insurance in the 70s" by the Canadian Chamber of Commerce; reprinted as Appendix A-5 in ibid.

104 Submission by the Canadian Labour Congress to the House of Commons Standing Committee on Labour, Manpower and Immigration on "Unemployment Insurance in the '70s," reprinted as Appendix A-11 in ibid.

105 Interview with Bryce Mackasey, Ottawa, February 1982.

106 Ibid.

107 Standing Committee on Labour, *Minutes*, 18 December 1970, No. 9.

108 Two key differences were inclusion of fishermen under the act even though the White Paper meant to exclude the self-employed from coverage and a slight change in the phase structure of the program.

109 Dingledine, *A Chronology of Response*, 72.

110 Canada, House of Commons, *Debates*, 1975, p. 8567.

111 Interview with Bud Cullen, Ottawa, February 1982.

112 Canada, House of Commons, Standing Committee on Labour, Manpower and Immigration, *Minutes of Proceedings and Evidence*, 18 November 1975, No. 22, 5-7.

113 Ibid., 17 May 1977, No. 22, 6-18.

114 Ibid., 23 November 1978, No. 6, 73-4.

115 Ibid., 20 November 1975, No. 23, 9.

116 The CMA and CLC maintained their joint opposition, but the Canadian Employment and Immigration Commission decided to discount it and proceed with pilot projects. See Canada Employment and Immigration Commission, *Minutes*, 28 October 1977.

117 Standing Committee on Labour, *Minutes*, Thursday, 28 April 1977, No. 16, 6-11.

118 Interview with senior official, Ottawa, April 1982.

119 The lack of prior consultation did not go unnoticed by private-sector groups. The Canada Employment and Immigration Advisory Council, in reacting to the task force's proposals, deliberately acted to reflect private-sector views. It recommended that "future fundamental changes in the UI program will be the result of more genuine consultation with the social partners. It is not enough to seek reactions to a package that was developed in camera. Labour and management have not fully participated in the formulation of the premises, i.e. the fundamental principles of the UI program as it has evolved over the years." Memorandum to Minister, "Unemployment Insurance in the 1980's," 10 November 1981.

120 Employment and Immigration Canada, *Unemployment Insurance in the 1980s*, 99.

121 Condensed from ibid., 100-1.

122 Ibid., 102-3.

123 CMA to Lloyd Axworthy, 16 September 1981.

124 See "Unemployment Insurance in the 1980s," Submission to the Minister of Employment and Immigration by the Canadian Chamber of Commerce, September 1981.

125 Canadian Labour Congress, "Response to the Report of the Task Force on Unemployment Insurance," September 1981, 2.

126 See, for example, Canadian Union of Public Employees, Response to "Unemployment Insurance in the 1980s," 4 November 1981. A more detailed breakdown and analysis of some 35 briefs shows the usual patterns among employer and employee organizations. See Canada Employment and Immigration Commission, "Summary and Analysis of Briefs Re 1981 Task Force." A notable feature of the briefs is the significant representation of women's groups.

127 This book went to press just as the report was released.

128 Canada Employment and Immigration Commission, "Summary of Various Non-Governmental Organizations' Briefs with Respect to the Unemployment Insurance Program (1971-1979)."

129 See Pelletier, *De la sécurité*, passim, for this type of argument.

CHAPTER FIVE

1 Krasner, *Defending the National Interest*, xi.
2 Ibid., 10. Alan Cairns has been the most consistent Canadian proponent of such an approach; see his "The Governments and Societies" and "The Embedded State."
3 Nordlinger, *On the Autonomy of the Democratic State*, 1.
4 Ibid., 14-15.
5 Ibid., 25.
6 Skocpol, *States and Social Revolutions*, 25.
7 Ibid., 27.
8 Ibid., chap. 2.
9 Skocpol, "Political Response to Capitalist Crisis." For an application of the concept of "state capacity" that deals with bureaux in a fashion similar to this chapter, see Skocpol and Finegold, "State Capacity and Economic Intervention."
10 Golembiewski, *Public Administration*, Part 1: *Perspectives*.
11 Holden, Jr, " 'Imperialism' in Bureaucracy," 944.
12 Seidman, *Politics, Position, and Power*, passim.
13 Rourke, *Bureaucracy, Politics, and Public Policy*, vii.
14 Ibid., 1-2.
15 Peters, *The Politics of Bureaucracy*, 173.
16 Allison and Halperin, "Bureaucratic Politics," 42. Also see chapter 5 in Allison's famous study of the Cuban missile crisis, *Essence of Decision*.
17 Allison and Halperin, "Bureaucratic Politics," 47-8.
18 Tullock, *The Politics of Bureaucracy*, 32.
19 Niskanen, Jr, *Bureaucracy and Representative Government*, 38.
20 Downs, *Inside Bureaucracy*, 2.
21 Ibid.
22 This discussion is drawn from ibid., chaps. 17-19.
23 Ibid., 213.
24 Ibid., 215.
25 This literature review has deliberately restricted itself to relatively narrow theories of bureaucratic autonomy in the policy process. Several neo-Marxist approaches in effect emphasize the same dynamics, but within a much broader social and political theory, making them difficult to assess here. For example, see Offe, *Contradictions of the Welfare State*, Block, "Beyond Relative Autonomy," and Mahon, *The Politics of Industrial Restructuring*. For a review of neo-Marxist theories of the state, see Carnoy, *The State and Political Theory*.
26 This is a somewhat broader understanding of bureaucratic politics, which more usually is seen as individualized bargaining among specific officials, as in Allison's model; see, for example, Schultz, *Federalism, Bureaucracy, and Public Policy*, 5-11.

27 See Nossal, "Allison through the (Ottawa) Looking Glass"; Atkinson and Nossal, "Bureaucratic Politics."
28 Struthers, *No Fault of Their Own*, chap. 1.
29 Canada, House of Commons, Select Standing Committee on Industrial and International Relations, *Final Report*, 1928, v.
30 Struthers, *No Fault of Their Own*, 87.
31 PAC, Bennett Papers, MG 26 K, memorandum from R.K. Finlayson to Bennett, n.d., pp. 504027-40.
32 Ibid., memorandum from G.D. Finlayson, 12 December 1932, p. 504014.
33 Ibid., p. 504015.
34 One might ask, then, why the actuarial ideology and not some other? The short answer is that by the time UI was being seriously considered in Canada, Britain's plan had begun to strain, and so financial considerations – an area of actuarial mastery – were uppermost. Moreover, the Canadian federal state had no notable social policy functions, and hence no organizational spokesmen of a non-actuarial approach. The Department of Insurance filled the void.
35 PAC, Bennett Papers, Bryce Stewart to W.C. Clark, 16 January 1933, p. 501799.
36 Ibid., memorandum from W.C. Clark to R.B. Bennett, 18 January, p. 501802.
37 Ibid., Holmes to Finlayson, 17 November 1933, pp. 502991-3036.
38 PAC, Department of Insurance Files, RG 40, vol. 24, file 3-25-1-1, memorandum from A.D. Watson to R.K. Finlayson, 3 April 1934.
39 Ibid., A.D. Watson, "Actuarial Report on the Contributions Required to Provide the Unemployment Insurance Benefits within the Scheme of the Draft of an Act Entitled The Employment and Social Insurance Act," 2 November 1934.
40 Ibid.
41 PAC, Department of Insurance Files, vol. 24, File 3-25-1-3, H. Wolfenden, "The Employment and Social Insurance Act: Actuarial Report on the Rates of Contribution for the Unemployment Insurance Benefits and the Provisions with Respect to Supplementary Unemployment Benefits," 1 February 1935.
42 Struthers, *No Fault of Their Own*, 121-2, adduces "non-actuarial" reasons for the act's restricted scope, such as the sheer expense of broad coverage and the political usefulness of driving a wedge between skilled and unskilled workers by having the former supported under UI and the latter under the more humiliating and less generous relief. This is plausible, but the logic of the restrictions can be easily explained by reference to the actuarial ideology alone.
43 PAC, Department of Insurance, vol. 24, file 3-25-1-5, A.D. Watson, "Memorandum re Brief of Canadian Bankers' Association against Inclusion of the Banks in Any General Scheme of Unemployment Insurance," 5 March 1938.
44 Canada, House of Commons, Special Committee on Bill No. 98 Respecting Unemployment Insurance, *Minutes of Proceedings and Evidence*, 26-7.
45 Ibid., 30.
46 Ibid., 33.
47 Ibid., 273.

48 Ibid., 274.

49 Ibid.

50 In fact, the commission in this period to the mid-1960s relied on the Department of Insurance for its actuarial advice. A.D. Watson continued as chief actuary to the mid-1950s and in that capacity was able to offer his views on every important aspect of the program.

51 Dingledine, *A Chronology of Response*, 20-1 and Appendix A.

52 PAC, Department of Labour Files, RG 27, vol. 912, file 8-9-104-1, part 1. The Interdepartmental Committee on Social Security consisted of senior representatives from the Bank of Canada and the departments of Finance, Labour, Health and Welfare, and Trade and Commerce. It was chaired by the secretary to cabinet and could invite other agency representatives as needed.

53 Ibid., minutes of Interdepartmental Committee on Social Security, 30 December 1949.

54 PAC, Privy Council Files, RG 2, 16, Cabinet Conclusions, 17 February 1950.

55 Dingledine, *A Chronology of Response*, 25.

56 PAC, Unemployment Insurance Commission Files, RG 50, vol. 53, quoted in minutes of meeting of the Unemployment Insurance Advisory Committee, 7-8 April 1952, p. 5.

57 PAC, Department of Labour, vol. 901, file 8-9-103-2-4-2, part 1, memorandum from UIC to Interdepartmental Committee on Unemployment Questions entitled "Extension of Unemployment Insurance Benefits," 25 February 1954, p. 3.

58 PAC, Department of Fisheries Files, RG 23, vol. 1136, file 721-64-3[1], Stewart Bates, deputy minister (DM) Fisheries, to Charles Cannon, 25 May 1950.

59 PAC, Unemployment Insurance Commission (UIC), vol. 53, "Survey of the Fishing Industry in Canada," April 1951, pp. 81-2; report attached to minutes of meeting of the Unemployment Insurance Advisory Committee, 9-10 July 1951.

60 PAC, Department of Fisheries, vol. 1136, file 721-64-3 [1], memorandum from UIC to Interdepartmental Committee on Extension of Unemployment Insurance to Fishing and Agriculture, 25 March 1954.

61 Ibid., memorandum from UIC entitled "Survey of Canadian Fishing Industry – 1954," October 1954; and vol. 1137, file 721-64-3 [3], two alternate plans for coverage attached to letter from W.R. Martin (assistant secretary to cabinet) to G.R. Clark (DM Fisheries), 23 January 1957.

62 PAC, Department of Labour, vol. 3390, file 8-4-18, vol. 2, memorandum entitled "Unemployment Insurance: Comparison of Recommendations of Gill Committee with Proposals regarding Unemployment Insurance Fund by Interdepartmental Committee on 1 March 1961 and by the Cabinet Committee on 15 May 1961," n.d., but ca. 1963, p. 1.

63 Ibid., memorandum from G.V. Haythorne to M. Starr (minister of labour), 14 January 1963, p. 3.

64 Ibid., p. 12.

65 Ibid., vol. 4, "Report of the Interdepartmental Committee on the Gill Committee Report," 23 October 1963, p. 1.

66 Canada, Department of Labour, *Unemployment Insurance in the 70's*, 11.
67 Canada, House of Commons, Standing Committee on Labour, Manpower and Immigration, *Minutes of Proceedings and Evidence* 15 September 1970, No. 10, 19.
68 Ibid., No. 11, 16 September 1970, 108.
69 Canada, Department of Labour, *Unemployment Insurance in the 70's*, 6.
70 Johnson, "Political Leadership," 104.
71 Canada, House of Commons, *Debates*, 27 October 1975, p. 8567.
72 Ibid.
73 Ibid., p. 8568.
74 Ibid., p. 8570.
75 Ibid., 1 February 1977, p. 2591.
76 Ibid.
77 Ibid., 9 November 1978, p. 983.
78 Ibid.
79 Employment and Immigration Canada, *Unemployment Insurance in the 1980s*, 37.
80 Hum, *Unemployment Insurance and Work Effort*.
81 Employment and Immigration Canada, "Rate of Misuse/Abuse," p. R-3.
82 Employment and Immigration Canada, Strategic Policy and Planning Branch, "Analysis of Misuse and Abuse of UI," p. L-7.
83 In this respect, my presentation of bureaucratic politics is structural, not personality-based.
84 PAC, William Lyon Mackenzie King Papers, MJ 26, J4, G.S. Harrington to Mackenzie King, 1 November 1935, pp. C151293-5.
85 Ibid., Harrington to King, 21 January 1936, pp. C151290-2.
86 Ibid., memorandum from E.A. Pickering to Mackenzie King, 2 April 1936, pp. C117209-11.
87 Ibid., Pickering to King, 18 May 1936, pp. C117211-12.
88 Ibid., "Memorandum re Unemployment Insurance Commission and National Selective Service," dictated by Mackenzie King, 20 August 1942, pp. C232056-8.
89 Ibid., p. C232057.
90 Ibid., p. C232058.
91 Ibid., "Memorandum for the Prime Minister re Unemployment Insurance Commission – transfer of functions to Department of Labour," 28 August 1942, p. C232060.
92 Ibid., p. C232061.
93 Ibid.
94 Ibid., p. C232063.
95 Ibid.
96 PAC, Department of Insurance, vol. 28, file 1-3, L.J. Trottier to L.S. St-Laurent, 16 March 1943.
97 Ibid., F.P. Varcoe to L.J. Trottier, 19 April 1943.
98 Ibid., R.J. Tallon to L.J. Trottier, 25 May 1943.
99 Ibid., Trottier to Mitchell, 22 June 1943.

100 Ibid., Mitchell to Trottier, 14 June 1943.

101 Pal, "Keynesian Commitment, Keynesian Illusion."

102 PAC, Department of Insurance, vol. 28, file 1-3, Mitchell to Trottier, 21 August 1945.

103 Ibid.

104 Ibid., Trottier to Mitchell, 27 August 1945.

105 Ibid.

106 PAC, King Papers, "Memorandum for the Prime Minister re Unemployment Insurance Commission," 5 March 1946, p. C232090.

107 PAC, King Papers, MG 26, J13, 7 March 1946.

108 *Unemployment Insurance Act*, SC 1955, c. 50, sec. 4.

109 PC 1980, 19 June 1947. In a letter to W.A. Mackintosh, chairman of the Unemployment Insurance Advisory Committee, MacNamara said: "The Minister is somewhat apprehensive because of the lack of departmental control realizing as he does that he will be the focal point for criticism if anything goes wrong." He added: "The pitfall we wish to avoid is to have the Secretary of the Board under the control of the Unemployment Insurance Commission." PAC, Department of Labour, vol. 886, file 8-9-26-1, part 3, MacNamara to Mackintosh, 5 July 1947.

110 PAC, Department of Labour, vol. 912, file 8-9-104-1, part 1, minutes of Interdepartmental Committee on Social Security, 29 December 1949.

111 Ibid., memorandum from A.H. Brown to A. MacNamara, 30 November 1949.

112 Ibid., vol. 912, file 8-9-104-1, part 1.

113 PAC, Privy Council, Cabinet Conclusions, 1 February 1950. Since Mitchell was away, the memorandum was presented by the minister of health and welfare, Paul Martin.

114 PAC, Department of Labour, vol. 912, file 8-9-104-1, part 1, minutes of Interdepartmental Committee on Social Security, 31 January 1950.

115 Ibid., minutes of Interdepartmental Committee on Social Security, 6 February 1950.

116 PAC, Department of Fisheries, vol. 1136, file 721-64-3 [1], Gushue to Bradbury, 23 October 1951.

117 Ibid., Bisson to McArthur, 20 July 1951; see handwritten note by Stewart Bates (DM Fisheries) at bottom.

118 Ibid., vol. 1137, file 721-64-3 [7], "The Scope and Effects of Unemployment Insurance Coverage for Fishermen," May 1962, p. i.

119 Ibid., vol. 1136, file 721-64-3 [1], memorandum from commission to the Interdepartmental Committee on the Extension of Unemployment Insurance to Fishing and Agriculture, 25 March 1954.

120 Ibid., minutes of Ad Hoc Committee on Unemployment Insurance, 5 April 1954.

121 Ibid., vol. 1137, file 721-64-3 [3], Martin to Clark, 23 January 1957.

122 Ibid.

123 Ibid., McArthur to Bates, 28 January 1957.

124 Doern and Phidd, *Canadian Public Policy*, 492.

125 PAC, Department of Labour, vol. 887, file 8-9-26-1, part 9, memorandum from A.H. Brown to G.G Cushing, 21 October 1960.

126 Ibid., vol. 3458, file 4-11, part 8, memorandum from W.R. Dymond to A.H. Brown, 1 November 1960.

127 The following is based on ibid., vol. 3390, file 8-4-18, vol. 2, "Memorandum to the Minister: Gill Committee's Recommendations re Organization," 30 January 1963.

128 Ibid, p. 3.

129 Ibid., p. 7.

130 Ibid.

131 Ibid., vol. 3390, file 8-4-18, part 5, memorandum from J.P. Francis to G.V. Haythorne, 23 December 1963.

132 Ibid.

133 Ibid., vol. 3458, file 4-11, part 9, memorandum from G.V. Haythorne to Allan MacEachen, 10 February 1964.

134 Ibid., vol. 3392, file 8-9-185, part 3, quoted in "Report to the Minister of Labour by the Interdepartmental Committee on Changes to the Unemployment Insurance Programme," 14 March 1966.

135 Ibid., memorandum from G. Schonning to G.V. Haythorne, 2 June 1967.

136 One of the members of this committee was Tom Kent, at that time the deputy minister of manpower and immigration. Committee minutes show that he was the originator of one of the 1971 act's most singular features – the "4 per cent trigger" – though he originally suggested 3 per cent. See ibid., minutes of meeting of Interdepartmental Committee of Officials on Unemployment Insurance, 15 June 1967.

137 Johnson, "Political Leadership," chap. 3. Johnson argues, on the basis of confidential interviews, that the commission "old guard" was frozen out of the policy process by Mackasey and his ally, the chief commissioner. This interpretation accords with the documentary evidence uncovered here, though Johnson perhaps places too much emphasis on Mackasey's personal role.

138 Department of Finance, file 6960-02, "Unemployment Insurance Act: New Coming Changes," 3 June 1974.

139 Department of Finance, file 6960-04, "Financing the U.I.C.," M.A. Cohen to T.K. Shoyama, 23 May 1975.

140 Unemployment Insurance Commission, *Annual Report 1972*, 13.

141 Ibid., *Annual Report 1974*, 1.

142 Department of Employment and Immigration files, Memorandum from J.W. Douglas to C.C. Tuck, 3 August 1976, p. 1.

143 Ibid., p. 2.

144 The term is from Pelletier, *De la sécurité*, 359.

145 Canada, House of Commons, *Debates*, 1 February 1977, pp. 2590-1.

146 Ibid., 21 October 1976, p. 339.

147 Ibid., p. 340.

148 Interview with Bud Cullen, Ottawa, February 1982.

149 Department of Finance, file 6960-04, "Financing the Unemployment Insurance Program," M. Chartier-Gauvin to E. Neufeld, 18 August 1978.

150 Ibid.

151 Pal, "The Fall and Rise of Developmental Uses of UI Funds."

152 Readers should note, however, that the commission had access to this book in manuscript form and cited arguments from this chapter to support its recommendations for a separate Unemployment Insurance Commission. See Commission of Inquiry on Unemployment Insurance, *Report*, 253, 255.

CHAPTER SIX

1 Banting, *The Welfare State*, 4.

2 Stevenson, *Unfulfilled Union*, 2.

3 Doern and Phidd, *Canadian Public Policy*, 63.

4 Smiley, *Canada in Question*, 18.

5 Wheare, *Federal Government*, 14.

6 The following is taken from Banting, *The Welfare State*, 39-44.

7 Ibid., 39.

8 Ibid., 41.

9 Ibid., 92.

10 Ibid., 42.

11 Ibid.

12 Ibid., 171-81.

13 Struthers, *No Fault of Their Own*, 9.

14 See Guest, *The Emergence of Social Security in Canada*.

15 Struthers, *No Fault of Their Own*, 10.

16 See Smiley, ed., *The Rowell-Sirois Report*, chap. 6.

17 Struthers, *No Fault of Their Own*, 14.

18 Banting, *The Welfare State*, 64.

19 As quoted in Struthers, *No Fault of Their Own*, 15.

20 Ibid., 19.

21 Ibid., 24.

22 Ibid., 27.

23 PAC, William Lyon Mackenzie King Papers, MG 26, J4, PC 3831, 7 October 1921, pp. C103165-6.

24 Struthers, *No Fault of Their Own*, 33.

25 PAC, King Papers, PC 220, 5 February 1923, p. C103167.

26 Struthers, *No Fault of Their Own*, 36.

27 See Russell, ed., *Leading Constitutional Cases*, 41.

28 Ibid., 55.

29 Ibid., 59.
30 Struthers, *No Fault of Their Own*, 24, asserts that in 1920 the only barrier to federal assumption of UI was political, not constitutional or legal. While his judgment for the 1920s is correct, he gives less weight to the trend of judicial decisions than he should when discussing policy-makers' views at the end of that decade. By 1928, the problem had indeed taken on a constitutional aspect and was not entirely political, though it must be conceded that Struthers persuasively shows the extreme political reluctance of the King government of those years to consider UI or even assistance for municipal relief.
31 See testimony by William S. Edwards, DM Justice, House of Commons, Select Standing Committee on Industrial and International Relations, *Minutes of Evidence*, 10 May 1928, No. 7, 113.
32 Ibid., *Final Report 1928*, 10.
33 Ibid., 10-11.
34 See Bryden, *Old Age Pensions*, 61-101.
35 Select Standing Committee, *Final Report 1928*, 11.
36 Ibid., *Minutes of Evidence*, 23 April 1929, No. 9, 56.
37 Struthers, *No Fault of Their Own*, 41.
38 Canada, House of Commons, *Debates*, 27 February 1930, p. 107.
39 Ibid., 8 September 1930, p. 4.
40 Ibid., 10 September 1930, p. 64.
41 Ibid., p. 65.
42 Struthers, *No Fault of Their Own*, 56.
43 Canada, House of Commons, *Debates*, 29 April 1931, pp. 1099-1100.
44 PAC, R.B. Bennett Papers, MG 26 K, "Memorandum for the Prime Minister," n.d., p. 504028.
45 Ibid., p. 504031.
46 Struthers, *No Fault of Their Own*, 86.
47 PAC, King Papers, pp. C151128-36.
48 Ibid., "Memorandum for the Prime Minister re – Unemployment Insurance," 22 April 1938, pp. C150839-41.
49 Ibid., pp. C150842-7.
50 Canada, House of Commons, *Debates*, 6 June 1938, p. 3561.
51 Struthers, *No Fault of Their Own*, 197.
52 PAC, King Papers, "Reasons for Introducing the Unemployment Insurance Bill during the War," n.d., pp. C231886-9.
53 Banting, *The Welfare State*, 81.
54 Struthers, *No Fault of Their Own*, 209-10.
55 For a view of the institutional machinery as it stood in July 1940, see Canada, House of Commons, *Debates*, 8 July 1940, at p. 1396.
56 Young, "Reining in James."
57 Canada, Department of Reconstruction, *Employment and Income*.
58 Ibid., 1.

59 Mackintosh, "Canadian Economic Policy."
60 See Granatstein, *Canada's War*, chap. 5.
61 Dominion-Provincial Conference on Reconstruction, *Proceedings*, 387.
62 Ibid., 102.
63 Ibid., 103.
64 Ibid.
65 Ibid., 104.
66 Ibid.
67 Ibid., 105.
68 Ibid., 509.
69 Ibid., 583-605.
70 Burns, *The Acceptable Mean*.
71 Federal-Provincial Conference, *Proceedings*, 102-4.
72 Dyck, "The Canada Assistance Plan."
73 See Simeon, *Federal-Provincial Diplomacy*.
74 See Phidd and Doern, *Politics and Management*, chap. 9.
75 Canada, Senate, Special Committee on Manpower and Employment, *Report*.
76 Brewis, *Regional Economic Policies*, chap. 6.
77 See chapter 5.
78 Though see Kesselman, *Financing Canadian Unemployment Insurance*, chap. 9.
79 Canada, Department of Labour, *Unemployment Insurance in the 70's*, 20-2.
80 Ibid., 18.
81 Canada, House of Commons, *Debates*, 19 April 1971, p. 5039.
82 *Unemployment Insurance Act*, SC 1970-72, c. 48, secs. 3(2)(e), 4(1)(d).
83 Ibid., secs. 29(s), 30(3).
84 Canada, Employment and Immigration Canada, *Unemployment Insurance Interprovincial Transfers*, 12.
85 Interview with Bryce Mackasey, Ottawa, February 1982.
86 Interview with Bud Cullen, Ottawa, February 1982.
87 Ibid.
88 Canada, House of Commons, Standing Committee on Labour, Manpower and Immigration, Fourth Session, Thirtieth Parliament, 30 November 1978. Ontario's objections focused less on increases in welfare costs than on lack of consultation.
89 For example, see Canada, House of Commons, *Debates*, 9 November 1978, p. 984. Cullen estimated that the 1978 changes would increase net provincial welfare costs 1979-81 by $68.8 million.
90 One partial measure relevant to the dispute is the increase in Canada Assistance Plan (CAP) expenditures. Total provincial CAP expenditures increased by $149.1 million between 1979 and 1981. Not all of this increase would have been due to UI cuts, but it does appear that Ottawa underestimated the effects of Bill C-14.

91 For data on UI's redistributive effects, see Canada, Employment and Immigration Canada, *Distributive and Redistributive Effects* and *Income Redistribution through UI*, Cloutier, *The Distribution of Benefits and Costs*, and Smith et al, *Poverty and Government Income Support*.

92 See Brown and Eastman, *The Limits of Consultation*.

93 Canada Employment and Immigration Commission, Report on Labour Market Issues.

94 Ibid., 7.

95 Interview with senior official, Ottawa, February 1982.

96 See, for example, Quebec's Commission of Inquiry on Health and Social Welfare, *Income Security*.

Bibliography

ARCHIVAL SOURCES

All the following are held at the Public Archives of Canada:

Department of Fisheries Files
Department of Insurance Files
Department of Labour Files
Privy Council Files
R.B. Bennett Papers
Unemployment Insurance Commission Files
William Lyon Mackenzie King Papers

GOVERNMENT DOCUMENTS

Canada

Canada Employment and Immigration Advisory Council. Memorandum to Minister, "Unemployment Insurance in the 1980's." 10 November 1981.
Canada Employment and Immigration Commission. *Minutes*, 28 October 1977.
– Report on Labour Market Issues Tabled at the November 1978 Meeting of First Ministers on the Economy. 1979.
– "Summary and Analysis of Briefs re 1981 Task Force." 1981.
– "Summary of Various Non-Governmental Organizations' Briefs with Respect to the Unemployment Insurance Program (1971-1979)." October 1980.
Commission of Inquiry on Unemployment Insurance. *Report*. 1986.
Committee of Inquiry into Unemployment Insurance. *Report*. 1962.
Department of Labour. *Unemployment Insurance in the 70's*. 1970.
Department of Reconstruction. *Employment and Income with Special Reference to the Initial Period of Reconstruction*. 1945.
Dominion-Provincial Conference on Reconstruction. *Proceedings*. 1946.

Economic Council of Canada. *First Annual Review*. 1964.
– *Second Annual Review*. 1965.
Employment and Immigration Canada. *Distributive and Redistributive Effects on the UI Program*. Task Force on Unemployment Insurance, Technical Study 10. August 1981.
– *Highlights of an Evaluation of Canadians' and Canadian Employers' Attitudes towards Unemployment Insurance, Canada Employment Centres and Immigration*. Minister of Supply and Services, 1981.
– *Income Redistribution through UI: An Analysis by Individual and Family Income Class in 1977*. Task Force on Unemployment Insurance, Technical Study 11. August 1981.
– *Labour Market Development in the 1980s*. Minister of Supply and Services, 1981.
– "Rate of Misuse/Abuse and Success of Control Measures in the Unemployment Insurance Program." October 1976.
– Strategic Policy and Planning Branch. "Analysis of Misuse and Abuse of UI Based on Investigation of a Random Sample of Claimants." August 1978.
– *Unemployment Insurance in the 1980s*. Minister of Supply and Services, 1981.
– *Unemployment Insurance: Interprovincial Transfers*. Task Force on Unemployment Insurance, Technical Study 9. August 1981.
Federal-Provincial Conference. *Proceedings*. 1955.
House of Commons. *House of Commons Debates*.
House of Commons, Select Standing Committee on Industrial and International Relations. *Final Report*. 1928 and 1929.
– *Minutes of Evidence*. 1928.
House of Commons, Special Committee on Bill No. 98 respecting Unemployment Insurance. *Minutes of Proceedings and Evidence*. 1940.
House of Commons, Standing Committee on Labour, Manpower and Immigration. *Minutes of Proceedings and Evidence*. Various years.
National Employment Commission. *Final Report*. 1938.
– *Interim Report*. 1937.
Royal Commission on Industrial Relations. *Report*. 1919.
Senate, Special Committee on Manpower and Employment. *Report*. 1961.
Unemployment Insurance Commission. *Annual Reports*.
– *Report of the Study for Updating the Unemployment Insurance Programme*. 1968.

Ontario

Ontario Commission on Unemployment. *Interim Report*. 1915.
– *Report of the Ontario Commission on Unemployment*. 1916.

Quebec

Commission of Inquiry on Health and Social Welfare. *Income Security*. 1971.

BOOKS AND ARTICLES

Abler, Jens. "Government Responses to the Challenge of Unemployment: The Development of Unemployment Insurance in Western Europe." In *The Development of Welfare States in Europe and America*, edited by Peter Flora and Arnold J. Heidenheimer. New Brunswick, NJ: Transaction Books, 1981, 151-83.

Abraham, David. *The Collapse of the Weimar Republic*. Princeton: Princeton University Press, 1981.

Adams, Leonard P. *Public Attitudes toward Unemployment Insurance*. Kalamazoo, Mich.: Upjohn Institute, 1971.

Allison, Graham T. *Essence of Decision*. Boston: Little, Brown, 1971.

Allison, Graham T., and Morton H. Halperin. "Bureaucratic Politics: A Paradigm and Some Policy Implications." In *Theory and Policy in International Relations*, edited by Raymond Tanter and Richard H. Ullman. Princeton: Princeton University Press, 1972, 40-79.

Althusser, Louis. *For Marx*. London: Penguin, 1969.

Althusser, Louis, and Etienne Balibar. *Reading Capital*. London: New Left Books, 1970.

Atkinson, Michael M., and Kim Richard Nossal. "Bureaucratic Politics and the New Fighter Aircraft Decisions." *Canadian Public Administration* 24 (Winter 1981): 531-62.

Atkinson, Michael M., and Marsha A. Chandler. "Strategies for Policy Analysis." In *The Politics of Canadian Public Policy*, edited by Michael M. Atkinson and Marsha A. Chandler. Toronto: University of Toronto Press, 1983, 3-19.

Aucoin, Peter. "Public-Policy Theory and Analysis." In *Public Policy in Canada*, edited by G. Bruce Doern and Peter Aucoin. Toronto: Macmillan, 1979, 1-26.

Banting, Keith G. *The Welfare State and Canadian Federalism*. Kingston and Montreal: McGill-Queen's University Press and the Institute of Intergovernmental Relations, Queen's University, 1982.

Becker, Joseph M. *The Problem of Abuse in Unemployment Benefits: A Study in Limits*. New York: Columbia University Press, 1953.

– "Twenty-five Years of Unemployment Insurance: An Experiment in Competitive Collectivism." *Political Science Quarterly* 75 (December 1960): 484-5.

Bentley, Arthur. *The Process of Government*. Chicago: University of Chicago Press, 1908.

Best, Fred. *Work Sharing: Issues, Policy Options and Prospects*. Kalamazoo, Mich.: Upjohn Institute, 1981.

Beveridge, William H. *Unemployment, A Problem of Industry*, 1909 and 1930. London: Longmans, Green, 1930.

Blaustein, Saul J. *Unemployment Insurance Objectives and Issues: An Agenda for Research and Evaluation*. Kalamazoo, Mich.: Upjohn Institute, 1968.

Blaustein, Saul J., and Isabel Craig. *An International Review of Unemployment Insurance Schemes*. Kalamazoo, Mich.: Upjohn Institute, 1977.

Block, Fred. "Beyond Relative Autonomy: State Managers as Historical Subjects." In *The Socialist Register*, edited by Ralph Miliband and John Saville. London: Merlin Press, 1980, 227-42.

Brewis, T.N. *Regional Economic Policies in Canada*. Toronto: Macmillan, 1969.

Brown, Douglas, and Julia Eastman. *The Limits of Consultation*. Ottawa: Minister of Supply and Services, 1981.

Brunelle, Dorval. *Le Code civil et les rapports de classes suivi d'une analyse sociologique de la loi canadienne de l'assurance-chomage*. Montreal: Les Presses de l'Université du Québec, 1975.

Bryden, Kenneth. *Old Age Pensions and Policy-Making in Canada*. Montreal and London: McGill-Queen's University Press and the Institute of Public Administration of Canada, 1974.

Burns, R.M. *The Acceptable Mean: The Tax Rental Agreements, 1941-1962*. Toronto: Canadian Tax Foundation, 1980.

Cairns, Alan C. "The Embedded State: State-Society Relations in Canada." In *State and Society: Canada in Comparative Perspective*, edited by Keith Banting. Toronto: University of Toronto Press, 1986, 53-86.

– "The Governments and Societies of Canadian Federalism." *Canadian Journal of Political Science* 10 (December 1977): 695-725.

Cameron, David R. "The Expansion of the Public Economy: A Comparative Analysis." *American Political Science Review* 72 (December 1978): 1243-61.

Carnoy, Martin. *The State and Political Theory*. Princeton: Princeton University Press, 1984.

Cloutier, J.E. *The Distribution of Benefits and Costs of Social Security in Canada 1971-1975*. Discussion Paper No. 108. Ottawa: Economic Council of Canada, February 1978.

Cohen, J.L. *The Canadian Unemployment Act: Its Relation to Social Security*. Toronto: Thomas Nelson, 1935.

Coleman, William. "Canadian Business and the State." In *The State and Economic Interests*, edited by Keith Banting. Toronto: University of Toronto Press, 1986, 245-89.

Crouch, Colin. "The State, Capital and Liberal Democracy." In *The State and Economy in Contemporary Capitalism*, edited by Colin Crouch. London: Croom Helm, 1979, 13-54.

Cuneo, Carl J. "State, Class and Reserve Labour: The Case of the 1941 Canadian Unemployment Insurance Act." *Canadian Review of Sociology and Anthropology* 16 (May 1979): 147-70.

– "State Mediation of Class Contradictions in Canadian Unemployment Insurance. 1930-1935." *Studies in Political Economy* No. 3 (Spring 1980): 37-63.

Cutright, Phillips. "Political Structure, Economic Development, and National Social Security Programs." *American Journal of Sociology* 70 (March 1965): 537-50.

Dahl, Robert A. *Dilemmas of Pluralist Democracy*. New Haven: Yale University Press, 1982.

- *Polyarchy: Participation and Opposition*. New Haven: Yale University Press, 1971.
- *Who Governs?* New Haven: Yale University Press, 1961.

Dawson, R. MacGregor. *William Lyon Mackenzie King*. London: Methuen, 1958.

Dingledine, Gary. *A Chronology of Response: The Evolution of Unemployment Insurance from 1940 to 1980*. Ottawa: Minister of Supply and Services, 1981.

Doern, G. Bruce, and Richard W. Phidd. *Canadian Public Policy: Ideas, Structure, Process*. Toronto: Methuen, 1983.

Domhoff, Gabriel. *Who Really Rules?* New Brunswick, NJ: Transaction Books, 1978.

Downs, Anthony. *Inside Bureaucracy*. Boston: Little, Brown, 1967.

Dyck, Rand. "The Canada Assistance Plan: The Ultimate in Co-operative Federalism." *Canadian Public Administration* 19 (Winter 1976): 587-602.

Feyerabend, Paul. *Against Method: Outline of an Anarchistic Theory of Knowledge*. London: Verso, 1978.

Finkel, Alvin. *Business and Social Reform in the Thirties*. Toronto: James Lorimer, 1979.

Flora, Peter, and Arnold J. Heidenheimer. "The Historical Core and Changing Boundaries of the Welfare State." In *The Development of Welfare States in Europe and America*, edited by Peter Flora and Arnold J. Heidenheimer. New Brunswick, NJ: Transaction Books, 1981, 17-34.

Garraty, John A. *Unemployment in History: Economic Thought and Public Policy*. New York: Harper and Row, 1978.

Gibbon, I.G. *Unemployment Insurance: A Study of Schemes of Assisted Insurance*. London: P.S. King and Son, 1911.

Gilbert, B.B. *The Evolution of National Insurance in Great Britain*. London: Michael Joseph, 1973.

Golembiewski, R.T. *Public Administration as a Developing Discipline*. Part 1: *Perspectives on Past and Present*. New York: Marcel Dekker, 1977.

Granatstein, J.L. *Canada's War: The Politics of the Mackenzie King Government, 1939-1945*. Toronto: Oxford University Press, 1975.

Grubel, Herbert G., and Michael W. Walker. "Moral Hazard, Unemployment Insurance and the Rate of Unemployment." In *Unemployment Insurance: Global Evidence of Its Effects on Unemployment*, edited by Herbert G. Grubel and Michael A. Walker. Vancouver: The Fraser Institute, 1978, 1-35.

Guest, Dennis. *The Emergence of Social Security in Canada*. Vancouver: University of British Columbia Press, 1980.

Haber, William, and Merrill G. Murray. *Unemployment Insurance in the American Economy: An Historical Review and Analysis*. Homewood, Ill.: Richard D. Irwin, 1966.

Habermas, Jürgen. *Legitimation Crisis*. Boston: Beacon Press, 1975.

Hammermesh, Daniel S. *Jobless Pay and the Economy*. Baltimore: Johns Hopkins University Press, 1977.

Hauser, Mark M., and Paul Burrows. *The Economics of Unemployment Insurance*. London: George Allen and Unwin, 1969.

Heclo, Hugh. *Modern Social Politics in Britain and Sweden: From Relief to Income Maintenance*. New Haven: Yale University Press, 1974.

Hennock, E. Peter. "The Origins of British National Insurance and the German Precedent, 1880-1914." In *The Emergence of the Welfare State in Britain and Germany, 1850-1950*, edited by W.J. Mommsen. London: Croom Helm, 1981, 84-106.

Hill, Michael. *Policies for the Unemployed: Help or Coercion?* Poverty Pamphlet 15. London: Child Poverty Action Group, 1974.

Hill, Polly. *The Unemployment Services: A Report Prepared for the Fabian Society*. London: George Routledge and Sons, 1940.

Hockin, Thomas A. *Government in Canada*. Toronto: McGraw-Hill Ryerson, 1976.

Holden, Matthew, Jr, "'Imperialism' in Bureaucracy." *American Political Science Review* 60 (December 1966): 943-51.

Holloway, John, and Sol Picciotto, eds. *State and Capital*. London: Edward Arnold, 1978.

Hum, Derek P.J. *Unemployment Insurance and Work Effort: Issues, Evidence, and Policy Directions*. Toronto: Ontario Economic Council, 1981.

International Labour Office. *Unemployment Insurance Schemes*. Studies and Reports, New Series, No. 42. Geneva: 1955.

Jackson, Robert J., et al, *Politics in Canada: Culture, Institutions, Behaviour and Public Policy*. Toronto: Prentice-Hall, 1986.

Johnson, Andrew F. "A Minister as an Agent of Policy Change: The Case of Unemployment Insurance in the Seventies." *Canadian Public Administration* 24 (Winter 1981): 612-33.

– "Political Leadership and the Process of Policy-Making: The Case of Unemployment Insurance in the 1970's." PHD dissertation, McGill University, 1983.

Kaim-Caudle, P.R. *Comparative Social Policy and Social Security: A Ten Country Study*. London: Martin Robertson, 1973.

Kealey, Greg, ed. *Canada Investigates Industrialism*. Toronto: University of Toronto Press, 1973.

Kelly, Laurence A. "Unemployment Insurance in Canada: Economic, Social and Financial Aspects." PHD dissertation, Queen's University, 1967.

Kesselman, Jonathan R. *Financing Canadian Unemployment Insurance*. Toronto: Canadian Tax Foundation, 1983.

Keynes, John Maynard. *The General Theory of Employment, Interest, and Money*. London: 1936. Reprint. New York: Harcourt, Brace and World, 1964.

Kincaid, J.C. *Poverty and Equality in Britain: A Study of Social Security and Taxation*. Rev. ed. London: Penguin, 1975.

Krasner, Stephen D. *Defending the National Interest: Raw Materials Investments and U.S. Foreign Policy*. Princeton: Princeton University Press, 1978.

Kuhn, Thomas S. "Logic of Discovery or Psychology of Research." In *The Philo-

sophy of Karl Popper, vol. 1, edited by P.A. Schilpp. Lasalle: Open Court, 1974, 798-819.

- "Second Thoughts on Paradigms." In *The Structure of Scientific Theories*, edited by Frederick Suppe. Urbana: Univeristy of Illinois Press, 1972, 459-82.
- *The Structure of Scientific Revolutions*. Chicago: University of Chicago Press, 1962.

Laclau, Ernesto. *Politics and Ideology in Marxist Theory*. London: New Left Books, 1977.

Lanphier, C. Michael, et al. *An Analysis of Attitudes toward Unemployment Insurance*. Toronto: Institute for Behavioural Research at York University, July 1970.

Lindblom, Charles E. *Politics and Markets*. New York: Basic Books, 1977.

Lowi, Theodore J. "American Business, Public Policy, Case-Studies, and Political Theory." *World Politics* 16 (July 1964): 667-715.

- *The End of Liberalism*. 2nd ed. New York: Norton, 1979.
- "Four Systems of Policy, Politics, and Choice." *Public Administration Review* 32 (July/August 1972): 298-310.

McConnell, Grant. *Private Power and American Democracy*. New York: Alfred A. Knopf, 1966.

McConnell, W.H. "The Judicial Review of Prime Minister Bennett's New Deal Legislative Programme." PHD dissertation, University of Toronto.

McDonald, G.P.A. "Labour, Manpower and Government Reorganization." *Canadian Public Administration* 10 (December 1967): 471-98.

McFarland, Andrew S. *Power and Leadership in Pluralist Systems*. Stanford, Calif.: Stanford University Press, 1969.

Mackintosh, W.A. "Canadian Economic Policy from 1945 to 1957 – Origins and Influence." In *The American Economic Impact on Canada*, edited by H.G.J. Aitken et al. Durham, NC: Duke University Press, 51-68.

Mahon, Rianne. "Canadian Public Policy: The Unequal Structure of Representation." In *The Canadian State*, edited by Leo Panitch. Toronto: University of Toronto Press, 1977, 133-98.

- *The Politics of Industrial Restructuring: Canadian Textiles*. Toronto: University of Toronto Press, 1984.

Manley, John F. "Neo-Pluralism: A Class Analysis of Pluralism I and Pluralism II." *American Political Science Review* 77 (June 1983): 368-83.

Marsden, Dennis. *Workless: Some Unemployed Men and Their Families*. London: Penguin, 1975.

Marshall, T.H. *Class, Citizenship and Social Development*. New York: Anchor Books, 1965.

Miliband, Ralph. *Marxism and Politics*. London: Oxford University Press, 1977.

- *The State in Capitalist Society*. London: Weidenfeld and Nicholson, 1969.

Mill, John Stuart. *Principles of Political Economy*. 2 vols. London: 1848. Rev. ed. New York: Co-Operative Publication Society, 1900.

Mishra, Ramesh. *Society and Social Policy: Theoretical Perspectives on Welfare*. 2nd ed. London: Macmillan, 1977.

Nelson, Daniel. *Unemployment Insurance: The American Experience, 1915-1935*. Madison, Wisc.: University of Wisconsin Press, 1969.

Nichols, David. *Three Varieties of Pluralism*. London: Macmillan, 1974.

Niskanen, William A., Jr. *Bureaucracy and Representative Government*. Chicago: Aldine-Atherton, 1971.

Nordlinger, Eric. *On the Autonomy of the Democratic State*. Cambridge, Mass.: Harvard University Press, 1981.

Nossal, Kim Richard. "Allison through the (Ottawa) Looking Glass: Bureaucratic Politics and Foreign Policy in a Parliamentary System." *Canadian Public Administration* 22 (Winter 1979): 610-26.

Offe, Claus. *Contradictions of the Welfare State*, edited by John Keane. Cambridge, Mass.: MIT Press, 1984.

Offe, Claus, and Volker Ronge. "Theses on the Theory of the State." *New German Critique* 6 (1975): 139-47.

Ogus, A.I. "Great Britain." In *The Evolution of Social Insurance 1881-1981: Studies of Germany, France, Great Britain, Austria and Switzerland*, edited by Peter A. Kohler et al. London: Frances Pinter, 1982, 150-264.

Olson, Mancur. *The Logic of Collective Action: Public Goods and the Theory of Groups*. Cambridge, Mass.: Harvard University Press, 1965 and 1971.

- *The Rise and Decline of Nations: Economic Growth, Stagflation, and Social Rigidities*. New Haven: Yale University Press, 1982.

Pal, Leslie A. "The Fall and Rise of Developmental Uses of UI Funds," *Canadian Public Policy* 9 (March 1983): 81-93.

- "Keynesian Commitment, Keynesian Illusion: The Politics of Canadian Fiscal Policy 1943-1963." PHD dissertation, Queen's University, 1981.

Paltiel, K.Z. "The Changing Environment and the Role of Special Interest Groups." *Canadian Public Administration* 25 (Summer 1982): 198-210.

Panitch, Leo. "Trade Unions and the State." *New Left Review* 125 (January-February 1981): 21-43.

Pelletier, Michel. *De la sécurité sociale a la sécurité du revenu: essais sur la politique économique et sociale contemporaine*. Montreal: Michel Pelletier, 1982.

Pentland, H. Clare. *Labour and Capital in Canada, 1650-1860*, edited by Paul Phillips. Toronto: James Lorimer, 1981.

Peters, B. Guy. *The Politics of Bureaucracy: A Comparative Perspective*. New York: Longman, 1978.

Phidd, Richard W., and G. Bruce Doern. *The Politics and Management of Canadian Economic Policy*. Toronto: Macmillan, 1978.

Popper, Karl R. *Conjectures and Refutations: The Growth of Scientific Knowledge*. New York: Harper and Row, 1963.

- *The Logic of Scientific Discovery*. 2nd ed. New York: Harper and Row, 1968.

- "The Logic of the Social Sciences." In *The Positivist Dispute in German*

Sociology, edited by Theodor W. Adorno. London: Heinemann, 1976, 87-104.
- *The Poverty of Historicism*. London: Routledge and Kegan Paul, 1957.
Poulantzas, Nicos. *Political Power and Social Classes*. London: New Left Books, 1975.
- *State, Power, Socialism*. London: New Left Books, 1978.
Pross, A. Paul. *Group Politics and Public Policy*. Toronto: Oxford University Press, 1986.
- "Pressure Groups: Talking Chameleons." In *Canadian Politics in the 1980s*, 2nd ed., edited by Michael S. Whittington and Glen Williams. Toronto: Methuen, 1984, 301-6.
- "Space, Function and Interest: The Problem of Legitimacy in the Canadian State." In *The Administrative State: Canadian Perspectives*, edited by O.P. Dwivedi et al. Toronto: University of Toronto Press, 1982, 107-29.
Pryor, Frederic L. *Public Expenditures in Communist and Capitalist Nations*. London: George Allen and Unwin, 1968.
Rea, Samuel A., Jr. "Unemployment Insurance and Labour Supply: A Simulation of the 1971 Unemployment Insurance Act." *Canadian Journal of Economics* 10 (May 1977): 263-78.
Rose, Michael E. "The Crisis of Poor Law Relief in England, 1860-1890." In *The Emergence of the Welfare State in Britain and Germany, 1850-195*, edited by W.J. Mommsen. London: Croom Helm, 1981, 50-70.
Rourke, Francis E. *Bureaucracy, Politics, and Public Policy*. Boston: Little, Brown, 1969.
Russell, Peter H., ed. *Leading Constitutional Cases*. 3rd ed. Ottawa: Carleton University Press, 1982.
Saywell, John, ed. *Canadian Annual Review of Politics and Public Affairs 1971*. Toronto: University of Toronto Press, 1972.
- *Canadian Annual Review of Politics and Public Affairs 1972*. Toronto: University of Toronto Press, 1974.
Schlozman, Kay Lehman, and Sidney Verba. *Injury to Insult: Unemployment, Class, and Political Response*. Cambridge, Mass.: Harvard University Press, 1979.
Schmitter, Philippe, and Gerhard Lembruch, eds. *Trends towards Corporatist Intermediation*. Beverly Hills, Calif.: Sage, 1979.
Schultz, Richard J. *Federalism, Bureaucracy, and Public Policy*. Montreal: McGill-Queen's University Press and the Institute of Public Administration of Canada, 1980.
Seidman, Harold. *Politics, Position, and Power: The Dynamics of Federal Organization*. 3rd ed. New York: Oxford University Press, 1980.
Simeon, Richard. *Federal-Provincial Diplomacy: The Making of Recent Policy in Canada*. Toronto: University of Toronto Press, 1972.
- "Studying Public Policy." *Canadian Journal of Political Science* 9 (December 1976): 548-80.
Skocpol, Theda. "Bringing the State Back In: Strategies of Analysis in Current Research." In *Bringing the State Back In*, edited by Peter B. Evans, Dietrich Rueschemyer, and Theda Skocpol. Cambridge: Cambridge University Press, 1985, 3-37.

- "Political Response to Capitalist Crisis: Neo-Marxist Theories of the State and the Case of the New Deal." *Politics and Society* 10 (1980): 155-201.
- *States and Social Revolutions: A Comparative Analysis of France, Russia, and China*. Cambridge: Cambridge University Press, 1979.

Skocpol, Theda, and Kenneth Finegold. "State Capacity and Economic Intervention in the Early New Deal." *Political Science Quarterly* 97 (Summer 1982): 255-78.

Smiley, Donald V. *Canada in Question: Federalism in the Eighties*. 3rd ed. Toronto: McGraw-Hill Ryerson, 1980.

Smiley, Donald V., ed. *The Rowell-Sirois Report*. Toronto: McClelland and Stewart, 1963.

Smith, A.M.M., et al, *Poverty and Government Income Support in Canada, 1971-1975: Characteristics of the Low Income Population*. Discussion Paper No. 130. Ottawa: Economic Council of Canada, April 1979.

Sproule-Jones, Mark. "Institutions, Constitutions, and Public Policies: A Public-Choice Overview." In *The Politics of Canadian Public Policy,* edited by Michael M. Atkinson and Marsha A. Chandler. Toronto: University of Toronto Press, 1983, 127-50.

Stevenson, Garth. *Unfulfilled Union: Canadian Federalism and National Unity*. Rev. ed. Toronto: Gage, 1982.

Struthers, James. *No Fault of Their Own: Unemployment and the Canadian Welfare State, 1914-1941*. Toronto: University of Toronto Press, 1983.

Suppe, Frederick. "Afterword." In *The Structure of Scientific Theories*, 2nd ed., edited by Frederick Suppe. Urbana: University of Illinois Press, 1977, 617-730.

Thompson, Fred, and W.T. Stanbury. "The Political Economy of Interest Groups in the Legislative Process in Canada." In *The Canadian Political Process*, 3rd ed., edited by Richard Schultz et al. Toronto: Holt, Rinehart, and Winston, 1979, 224-49.

Truman, David. *The Governmental Process*. New York: Alfred A. Knopf, 1951.

Tullock, Gordon. *The Politics of Bureaucracy*. Washington, DC: Public Affairs Press, 1965.

Wheare, K.C. *Federal Government*. 4th ed. New York: Oxford University Press, 1964.

Wilson, V. Seymour. *Canadian Public Policy and Administration*. Toronto: McGraw-Hill Ryerson, 1981.

Wolfenden, Hugh H. *The Real Meaning of Social Insurance: Its Present Status and Tendencies*. Toronto: Macmillan, 1932.
- *Unemployment Funds: A Survey and Proposal*. Toronto: Macmillan, 1934.

Wright, Erik Olin. *Class, Crisis and the State*. London: New Left Books, 1978.

Yin, Robert K. *Case Study Research: Design and Method*. Beverly Hills, Calif.: Sage, 1984.

Young, Robert A. "Reining in James: The Limits of the Task Force." *Canadian Public Administration* 24 (Winter 1981): 596-611.

Zukav, Gary. *The Dancing Wu Li Masters: An Overview of the New Physics*. New York: William Morrow, 1979.

Index